CREATIVE
ALCOHOL INK
Flowers

Quarto.com

© 2026 Quarto Publishing
Artwork & text © 2026 Anne Roos Art

First Published in 2026 by Quarry Books,
an imprint of The Quarto Group,
100 Cummings Center, Suite 265-D, Beverly, MA 01915, USA.
T (978) 282-9590 F (978) 283-2742

EEA Representation, WTS Tax d.o.o.,
Žanova ulica 3, 4000 Kranj, Slovenia.
www.wts-tax.si

Quarry Books titles are also available at discount for retail, wholesale, promotional, and bulk purchase. For details, contact the Special Sales Manager by email at specialsales@quarto.com or by mail at The Quarto Group, Attn: Special Sales Manager, 100 Cummings Center, Suite 265-D, Beverly, MA 01915, USA.

10 9 8 7 6 5 4 3 2 1

ISBN: 978-0-7603-9780-0

Digital edition published in 2026
eISBN: 978-0-7603-9781-7

Library of Congress Cataloging-in-Publication Data

Names: Smink, Anne Roos, 1990- author
Title: Creative alcohol ink flowers : a step-by-step guide to 20 stunning
  floral designs / Anne Roos Smink.
Description: Beverly, MA : Quarry Books, 2026. | Includes bibliographical
  references and index.
Identifiers: LCCN 2025023474 (print) | LCCN 2025023475 (ebook) | ISBN
  9780760397800 paperback | ISBN 9780760397817 ebook
Subjects: LCSH: Flowers in art | Ink painting--Technique | Alcohol ink.
Classification: LCC ND1400 .S65 2026 (print) | LCC ND1400 (ebook) | DDC
  751.42/5--dc23/eng/20250625
LC record available at https://lccn.loc.gov/2025023474
LC ebook record available at https://lccn.loc.gov/2025023475

Design and Page Layout: Laura McFadden Design, Inc.

Printed in Guangdong, China TT082025

CREATIVE ALCOHOL INK

Flowers

A Step-by-Step Guide to 20 Stunning Floral Designs

Anne Roos Smink

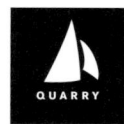

contents

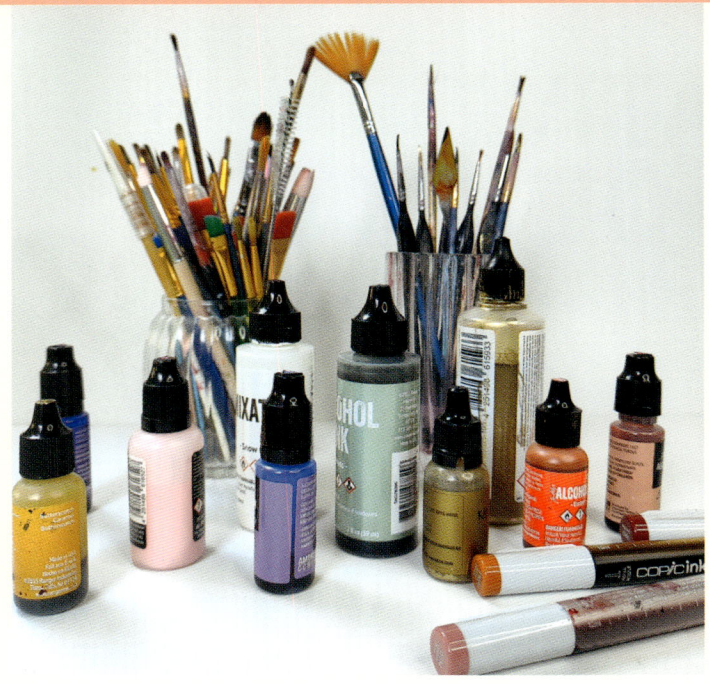

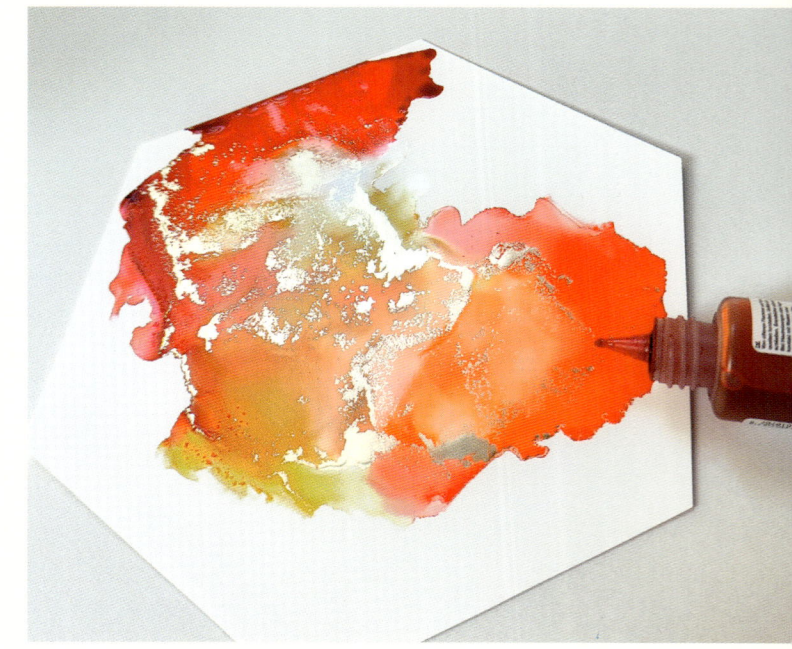

CHAPTER
3

flower projects 47

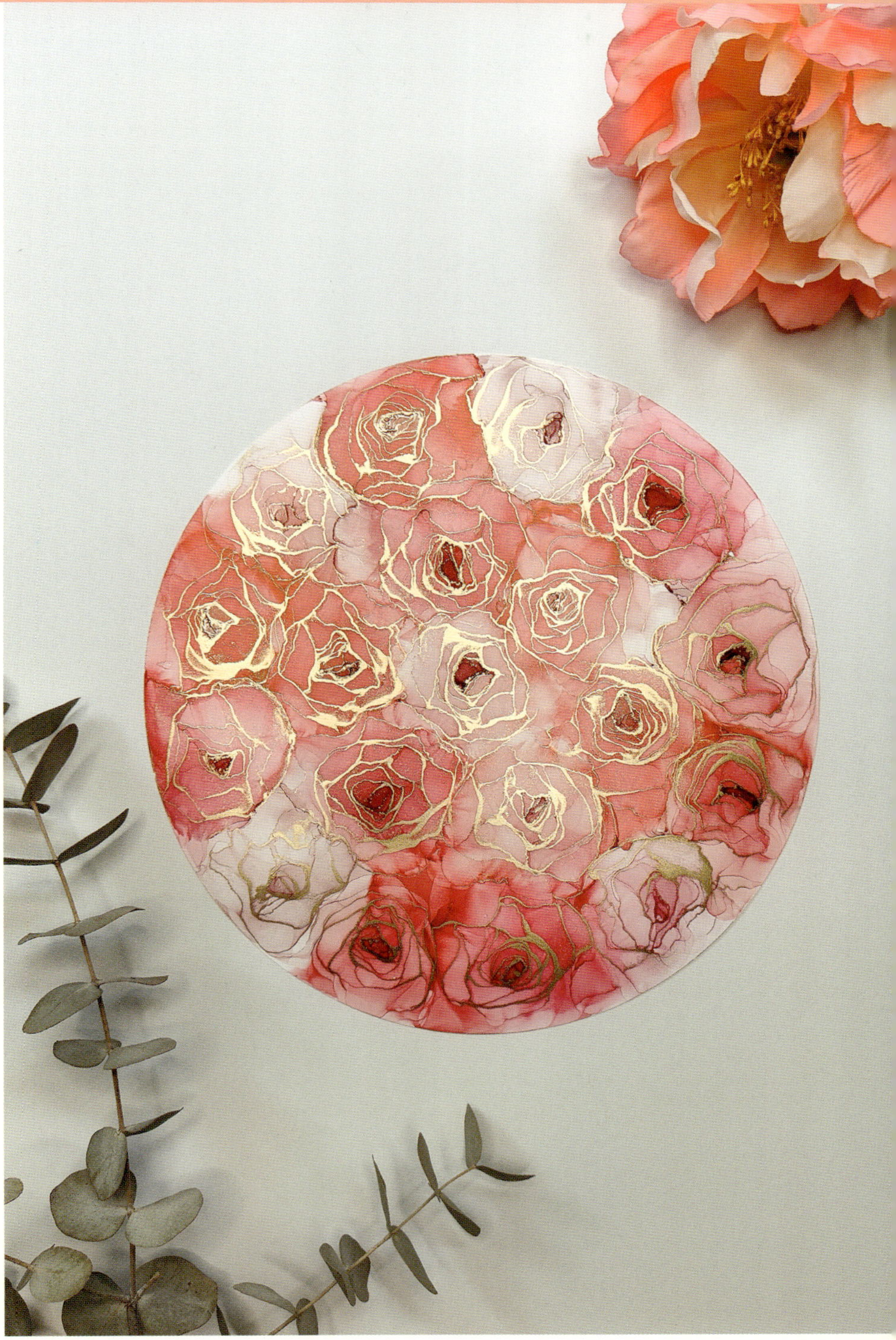

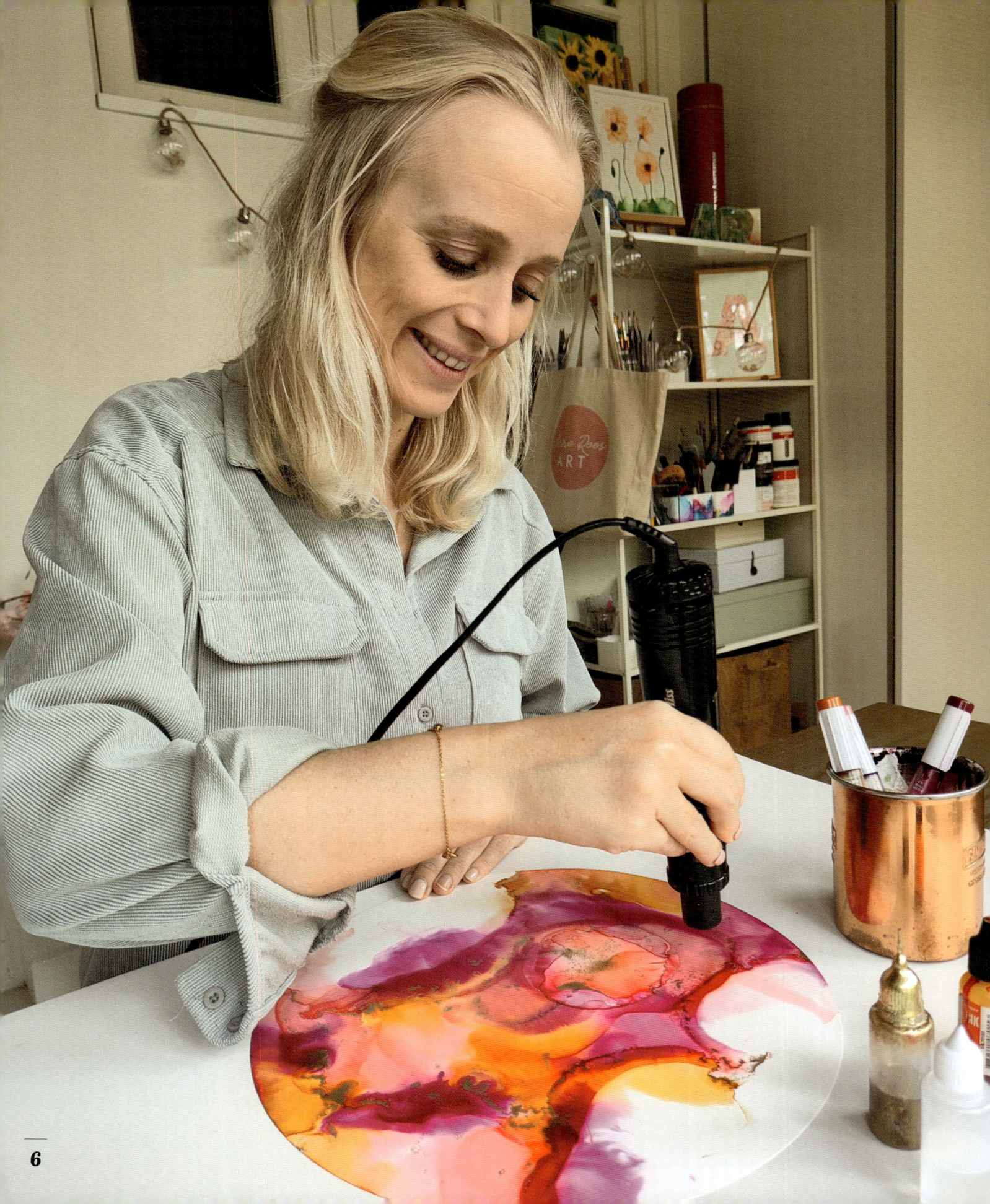

introduction

I'm so excited you decided to pick up this book and dive into *Creative Alcohol Ink Flowers* with me! Whether you're brand new to alcohol inks or already proficient, this book is full of floral inspiration to get creative and guide you on your alcohol ink journey.

In this book, you will learn how to transform simple blobs of ink into stunning floral compositions. We'll start with the basics: everything you need to know about tools, materials, and my favorite supplies. Then, I'll share my best tips and tricks on how to work with alcohol inks, including warm-up exercises to help you gain confidence in controlling and manipulating the inks. Finally, we'll dive into the most exciting part: **20 flower projects** that will guide you step-by-step through creating a variety of blooms—from delicate poppies and bold daisies to dreamy abstract florals and my signature roses. You'll also find QR codes to videos showing various techniques throughout the book. To access them, scan the QR code below to create a free log-in on my website. Once you're logged in, you'll be able to access all videos directly or via the QR codes. With projects ranging from beginner to advanced level, exploring different techniques and tools, there's something for everyone!

Alcohol inks are a magical medium, the way the inks flow and blend into each other to create interesting and unexpected patterns and textures is mesmerizing. When I first started working with alcohol inks, I was drawn to their unpredictability, and I quickly discovered how much joy and positive energy they brought me. They became my creative escape, a way to let go and simply enjoy the process. I hope this book sparks that same joy and creativity in you and encourages you to let go, experiment, and embrace the magic of alcohol inks to create beautiful flowers.

While it's true that alcohol inks have a mind of their own and can be difficult to control, with practice, play, and a bit of patience, you'll learn how to master alcohol inks in your own style. Let this book be your guide and source of inspiration, but most importantly, let your own intuition and imagination guide your creative process—and don't forget to enjoy the journey!

Let your creativity bloom!

Anne Roos Smink

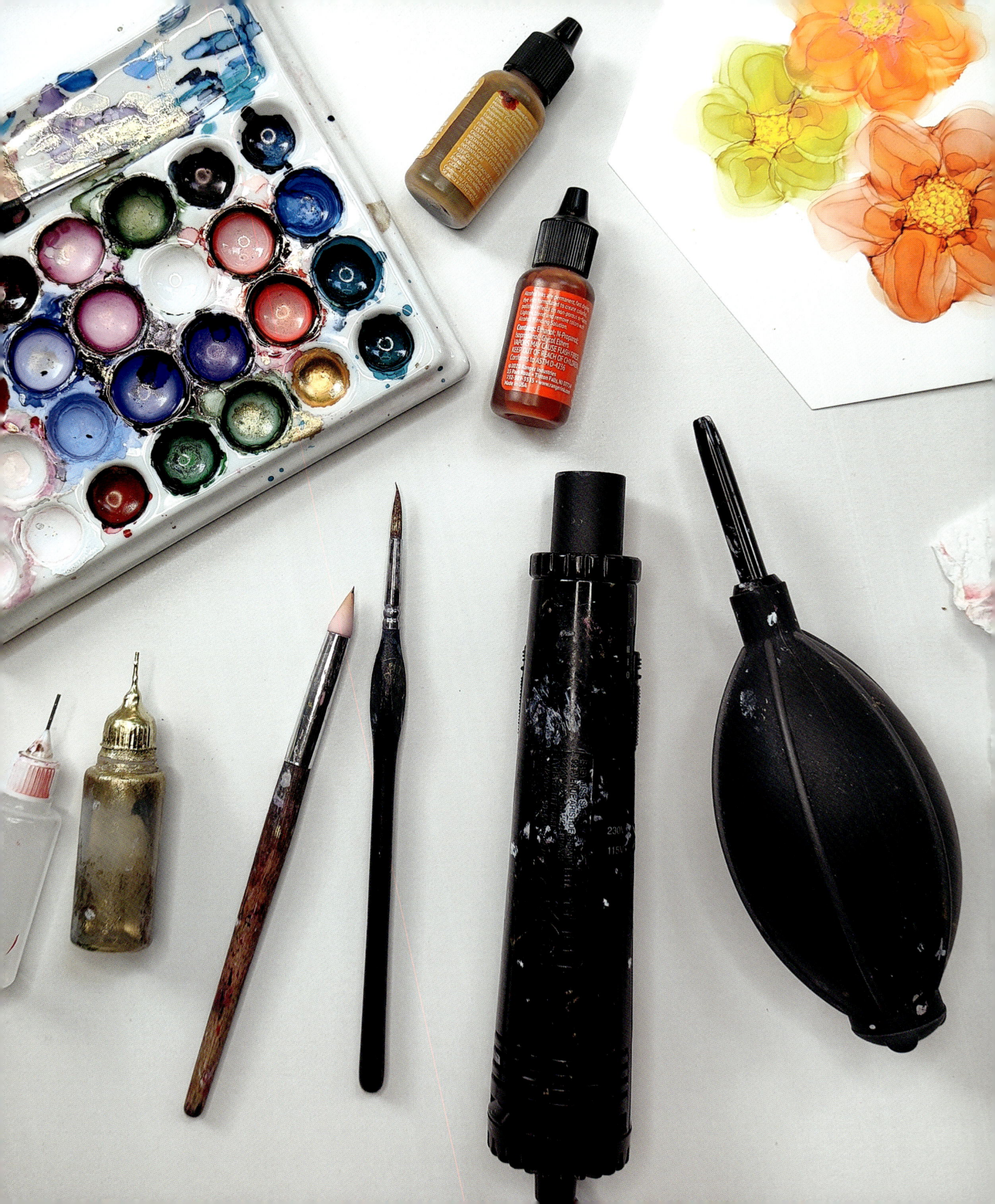

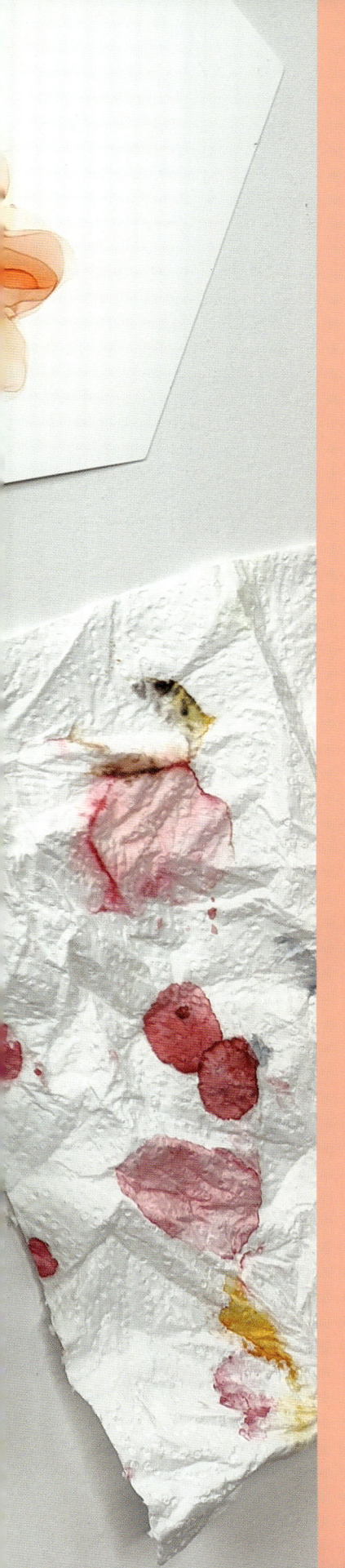

tools and materials

Alcohol ink art requires specific tools and materials to take advantage of the fluidity of the medium to create beautiful designs, like flowers. In this chapter, I'll go over the basic tools you'll need—such as the alcohol inks, isopropyl alcohol, and a nonporous surface—so you can discover the magic of this medium for yourself. I'll wrap things up with a shopping list to give you a clear overview of what you'll need to get started!

alcohol inks

Alcohol inks are alcohol- and dye-based inks (a mixture of alcohol, dyes, and more) that can be used on smooth, nonporous surfaces. While there are different types of alcohol inks available, most alcohol inks are transparent. Because they are alcohol-based, they can be diluted with isopropyl alcohol (or a blending solution) to increase the transparency of the alcohol ink colors and create fluidity. Besides the alcohol base, there are four other key features that set this medium apart and make it so addictive to work with!

Key Features of Alcohol Inks

Fluidity: Alcohol inks are fluid in nature. The fluidity of the medium is used to move the inks in certain patterns using a manipulation tool like an ink air blower or a heat tool. In the process, the alcohol will evaporate, and the inks will dry on the surface, creating beautiful patterns and textures. In this book, the fluidity of alcohol inks is used to turn them into picturesque flowers.

Air manipulation: The most exciting and mind-blowing thing about alcohol inks is that instead of using a brush, the air flow from an ink air blower or heat tool can be used to manipulate the inks. By moving the air around, the inks will dry in a pattern, creating the art. If you're new to alcohol inks, I'll warn you, controlling these inks is more difficult than it looks! But in this book, I'll give you tips to help you gain (some) control over them. Part of the beauty of this medium is that with the fluidity comes some uncontrollable spontaneity.

Color vibrancy: Alcohol ink colors are very vibrant, and because of the high saturation of the dye-based ink, very little ink is needed for a saturated and vibrant look. Unlike many other media, the colors also tend to keep their vibrancy when dry. When different colors of alcohol ink are used together, they will mix and beautifully blend into each other. It's also important to note that alcohol inks tend to produce a lot of undertones. For example, a black

ink may produce blue, purple, or pink undertones. This is another feature that adds to the magical look of alcohol inks. Metallic inks can add mesmerizing golden details to your art.

Reactivating: One of the best features of alcohol inks is that they can be reactivated each time isopropyl alcohol is added to the surface. This creates endless possibilities to manipulate the inks using the different techniques and tools that you will discover in this book. When using a nonstaining surface, the inks can even be completely removed, and you can just start over. The hardest part might be knowing when to stop!

Types of Alcohol Inks

Transparent: Transparent alcohol inks are the most common. The more isopropyl alcohol it contains, the lighter, more transparent, and fluid it will be. This ink will be used for most projects in this book.

Opaque: Opaque alcohol inks come in white and pastel colors and are nontransparent, although when isopropyl alcohol is added they can still create a semitransparent look. White alcohol ink can be mixed with transparent alcohol inks to create pastel colors. Unlike transparent inks, opaque inks are visible on black surfaces. They are much thicker and therefore less fluid than transparent inks. While their thickness can make them more difficult to work with, opaque inks can be great for adding details to flowers or adding texture in the flower petals.

Metallic: Metallic inks come in gold, bronze, silver, and copper and are some of the most exciting inks to work with. Metallic inks are made from small metallic particles that create beautiful reflective textures and lines. Only specific alcohol ink brands and colors give this much sought-after effect, so be sure to see my brand recommendations below.

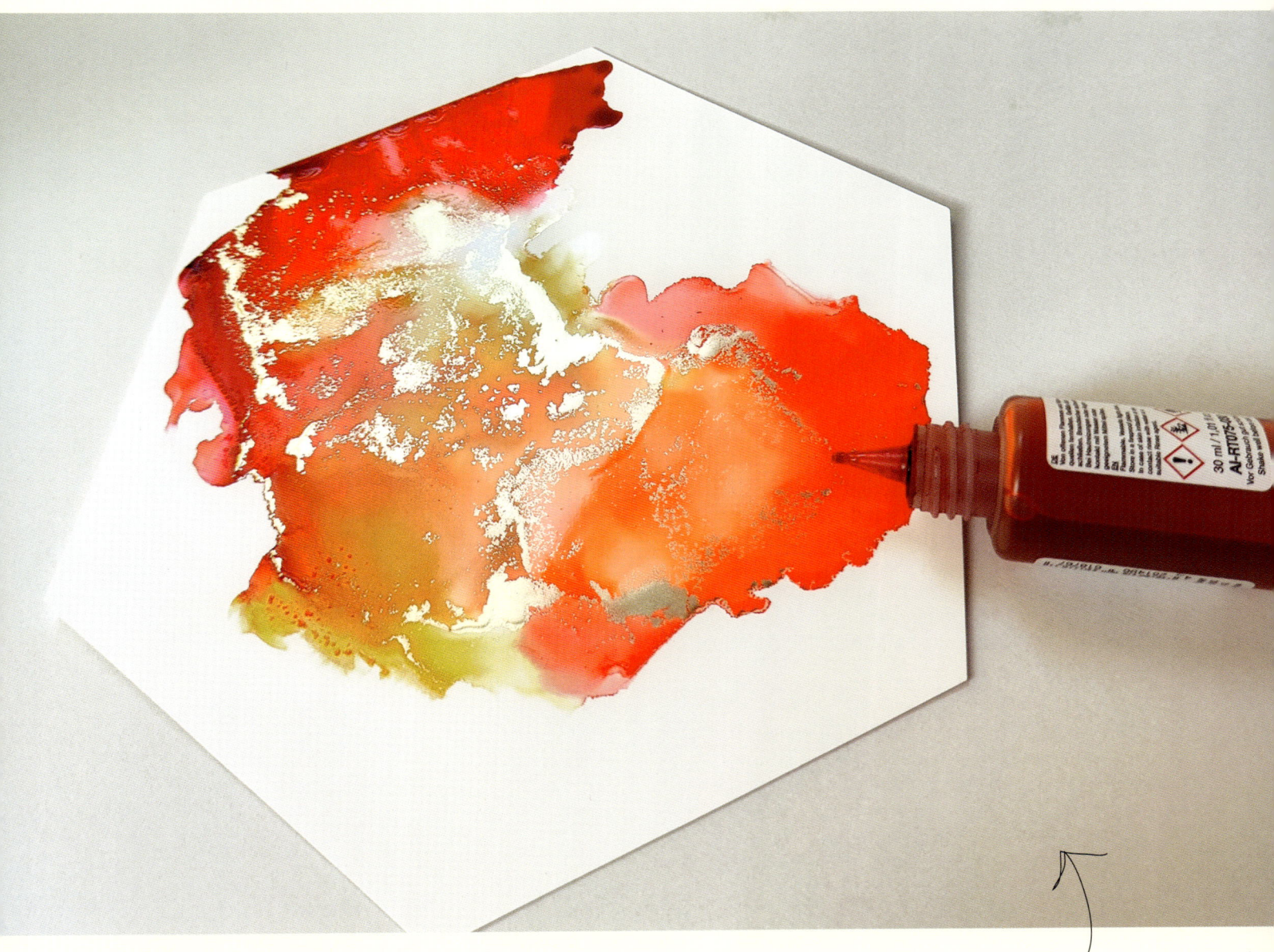

Pearl/Shimmering: Pearl inks will give a shimmery, pearlescent look to the inks that is visible on white and black surfaces. White pearl inks can be mixed with transparent inks to create different pearlescent colors. Some shimmering inks even shift color depending on the angle at which you look at them.

Alcohol inks are a very exciting medium to work with because of their vibrancy and other key features.

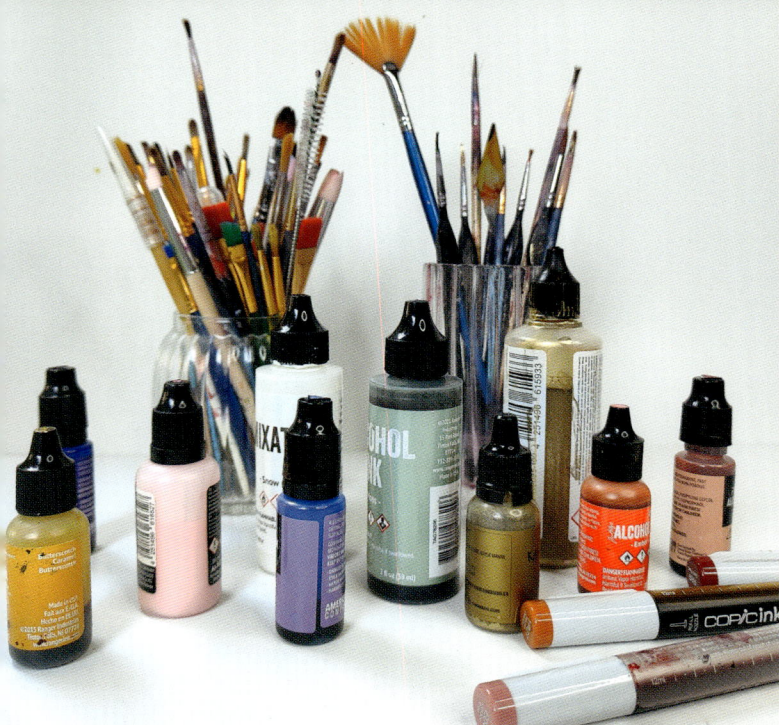

Metallic Alcohol Ink Brands

Every metallic ink behaves differently, and to produce those beautiful golden edges, there are specific alcohol inks I recommend using, in order of preference:

- Octopus Fluids *Gold Rush* (only available in Europe)
- Jacquard Piñata *Brass* (**not** gold)
- Kamenskaya Ink *Bronze* (**not** gold)
- PIXISS Alcohol Ink *Gold*
- Ranger Tim Holtz *Alloys Statue*

It's very difficult finding the same quality in silver or copper inks. For silver, here are the inks I recommend:

- Octopus Fluids *Silver Mine*
- MOLOWTOW *LIQUID CHROME* (refill)

For copper, I recommend Octopus Fluids *Coin Copper*.

Alcohol Ink Brands

Nowadays, there are many different brands available offering a large range of colors and types of alcohol ink. Quality of inks and colors can differ between and within brands. For example, some ink colors tend to stain more than others, and some colors are more saturated (which means you need less of it) than others. The best way to discover this is through experimentation.

Here's a list of some of the brands I personally use and recommend. It's better to invest in a couple of good alcohol inks than to purchase some of the cheaper off-brand inks as they will last you much longer and produce much better effects. The availability and price of each brand will depend upon your location.

- Ranger Tim Holtz Alcohol Inks
- Jacquard Piñata Colors
- Copic Ink
- Octopus Fluids Alcohol Inks
- Kamenskaya Ink
- PIXISS Alcohol Inks
- NARA Alcohol Inks

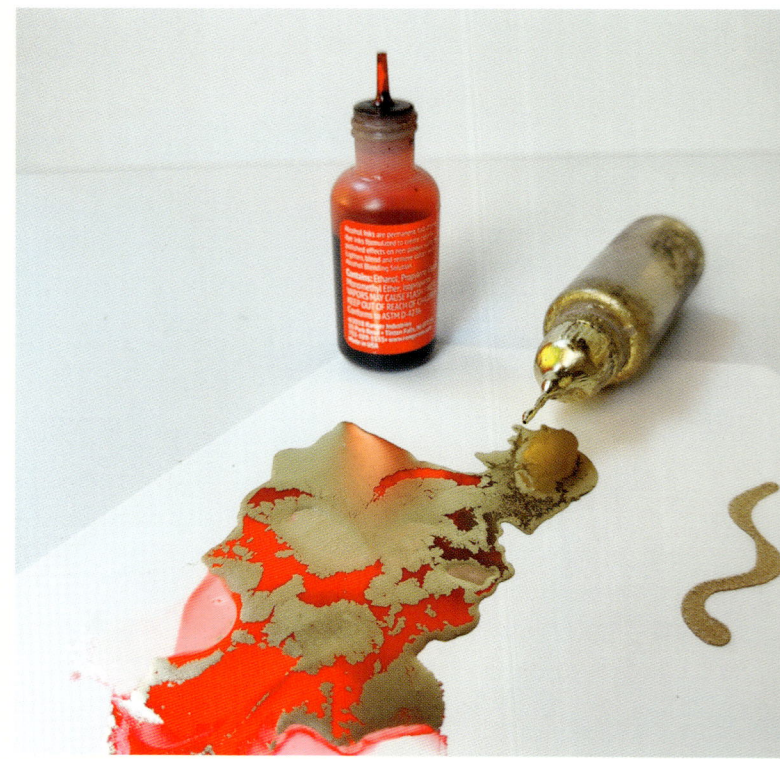

Overview of Brands

	RANGE	INK TYPES	SIZE	AVAILABILITY	NOTES
Ranger Tim Holtz Alcohol Inks	116 inks	85 transparent inks 1 opaque ink (white) 12 metallic inks 18 pearl inks	0.5 oz (14 ml) 2 oz (59 ml)	Widely available	These are my personal favorite for transparent inks. I love the beautiful undertones in these inks.
Jacquard Piñata Colors	29 inks	22 transparent inks 1 opaque ink (white) 5 metallic inks 1 pearlescent ink	0.5 oz (14.79 ml) 4 oz (118.29 ml)	Widely available	These are highly saturated inks. The metallic *Brass* is popular, and *Opal* is a color-shifting iridescent ink.
Copic Ink	358 inks	358 transparent inks	0.4 oz (12 ml)	Widely available	The range of colors from Copic is unmatched. They're generally higher priced, but are very good quality inks.
Octopus Fluids Alcohol Inks	50 inks	30 transparent inks 14 opaque inks 6 metallic inks	1 oz (30 ml) 3.4 oz (100 ml)	Germany—international shipping available	Octopus Fluids metallics are my favorite to work with and their starter kits are great for beginners.
Kamenskaya Ink	99 inks	33 transparent inks 17 opaque inks 3 metallics 6 shimmering inks 40 delaminating inks	0.5 oz (15 ml)	Europe—ships worldwide	These are good quality alcohol inks with some cool inks like their metallic *Bronze* and shimmering inks.
PIXISS Alcohol Inks	48 inks	32 transparent inks 1 opaque ink 5 metallic inks 10 shimmering inks	0.5 oz (15 ml) 4 oz (118 ml)	US—ships worldwide	PIXISS inks are relatively affordable, although quality can differ between colors. Their color-shifting inks are awesome.
NARA Alcohol Inks	48 inks	39 transparent inks 7 opaque inks 2 metallic inks	0.5 oz (15 ml)	India—ships worldwide	NARA offers a range of bright and earthy colors.

isopropyl alcohol

Isopropyl alcohol is used to dilute and enhance the fluidity of alcohol inks. Think of it this way: What water is to watercolor paint, isopropyl alcohol is to alcohol inks. To work with alcohol inks, you need either 91% or 99% isopropyl alcohol, which can generally be found in drugstores.

Alcohol inks can either be premixed with isopropyl alcohol or applied directly from the bottle. I use both methods. For transparent inks, I usually drop a few drops of inks straight from the bottle and add isopropyl alcohol on top to dilute it directly on my surface. For metallic and opaque inks, premixing with isopropyl alcohol is recommended.

small needle tip bottles

Since isopropyl alcohol comes in big bottles, it's useful to transfer the alcohol to a small needle tip bottle, allowing you to carefully apply it. An alternative is to use a plastic cup with a pipette, but I prefer a needle tip bottle as it's less likely to spill. Needle tip bottles can easily be found online or in craft stores.

blending solution

Many alcohol ink brands also offer a blending solution. Blending solutions contain isopropyl alcohol with additives like protective resins (just like alcohol inks). Blending solutions are meant to blend the inks while maintaining their vibrancy and provide a glossier finish than isopropyl alcohol. However, they are more difficult to work with, as the substance is much thicker, creates less fluidity, and makes it harder to reactivate inks after drying. For the techniques in this book, isopropyl alcohol will work much better than blending solution, and it's also much more affordable.

surfaces

Alcohol inks work best on a nonporous surface to utilize the fluidity of the medium. On normal paper or canvas, the inks will sink into the surface right away, making it difficult to move the inks around and create those beautiful fluid designs. Therefore, you need synthetic paper or other nonporous surfaces that allow the inks to float on top of the surface.

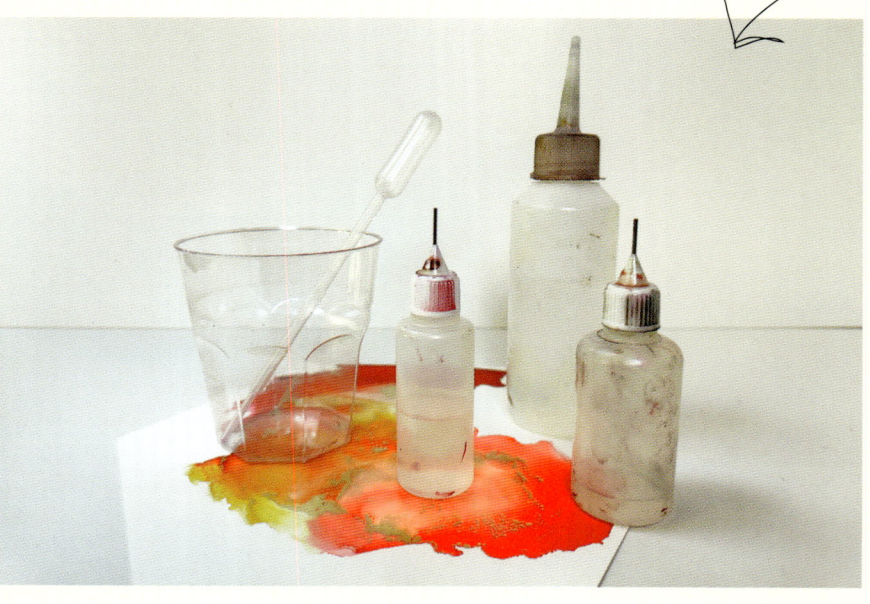

Small needle tip bottles and pipettes offer control as you apply the inks.

Synthetic Paper

Synthetic paper is a nonabsorbent, plastic-like paper designed to be used with alcohol inks. Because it's made of synthetic materials, it won't tear like normal paper, and the inks will float on top of the paper instead of soaking into it. This is the best surface to use for alcohol ink art and will be used for the projects in this book.

Many alcohol ink brands offer synthetic paper, but they aren't all alike. I recommend using **nonstaining** synthetic paper because this paper allows the inks to be reactivated multiple times without leaving any stains. You can even completely remove unwanted areas without leaving behind any residue or stains. This makes the paper very forgiving and economical, as you can rework and correct mistakes without it showing through. For the floral techniques used in this book, we will be reactivating the inks multiple times, and a nonstaining surface is best for this. Brands that offer nonstaining synthetic paper are **Grafix Arts Plastics** (Dura-Bright), **NARA** (NARA Synthetic Paper), and **Kamenskaya** (Alcohol Ink Paper).

YUPO is also a very well-known synthetic paper brand (YUPO Paper) for alcohol inks. While it can also be used for the techniques in this book, the inks will stain on the paper after they are dry. This reduces the ability to erase or lift the ink and will leave visible marks of where the inks were reactivated.

Synthetic paper comes in many sizes, shapes, weights, and even colors. To start out, it's best to work on a smaller sized paper (but not too small) like 8 to 12 inches (20 to 30 cm) wide. You can purchase synthetic paper in rectangular and square shapes and also round and hexagon shapes. I personally love working on round synthetic paper for my floral art. You can buy these precut or cut them yourself. The higher the weight of the paper, the sturdier and stronger the paper is. Synthetic paper generally comes in white but is also available in black. For the Flower Projects, we will be using white synthetic paper.

Before starting any project, **always clean your synthetic paper with isopropyl alcohol and a paper towel**. This will prevent any moisture or dust from affecting the inks when applied to the paper.

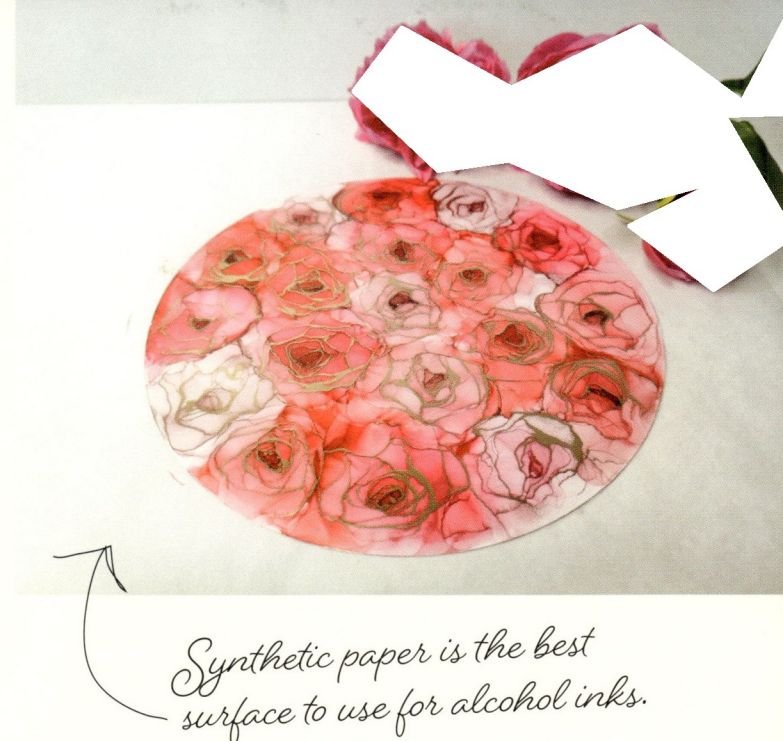

Synthetic paper is the best surface to use for alcohol inks.

Other Surfaces

Glazed ceramic tiles: Ceramic tiles are great to practice on. They are very forgiving and easy to wipe clean and start over. I recommend getting a tile to practice each flower on before moving on to synthetic paper. Make sure to get the glazed ones, as unglazed tiles are not suitable for alcohol inks. Small tiles can also be turned into beautiful coasters by varnishing them and covering them with resin.

Acrylic blanks: Acrylic blanks are a great alternative to synthetic paper. They are offered in many different shapes suitable as coasters, ornaments, earrings, and much more. Many companies now offer custom-made designs using a laser cutter.

Art board: Some brands offer specific art boards with a smooth nonabsorbent surface suitable for alcohol inks. Usually, these are primed MDF boards and will give a professional look to your finished artwork.

Primed canvas: While canvas is not the best surface for alcohol ink art, when primed with white latex primer, the surface becomes smoother and can be used with alcohol inks.

manipulation tools

Alcohol inks can be manipulated using an ink air blower, heat tool, or a brush. The ink air blower and heat tool techniques are the most widely used, but a brush can also create some fun effects when reactivating the inks or adding details. I often use a mix of these tools.

Ink Air Blower

An ink air blower is a rubber squeeze bulb that helps spread alcohol inks in a controlled manner by squeezing the bulb with your hand. This is a safer alternative to blowing the inks around by mouth, as it prevents inhalation of the ink and alcohol fumes. The tool is great to softly manipulate and blend the inks into each other, and it's one of my favorite ways to create flower petals, as we will explore in some of the projects in this book. I recommend getting the Tim Holtz Alcohol Ink Air Blower from Ranger Ink that's made specifically for alcohol inks.

Heat Tool

The most interesting way to manipulate alcohol inks is by using a heat tool. For alcohol ink art, you'll need a heat tool with a medium heat that doesn't get so hot that it warps the synthetic paper. The back of a hot air brush styler is recommended for this (a hair dryer with detachable brush), as it creates a more precise airflow than a normal hair dryer will, allowing for more control over the alcohol inks. When choosing a heat tool, look for one with multiple heat settings, lower wattage (200W–800W), and a detachable, smaller top for more focused and detailed work. I work with the BaByliss Shape & Smooth AS82E (800W) or the very focused BaByliss Smooth Boost 668E

(300W). The Revlon All-In-One Style Hot Air Kit is a good alternative if the others are not available to you.

Other Air Tools

Embossing/heat gun: An embossing or heat gun will easily warp synthetic paper when held in one position for a longer period of time, and the paper will not flatten out after. For the heat tool techniques in this book, an embossing or heat gun is **not** suitable; however, ceramic tiles or acrylic blanks can take the heat of an embossing gun.

Air brush: The air flow of an air brush can also be used to work with alcohol inks. Since air brushes use cold air, they are not suitable for all the techniques described in this book. For example, the roses technique needs the drying power of the heat tool.

Hair dryer: While hair dryers can be used to spread the inks around, they are generally not narrow enough, and the air flow is too strong to allow control over the inks.

Brushes

In addition to air tools, brushes are incredibly versatile when working with alcohol inks. You can use them to apply ink to the surface, add details to flowers, lift ink, or create texture through dabbing and stroking (see page

I often use a mix of these tools.

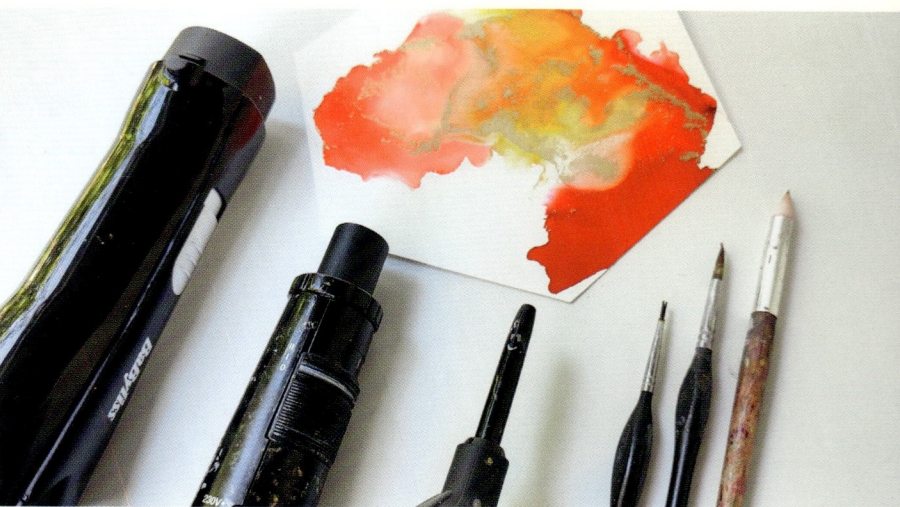

38 for more on working with brushes). One of my favorite techniques is splattering ink for a playful finishing touch. I advise getting a set of miniature round brushes in various sizes from 000 (0.4 mm) to 4.0 mm (fine to large) as well as a fan brush. It's best to use synthetic round brushes for alcohol inks. Synthetic brushes absorb less ink than natural ones, providing better control and durability, and they're less likely to stain or be damaged by the alcohol. You can clean brushes by soaking them in isopropyl alcohol.

sealants

To protect your work from moisture and color fading, it's important to seal your artwork. The best way to protect alcohol inks is using a varnish suitable for alcohol inks. Since alcohol inks are not lightfast, their color can fade over time, so it's important to use a varnish that also has an ultraviolet radiation (UV) sealant or use a separate UV protector.

Please note there are specific varnishes that work well with alcohol inks. Many varnishes will damage or reactivate the inks because they contain alcohol and will leave spots on your artwork. I personally like to use a glossy spray varnish for the best finish. The best varnishes for alcohol ink art are the following:

Krylon Kamar Varnish: This is the most well-known spray varnish for protecting alcohol ink art. However, it's not easily available outside the United States. Apply three even, thin coats of varnish and let it dry in between.

Krylon UV-Resistant Clear Coating: Combine with Kamar Varnish for a UV-resistant layer. Apply after Kamar Varnish with three even, thin layers.

Montana Varnish: This is a good alternative if Kamar is not available. It's a spray varnish with UV protection, and it comes in matte, glossy, and semi-gloss. I prefer gloss with alcohol ink art. Apply three even, thin, coats.

Talens Acrylic Varnish Glossy: This spray varnish is suitable to seal alcohol inks but does not have UV pro-tection. Apply three, even thin coats. It can be combined with Winsor & Newton Professional Gloss Varnish for a glossy UV-protective finish.

Winsor & Newton Professional Gloss Varnish: This spray varnish with UV protection can be used **only** as the final coat for a beautiful glossy finish. Apply one even coat of varnish as the final layer after sealing it with another varnish (applying it as the first coat might leave spots).

Piñata High Gloss Varnish: This brush-on varnish is developed specifically for alcohol inks. It needs one even coat of varnish using a brush. Because it's a brush-on varnish, a brush might sometimes damage the inks on the surface as they can scratch or fade when touched with a brush. Moreover, it can be difficult to apply a brush-on varnish evenly without any brushstrokes showing.

Kamenskaya Alcohol Varnish: This additive can be mixed with isopropyl alcohol to use during the creation process to give your artwork better fixation, a satin finish, and extra protection against moisture. It also helps make the inks more lightfast. I personally like to still use a spray varnish after to be safe.

Resin: The most professional way to finish your alcohol ink art is using a final coat of resin. Resin gives a glossy, glass-like coat to an alcohol ink artwork and makes the colors and metallics shine extra bright. Be aware that resin is a tricky process and requires specific safety mea-sures. Resin can only be applied after sealing with varnish and does not work with all varnishes. Always test that the resin doesn't cause the ink colors bleed. To work with resin, you need to apply your alcohol ink art on a sturdy surface like ceramic or apply your synthetic paper to a wooden panel. ArtResin is a high-quality resin brand that can be used for alcohol inks.

If none of these are available to you, search for an **acrylic** varnish. There might be other varnishes suitable for alcohol inks too. Always test your varnish on a practice piece before applying it to your artwork. Learn about the step-by-step process of sealing alcohol inks with spray varnish on page 40.

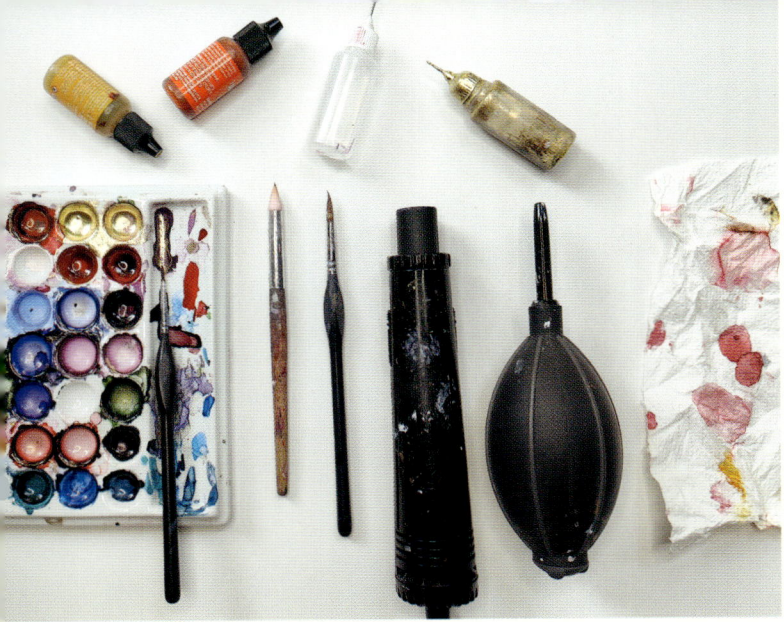

other tools and materials

Acrylic paint markers: Water-based acrylic paint markers are highly opaque and great to add white outlines and details to flowers. Not all brands provide as much coverage; therefore, I recommend using POSCA markers for alcohol inks.

Gold paint markers: Gold paint markers are used to outline and to add detail. I suggest having a range of fine point (0.8 mm) to medium and broad (1 to 2 mm). I recommend edding, DecoColor, and Sakura brands.

Silicone tip tool: I prefer to use a silicone tip tool over a brush because the silicone tip will not soak in any of the inks. This makes it a very versatile tool to manipulate the inks without affecting them. Silicone tip tools can be found for painting as well as for clay sculpting and manicuring.

Palette: A paint palette is useful to apply small amounts of inks in the process, to add ink to your surface, or to add small details using a brush. A ceramic or porcelain palette with small wells is best for alcohol inks as it can be cleaned more easily and will not stain. Ranger Ink also offers a plastic palette, the Tim Holtz Alcohol Ink Palette, designed specifically for alcohol inks.

Parchment paper: I love to use parchment paper as protection for my table and also to directly apply and mix small amounts of inks on when I'm creating flowers.

Paper towels: Paper towels easily lift parts of your inks from your surface and correct mistakes.

Cotton swabs: A cotton swab can be used to add details to an alcohol ink painting and to lift ink more precisely.

Painter's tape: This is useful for making sure the synthetic paper is unable to move around and for achieving clean white edges to your paper. Press down firmly to ensure it adheres well.

Masking fluid: Masking fluid can be used to intentionally leave parts of the synthetic paper white. Applying the liquid in a specific shape (e.g., flower petals) and letting it dry will prevent inks from adhering to the paper in that area. After applying and drying the inks, the masking fluid can be removed to reveal the white background underneath. I recommend using Winsor & Newton Art Masking Fluid for watercolor.

Relief paint and 3D liners: Relief paint or 3D liners come in small tubes with a precise nozzle to apply small, elevated lines that provide a 3D effect on an artwork. For example, they can be used to highlight the outer edges of a petal with beautiful, raised lines. I recommend using relief paint from Amsterdam All Acrylics or Pebeo, or 3D liners from Sennelier.

Gel medium: Gel medium can be used to glue synthetic paper together, for example when using a collage technique.

Decoupage glue: This is specially formulated glue used for decoupage projects where materials are layered with glue to create texture. I recommend the Mod Podge brand.

safety supplies & tips

When working with alcohol inks and isopropyl alcohol, it's very important to protect yourself as the alcohol in inks and isopropyl alcohol can release fumes and are highly flammable. Please note that you won't always see me wearing protective gear for the sake of the images in this book, but I do use safety precautions when creating my art and you should too.

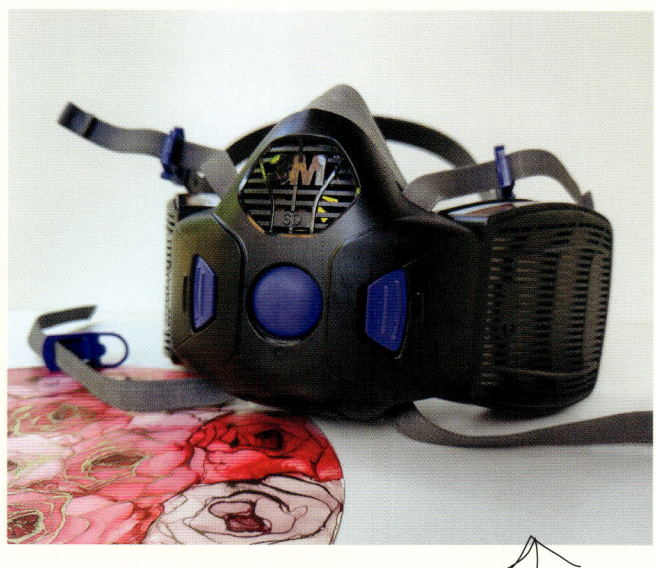

Protect your lungs. Wear a respirator for safety!

1. **Work in a well-ventilated room.** Make sure you work in a well-ventilated room so fresh air can come in, such as via an open window, or if possible, work outside. An air purifier can help filter the air.

2. **Wear protective gear.** When working with inks for long periods, consider wearing a **respirator**. A 3M 6000 mask with 3M 6055 filters for fumes is suitable to work with alcohol inks and isopropyl alcohol. Wear **safety goggles** to protect your eyes and **nitrile gloves** to protect your hands from staining from the inks.

3. **Keep your inks away from heat sources.** Because inks are highly flammable, keep them away from open flames or other devices that could cause sparks.

4. **Protect others.** Work alone and don't let your family members (including pets) breathe in the fumes.

5. **Protect your workspace.** Alcohol ink stains can be difficult to remove from your table, so make sure you protect it with a glass mixed media mat, parchment paper, or anything else that the inks cannot leak through.

shopping list

- Alcohol inks in various transparent colors such as yellow, orange, red, purple, lilac, pink, green, and gold metallic ink (see Alcohol Ink Brands on page 12 and each flower project for specifics)
- 91% or 99% isopropyl alcohol
- Synthetic paper
- Glazed ceramic tile for practicing (optional)

- Manipulation tool (ink air blower and heat tool)
- Set of miniature round synthetic brushes, 000 to 4.0 mm, plus a fan brush
- Palette or parchment paper
- Paper towels
- Varnish for protecting work (optional)
- Safety supplies (nitril gloves, protective glasses, and respirator)

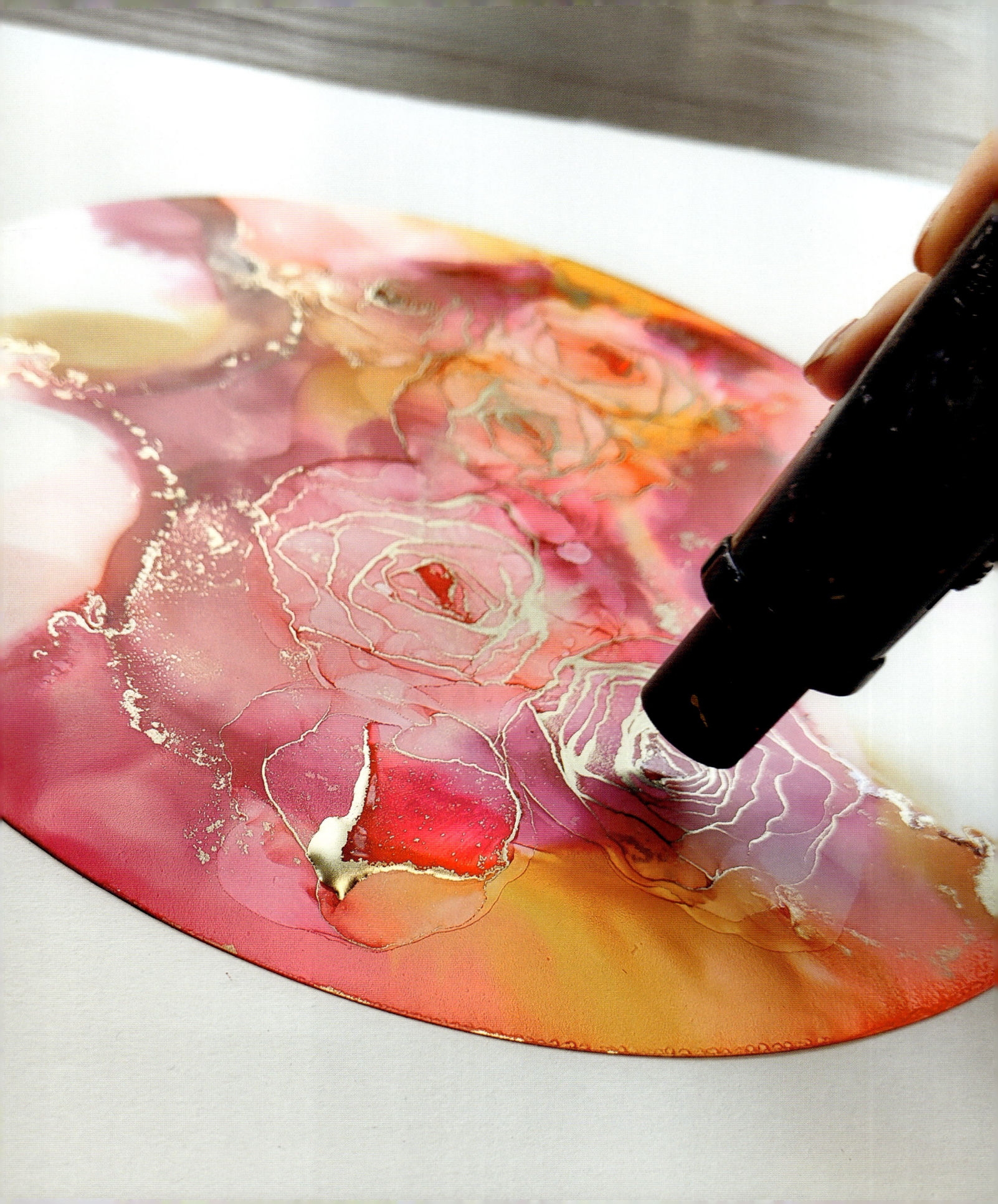

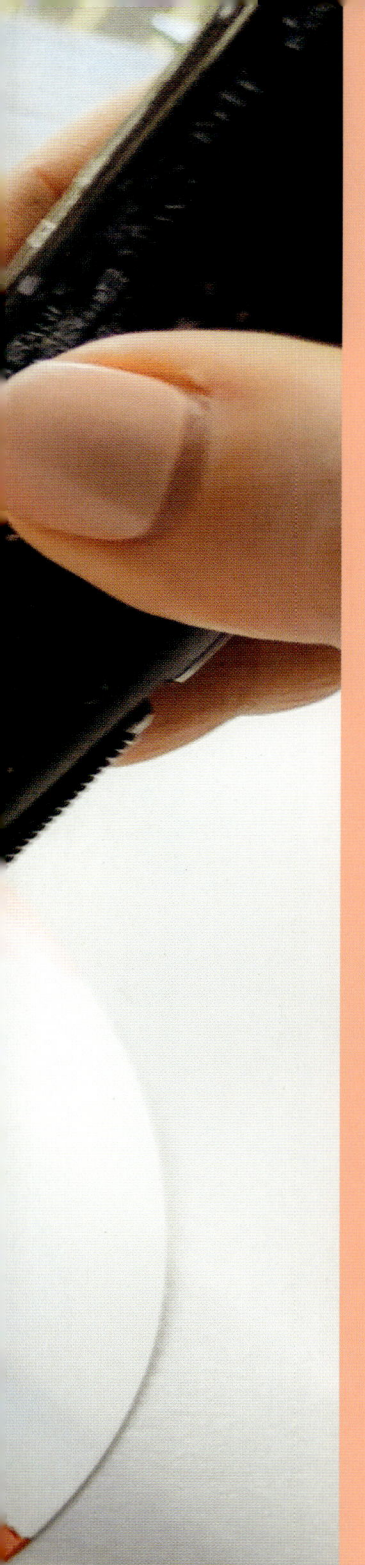

how to work with alcohol inks

This chapter covers everything you need to know about how to work with alcohol inks: from choosing the perfect color palettes to sealing your final piece. You'll find practical tips on using different manipulation tools, working with alcohol inks, and creating stunning floral compositions that draw the viewer in. The warm-up exercises will help you get comfortable with the tools and materials from the previous chapter so you'll be ready to dive into the Flower Projects with confidence!

choosing a color palette

Choosing a color palette is a highly personal choice. You can choose colors based on traditional color theory and the classic color wheel or take a more intuitive approach by experimenting with different ink combinations to discover unique and unexpected palettes. Personally, I love the process of testing colors to see how they interact and blend in surprising ways. Since this book focuses on floral art, many of the palettes in the next section are also inspired by the color palettes found in nature. Explore different methods and see which approach helps you create color combinations that resonate with you!

Color Palettes Inspired by the Color Wheel

While alcohol inks don't follow a standardized color system like acrylics or watercolors, the color wheel (2.1) is still a great source of inspiration for creating beautiful palettes. Because of the fluid nature of alcohol inks, colors naturally blend and merge, making harmonious color combinations easier to work with than high-contrast pairings. While contrasts can still be used, they require more control to avoid muddy tones.

THE COLOR WHEEL

There are several ways to build a color palette with alcohol inks using the color wheel as a guide. The color wheel is made up of primary, secondary, and tertiary colors. Across from any color is its complementary color and next to any color is its analogous color. The color wheel can be separated into warm and cool colors.

Primary colors: The color wheel is built around three primary colors: red, yellow, and blue.
Secondary colors: The primary colors mix into the secondary colors: orange, green, and purple.
Tertiary colors: Further blending creates tertiary colors, such as red orange, blue green, and yellow green.

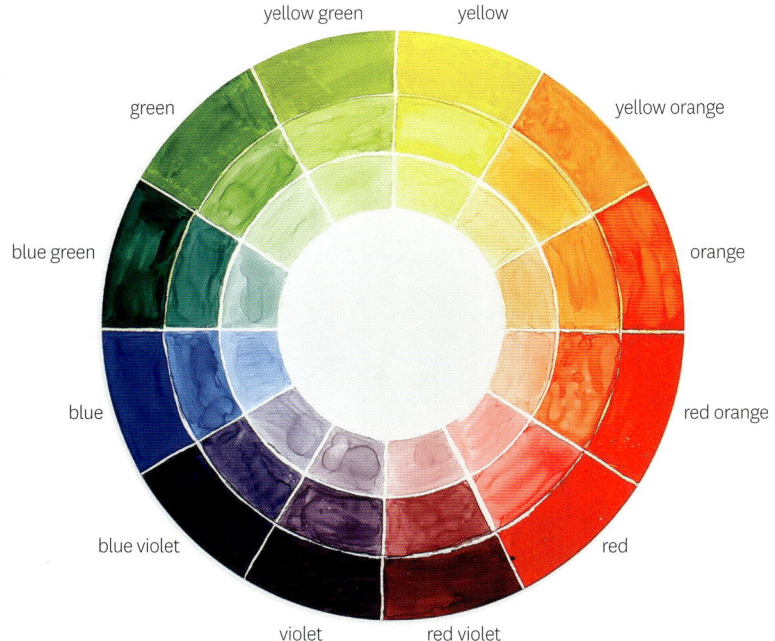

This color wheel was created with alcohol inks, from full saturation to progressively thinned with isopropyl alcohol for lighter tones.

2.1 Color wheel

ANALOGOUS COLOR PALETTE

These are colors that are adjacent to each other on the wheel, such as red, red violet, and violet as shown below (2.2). These colors easily blend and create a harmonious color palette together. It's the safest choice when working with alcohol inks.

COMPLEMENTARY COLOR PALETTE

Complementary colors are opposite colors on the wheel, such as blue and orange or red and green (2.3). In nature, you will often see complementary colors together, like bright red poppies with green stems and leaves. With alcohol inks, these create strong contrast but can turn muddy if mixed.

MONOCHROMATIC PALETTE

A monochromatic palette involves variations of a single color, such as different shades of red (2.4). You can create beautiful variations of one ink color by simply diluting the ink with isopropyl alcohol. For example, diluting red ink with isopropyl alcohol will turn it into pink.

WARM OR COOL COLOR PALETTE

The color wheel can be separated into warm and cool colors. The warm colors (2.5) are on the right of the color wheel: yellow, orange, and red shades, and the cool col-ors (2.6) are on the left: blue, green, and violet shades. By combining colors on the right, you can create a warm color palette, or you can combine colors on the left for a cool color palette.

MIXING COLORS

Alcohol inks can be mixed to achieve new colors (2.7):

Isopropyl alcohol: When mixing alcohol ink with isopropyl alcohol, colors will lose saturation the more isopropyl alcohol is added. This will sometimes produce additional undertones.

White ink: Mixing alcohol ink with a white ink will create pastel colors with a matte finish, but it will make the ink more opaque and thick.

Black ink: Mixing inks with black ink will create darker shades, but black inks tend to produce undertones of blue, purple, and pink.

Color wheel: If you are familiar with mixing colors using the color wheel to achieve a specific color (e.g., red and blue makes purple), you can do this with alcohol inks, but keep in mind that these may not always perfectly match the color system.

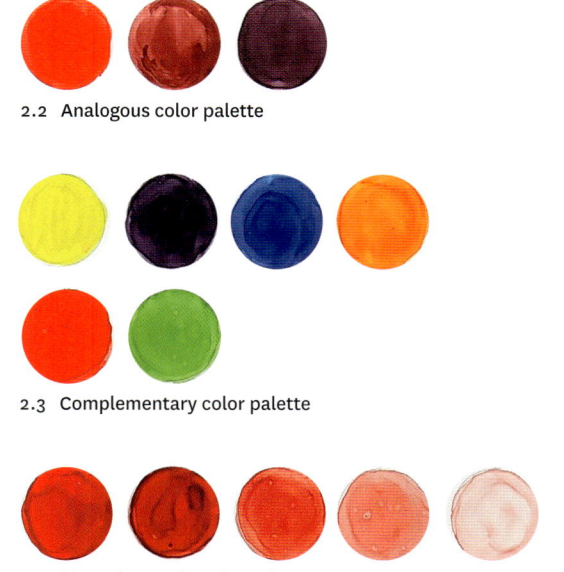

2.2 Analogous color palette

2.3 Complementary color palette

2.4 Monochromatic color palette

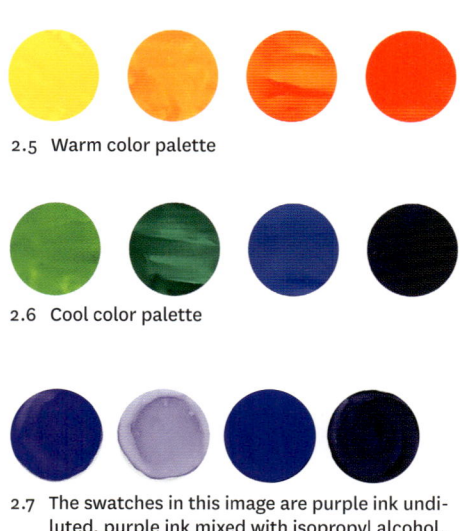

2.5 Warm color palette

2.6 Cool color palette

2.7 The swatches in this image are purple ink undi-luted, purple ink mixed with isopropyl alcohol, purple ink mixed with white ink, and purple ink mixed with black ink.

Color Palettes Inspired by Nature

Since this book focuses on floral art, nature is a great source of inspiration for your color palette! Go outside, take pictures of flowers, and take inspiration from the colors or use Pinterest images of flowers for color inspiration. Look into your alcohol ink collection for similar colors. Swatches can be useful to combine several colors to get an idea of how well they fit together. Of course, that doesn't mean you always need to create floral art with color palettes true to nature. Art allows us to create our own imaginary florals in our own imaginary colors!

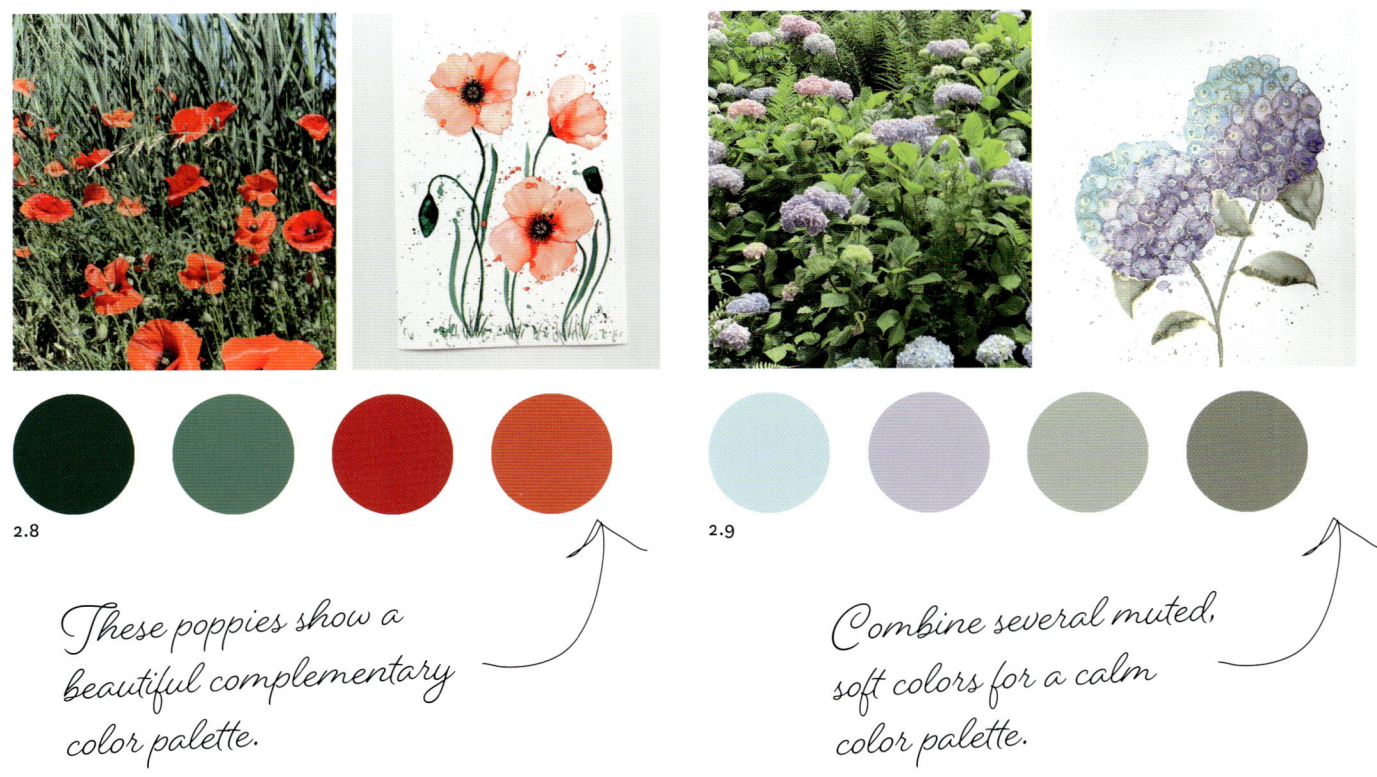

2.8

2.9

These poppies show a beautiful complementary color palette.

Combine several muted, soft colors for a calm color palette.

COMPLEMENTARY COLOR PALETTE

These bright red poppies against the greens stems and leaves show a beautiful complementary color palette that I matched for the poppy artwork (2.8). In the artwork, the inks are applied separately rather than mixed, preserving their bold contrast without creating muddy tones.

CALM COLOR PALETTE

These soft pastel-colored hydrangea flowers with bright green foliage provide a calming, cool color palette (2.9). I used the soft pastel blue and purple for the hydrangea flowers and chose a more muted soft green for an overall calm color palette.

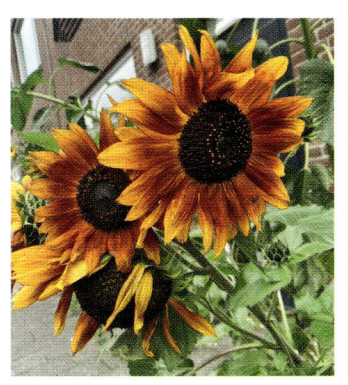
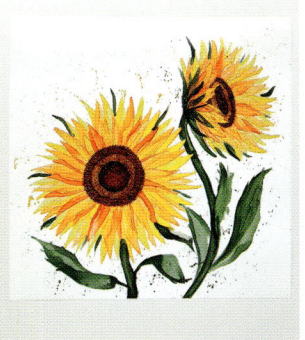

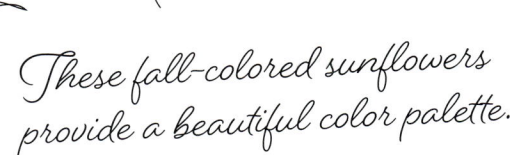

These fall-colored sunflowers provide a beautiful color palette.

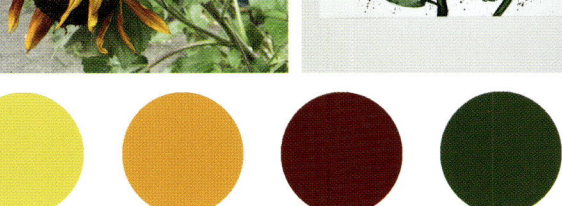

2.10

ANALOGOUS COLOR PALETTE

These saturated fall-colored sunflowers provide an analogous color palette blending warm yellows, oranges, and browns with some cooler green colors (2.10). The artwork reflects this color palette, using variations of these hues to enhance depth and warmth.

tip

Create swatches of your ink collection

Swatches are a great way to document all the colors in your collection and are useful to select a color palette by combining different swatches to get a feel for which colors work together. You can also use swatches to match a specific color palette from a photo. After matching the swatches, I often create a blend of the colors on some scrap paper by mixing each color with a few drops of isopropyl alcohol and softly blending them into each other to see whether they also match when mixed.

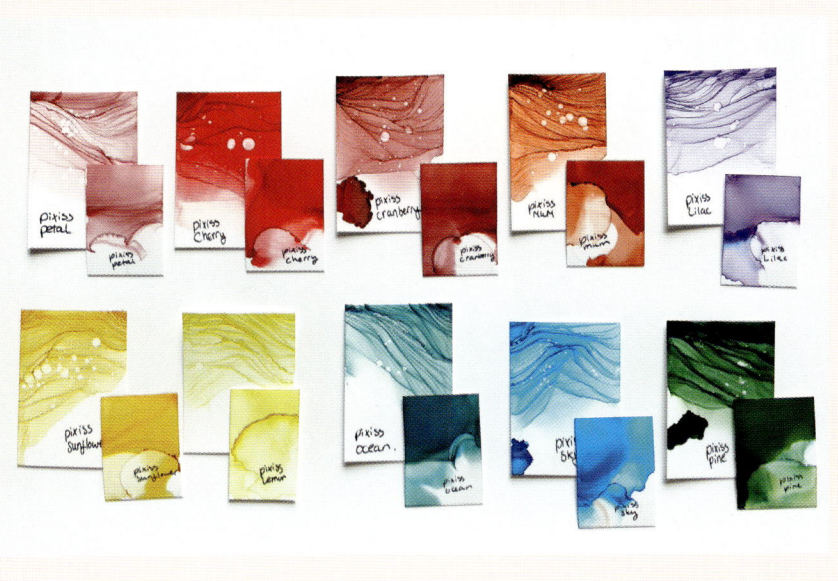

My Favorite Color Palettes

The beauty of alcohol inks is that they will naturally create different shades of one ink color when they are diluted with isopropyl alcohol. The undertones they sometimes produce adds to the charm of alcohol ink art, as you can achieve unexpected, but beautiful effects! The key is to embrace the unexpected and experiment with different ink combinations to discover unique palettes. Here are some of my personal favorite color palettes to work with.

HARMONIOUS COLOR PALETTE

Using two analogous colors (close to each other on the color wheel) in a light, bright, and dark shade creates a beautiful color palette (2.11) as the different shades give contrast and depth to the artwork. This is my favorite color palette to use for alcohol inks! In this example, I used red and pink as analogous colors and chose a light muted pink, a bright pink, and a dark (burgundy) red that produce a beautiful romantic color palette.

SOFT PASTEL COLOR PALETTE

I love combining several soft, pastel shades together for a spring-like feel to the floral artworks. In this example (2.12), I'm using a soft green, combined with light pink.

BOLD COLOR PALETTE

Combining several highly saturated vibrant colors close to each other on the color wheel will instantly bring a lot of life to an artwork. In this example (2.13), I'm using very saturated deep pink as well as orange combined with bright pink for a summerlike exotic color palette.

MONOCHROMATIC PALETTE

I love to combine several inks of one color to achieve a monochromatic palette. Adding isopropyl alcohol even adds more shades to the colors creating a beautiful palette, especially when blended with gold alcohol ink, like in this pink example (2.14).

A POP OF CONTRAST

If you used an analogous color palette and you feel it misses that extra touch, it can be a great idea to add a small touch of a complementary color to give it a pop of contrast and add interest to the artwork. In this example, I used pink and purple tones, combined with a touch of bright yellow for contrast (2.15).

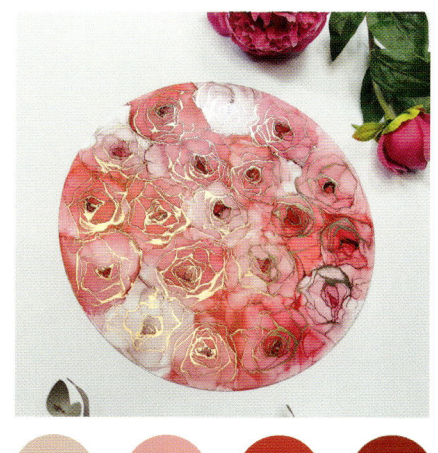

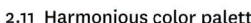

2.11 Harmonious color palette

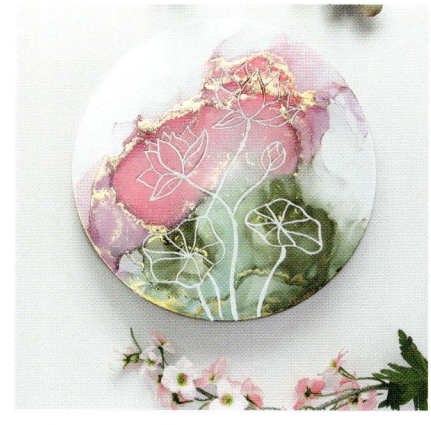

2.12 Soft pastel color palette

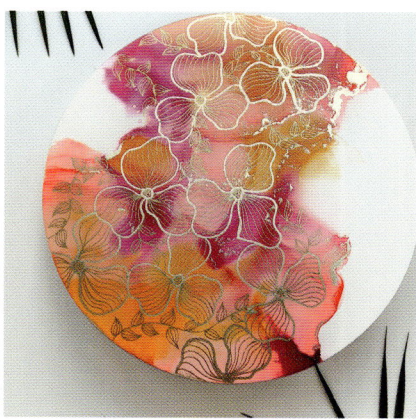

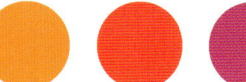

2.13 Bold color palette

Finding surprising color palettes

This is one of my favorite ways to experiment with new and surprising color palettes.

1. **Prepare:** Cut a few small pieces of synthetic paper (e.g., four 4 × 6-inch [10 × 15 cm] pieces) and gather your alcohol inks.

2. **Choose Colors:** Create four different color palettes by selecting three to four inks per combination. Experiment with a mix of analogous, complementary, cool, and warm colors or pick them randomly for a surprise! Don't overthink it.

3. **Test the Palette:** Cover the paper with isopropyl alcohol, add your inks, and use an ink air blower to spread them. Let colors touch rather than fully mix, especially with contrasting shades.

4. **Evaluate:** Repeat for all combinations and see what works. Not every mix will be perfect, but you'll likely find unexpected color pairings that inspire your next piece!

Here are color samples I created using this exercise.

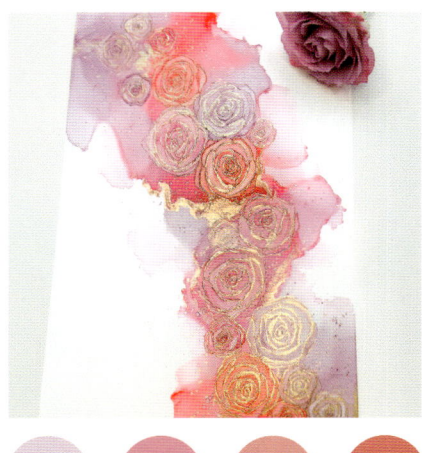

2.14 Monochromatic color palette

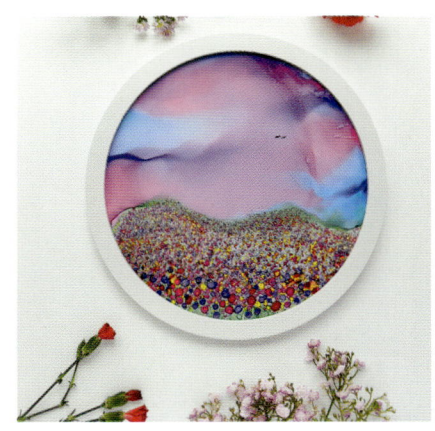
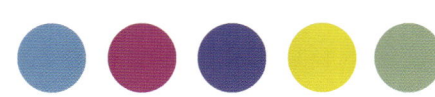

2.15 A pop of contrast color palette

working with an ink air blower

The ink air blower is a very versatile tool to manipulate alcohol inks and one of the simplest methods to push the inks around a surface. An ink air blower is great for softly blending inks into each other, guiding the inks in the right direction, and for creating various delicate flower petals. It's also a great beginners' tool as it's easier to control than a heat tool.

Best Uses for an Ink Air Blower

Guiding the ink flow: An ink air blower softly squeezes out air that helps guide the flow of the alcohol and ink mixture. Using cold air with a soft air flow, it doesn't immediately dry the inks like a heat tool would. This makes it suitable for guiding the inks in the desired direction without creating ripples and strong edges. The soft air flow makes it easier to control compared to a heat tool and offers a calmer method for manipulating the inks, making it a beginner-friendly tool.

Soft blends, color transitions, and fades: By applying multiple colors next to each other, the ink air blower can softly push them into each other to create smooth color transitions. Soft fades (2.16) can be created by pushing clear isopropyl alcohol into the ink colors. In the next chapter, we'll use this to our advantage to create beautiful abstract ink backgrounds for our floral art.

Creating organic (petal) shapes: The ink air blower can be used to push the ink into natural petal shapes. Each petal will look different, making it a great tool for replicating the imperfect shapes seen in nature, which may sometimes be challenging to achieve with a brush.

How to Use an Ink Air Blower

Air pressure: How hard you squeeze the bulb of the ink air blower controls the air flow strength. Soft squeezes blend inks gently, while hard squeezes push inks away, drying them from the inside, which may create splatter effects and ripples. Generally, a moderate squeeze works well, but it depends on the desired effect.

Positioning and angle: For most techniques, it's best to hold the ink air blower at a diagonal angle to the direction where the inks should go and keep a small distance from the inks, pushing them from the side. For other techniques, hold the ink air blower at a vertical angle and push directly on the inks. We'll explore these techniques in the Flower Projects.

Working time: As the alcohol and ink mixture will start drying relatively quickly, your working time is limited. With sufficient ink flow, the ink air blower can produce smooth transitions; however, once drying starts, it can create ripples and textures.

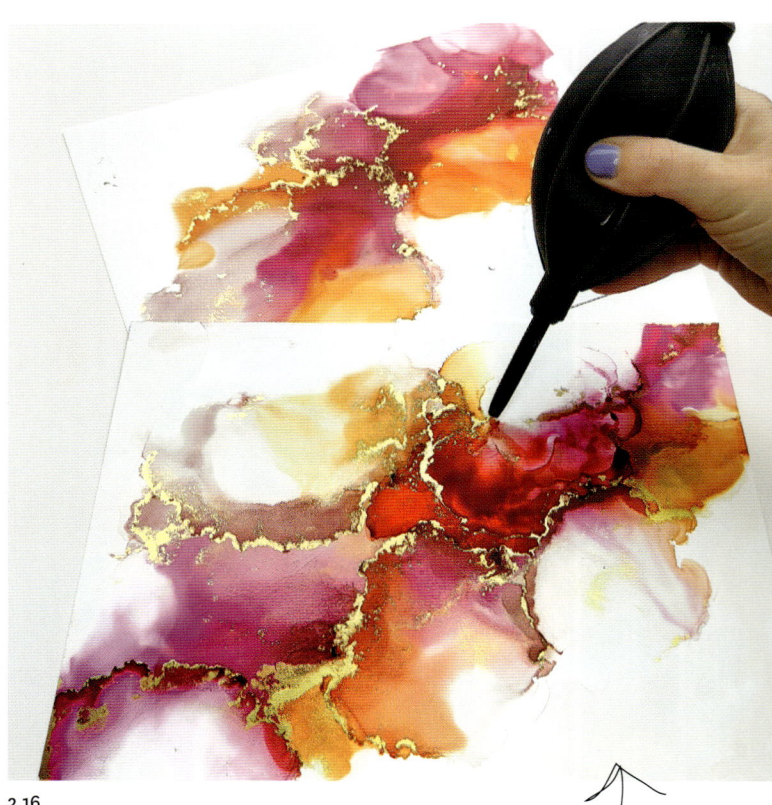

2.16

A soft fade is created by pushing clear alcohol into the colored inks.

Creating and manipulating flower shapes

The ink air blower is a great tool to create various flower petal shapes. In this warm-up, let's practice creating petal shapes to get a feel for how to use the ink air blower. We'll explore this technique further in the Flower Projects.

Materials

- Alcohol ink in one color
- 91% or 99% isopropyl alcohol in a needle tip bottle
- Synthetic paper or glazed ceramic tile
- Small brush
- Ink air blower
- Paper towels
- Safety supplies

Step 1

Clean the synthetic paper with isopropyl alcohol and a paper towel and make sure it's dry before continuing. Load your large brush with ink and paint six evenly spaced small circles on your synthetic paper (or tile). Dry them with your heat tool or wait for them to air-dry. To create the first petal, add two drops of isopropyl alcohol at the edge of one of your circles to reactivate the ink. Wait 2 to 3 seconds for the alcohol to spread, then angle your ink air blower on a diagonal to push the ink outward from the circle in the direction of the petal. Using moderate pressure, squeeze the blower briefly. After blowing out the petal, allow the ink to air-dry as it will continue to spread andchange shape naturally. Practice this twice more on the next two ink circles and experiment with the pressure.

Step 2

Follow step 1 but add three drops of alcohol in the next circle, then four drops, and then five drops. The more isopropyl alcohol, the bigger the petal shape will become. For the bigger petals, you may need to give the ink air blower two or three soft squeezes to get the desired petal shape. Experiment with this. Be careful not to overmanipulate the petals. Repeat this exercise as much as you like until you feel comfortable with the technique!

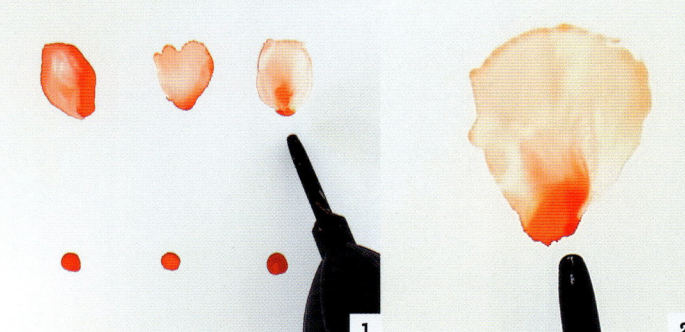

tip

Troubleshooting tips

- **Unwanted splattering:** If splattering or ink fingers appear, squeeze the ink air blower more gently and from a diagonal angle (not on top). A silicone tip tool or a brush can be used after blowing out the petals to adjust the shape if needed.
- **Unwanted ripples:** If unwanted ripples appear within the petal shape, avoid overmanipulating the inks but allow the ink to spread and change shape naturally after one or two squeezes.
- **Ink stains:** If ink stains occur or the inks behave strangely, try switching to another ink as different colors and brands may behave differently.
- **Mistakes:** If you mess up, you can simply use a paper towel with isopropyl alcohol to remove the petal shape before creating it.

Creating an abstract ink background

This exercise is great to get a feel for how to work with an ink air blower to create beautiful color blends and transitions and to add fades. This is a fast and intuitive technique, and the result will come out completely different each time. Have fun and keep an open mind. This technique will be used to create beautiful abstract backgrounds for the flowers in some of the Flower Projects.

Materials

- Alcohol ink in three colors
- Gold alcohol ink (optional)
- 91% or 99% isopropyl alcohol in a needle tip bottle
- Synthetic paper
- Ink air blower
- Paper towels
- Painter's tape
- Safety supplies

Step 1

First clean the synthetic paper with isopropyl alcohol and a paper towel and make sure it's dry before continuing. Ensure the paper is flat or tape it down with painter's tape. You'll create a background composition by layering your inks in a diagonal line over the paper. Start at the top-left corner and add a small puddle of isopropyl alcohol. Add three drops of your first color ink, one or two drops of gold alcohol ink (optional), and more drops of isopropyl alcohol to have enough ink flow. Use an ink air blower and softly squeeze it to spread the inks out.

Step 2

Repeat step 1 with your second ink color near the first wet ink puddle. Now, use your ink air blower to softly blend it into the first ink puddle (2a). Then, add a third ink color next to the other two and softly blend them together (2b).

tip

Abstract ink background technique

Need to see how to create an abstract ink background in action? Scan the QR for a video of this technique.

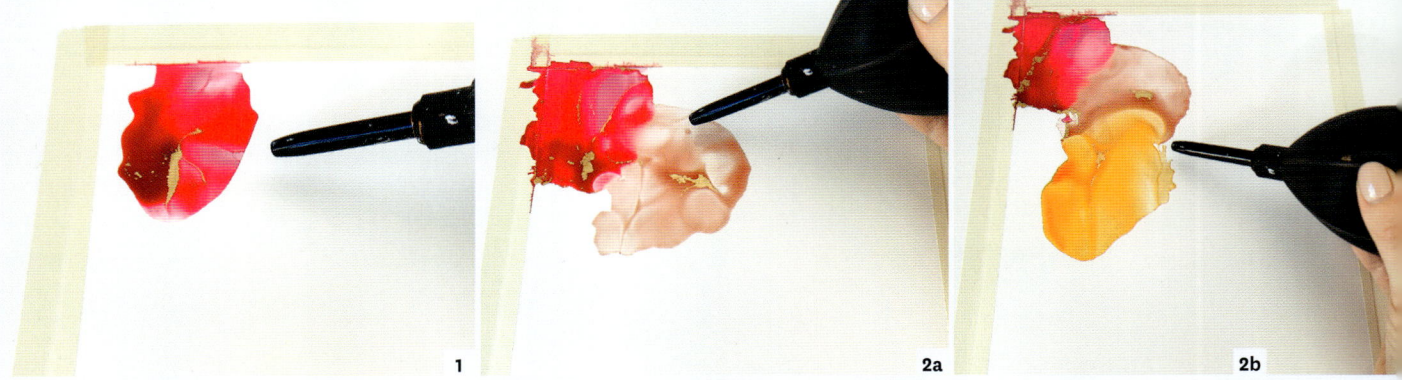

1   2a   2b

tips

Troubleshooting tips

Even with practice, ink behaves unpredictably. Here's how to fix common issues:

- **Ink pools:** If too much ink builds up in one area, use a paper towel to remove some of the ink. Make sure the surface is level and the paper is flat.

- **Unwanted splattering:** Squeeze the ink air blower more gently for a softer air flow to avoid splattering. Work more from the sides at a diagonal angle instead of directly on top of the inks.

- **Unwanted edges/ripples:** Avoid manipulating the inks while they are already drying. Try using more isopropyl alcohol and create enough ink flow.

- **Muddy colors:** Avoid overmixing colors. Either try manipulating the inks less or choose a more analogous color palette next time. Use a paper towel to lift the muddy color and add more of another color instead.

Step 3

Next add isopropyl alcohol to the edges of the ink puddles and push it inward to create a faded effect on the outside.

Step 4

Keep repeating steps 1 to 3. Vary the ink colors and layer them next to each other in a diagonal line (4a) until you reach the bottom-right corner (4b). By now, the top may have already started drying. If it's still wet, you can further manipulate the inks with more fades but try and keep it to a minimum and let the inks do their thing.

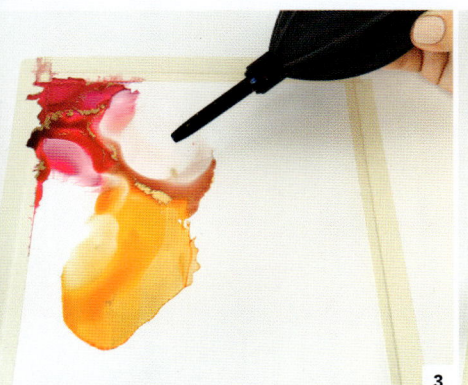
3

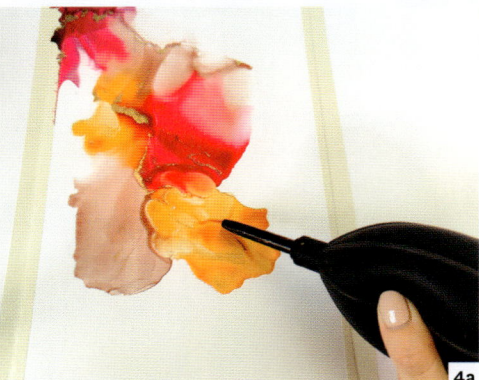
4a

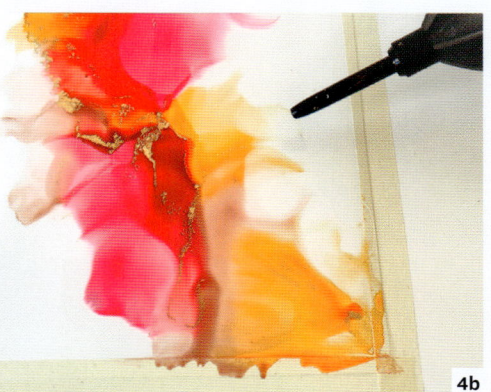
4b

working with a heat tool

The heat tool is one of the most popular tools to manipulate alcohol inks because of the beautiful textures that can be created in the drying process, especially when making mesmerizing golden ripples. However, it's also a much more advanced tool to work with—the process is fast, and it can be difficult to control the ink. While it may take some practice to master, the results are stunning and well worth the effort.

Best Uses for a Heat Tool

Guiding the ink flow: While the heat tool is not as gentle as an ink air blower, it can still be used to guide the ink flow. By controlling the direction and intensity of the heat tool, you can influence the movement of the inks, creating wispy and fluid petal shapes.

Ripples and textures: The heat tool is great for achieving ripples and textures. By directing the heat from different angles, you can create unique patterns and textures in the drying process. The heat will cause the outer edges of the ink to dry, and the wet ink will create patterns when it hits the dry ink.

Golden edges: Adding gold alcohol ink to the process will cause the golden particles to stick to the dry edges, creating the much sought-after golden edges (2.17). You'll learn this technique in the Bouquet of Roses project (page 79).

Speeding up the drying process: The heat tool is also a very practical tool as it helps to speed up the drying process. In the Flower Projects, we will combine the heat tool with ink air blower techniques to dry inks between steps.

How to Use a Heat Tool

Heat setting: For tools with multiple heat settings, a medium heat setting is best for most techniques. However, the heat level may differ by tool. The air should not be so hot that it warps the synthetic paper. Check my recommendations for heat tools in Tools and Materials on page 16.

Distance: The distance at which to keep the heat tool depends on the strength of the heat tool. The lower the wattage, the less strong the air pressure is and the closer it can be held to the surface. Generally, keep the heat tool 1 to 4 inches (3 to 10 cm) away from the wet ink.

Angle: For most techniques, it's best to hold the heat tool at a vertical angle to the synthetic paper, not diagonally, and position the heat tool next to the wet ink, not on top.

Speed of movement: The heat tool needs to be moved slowly so you see the outer edges of the ink drying. The faster you move, the smaller the ripples will be and vice versa. However, if you move too fast, there's no time for the inks to dry and no ripples will appear.

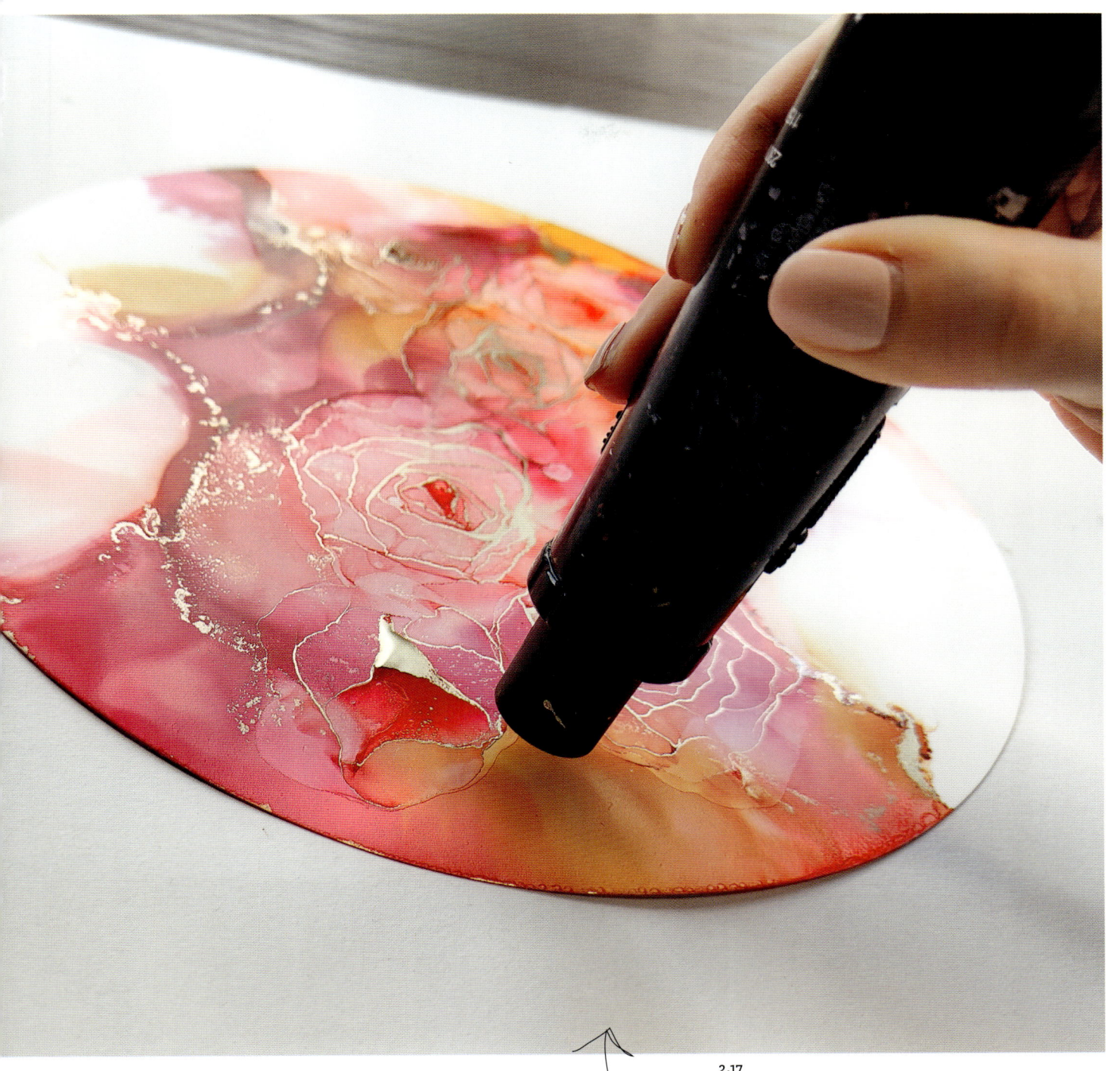

2.17

Roses are created by moving the heat tool in a round motion.

Creating fade-out effects

In this exercise, you'll practice using the heat tool to create fades, working from the inside to the outside. This exercise helps to get a feel for the strength of your heat tool and how to handle it. Remember, it takes time and practice to learn and control the inks!

Materials

- Alcohol ink in three colors
- 91% or 99% isopropyl alcohol in a needle tip bottle
- Synthetic paper or glazed ceramic tile
- Small brush
- Heat tool
- Paper towels
- Safety supplies (page 19)

Step 1

Clean the synthetic paper with isopropyl alcohol and a paper towel and make sure it's dry before continuing. Load your small brush with ink and paint small circles about ½ inch (13 mm) wide on your synthetic paper (or tile) in a diagonal line from the top left to bottom right. Create an even distribution of the three colors across the diagonal line. It's best to use saturated colors for this technique. Leave some negative space in the corners. Dry the circles with your heat tool or wait for them to air-dry.

Step 2

To create a fade-out effect, apply a line of isopropyl alcohol from the middle of the circle outward to the right side of the paper in a diagonal line. Use five to ten drops of isopropyl alcohol. Give it 2 to 3 seconds to reactivate the ink and then use the heat tool to blow the ink from the base outward (2a). Keep the heat tool 3 to 4 inches (8 to 10 cm) away from the paper.

Move slowly to dry the wet ink from the diagonal line outward and keep enough distance to dry it slowly. Keep going until all the ink has dried and use a paper towel to lift the excess ink at the edge of the paper if needed (2b). Don't worry about messy edges, these can be trimmed off later. Repeat this process on the left side of the paper.

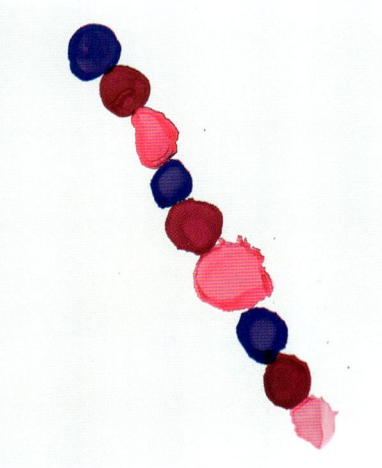

1

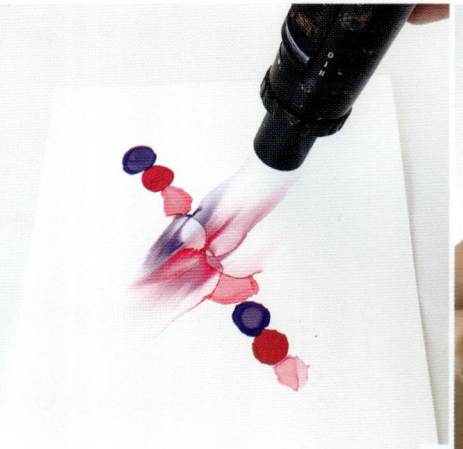

2a

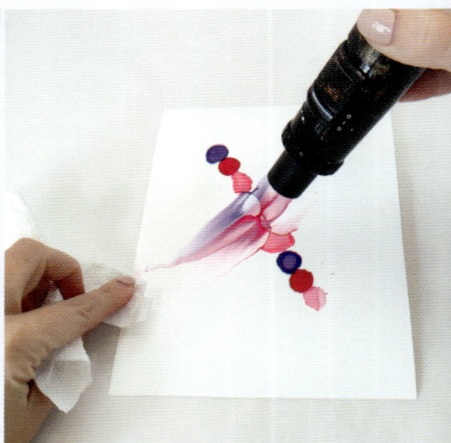

2b

Heat tool troubleshooting tips

Here's how to fix common issues:

- **Excess ink:** If you end up with too much isopropyl alcohol and ink, use a paper towel to absorb some of it.

- **Paper warping:** If your paper is warping and does not flatten out, your heat tool is too hot. Check my recommendations for heat tools in Tools and Materials on page 16.

- **Unwanted splattering:** Try moving further away from the wet ink to avoid splattering. Work more from the sides of the wet inks and at a vertical angle instead of directly on top of the inks.

- **No ripples are appearing:** Add more isopropyl alcohol if it's drying too quickly and move slower with your heat tool.

- **Sticky gold alcohol ink:** Gold alcohol ink that immediately sinks to the bottom or sticks to the paper may need the help of a brush to loosen it up and more isopropyl alcohol to make it float.

- **Muddy colors:** Avoid overmixing colors. Either try manipulating the inks less or choose a more analogous color palette. Use a paper towel to remove the muddy color.

- **Ink stains:** If ink stains occur or the inks behave strangely, try switching to another ink as different colors and brands may behave differently. Some synthetic papers like YUPO can cause stains.

Heat tool fade out technique

Need to see the fade out technique in action? Scan the QR for a video of this technique.

Step 3

Repeat step 2 to create multiple fades on both sides of the diagonal line and add fades toward the top and bottom of the paper to fill the entire paper. Repeat step 1 to add more ink in the process if needed. Experiment with the tips from "How to Use a Heat Tool" on page 32 and the troubleshooting tips above to refine your control over the heat tool. Experiment with different amounts of isopropyl alcohol to reactivate larger or smaller areas. You can also move over a fade a second time. After finishing, trim off any messy edges if needed and use a brush to add some ink splatters as a finishing touch.

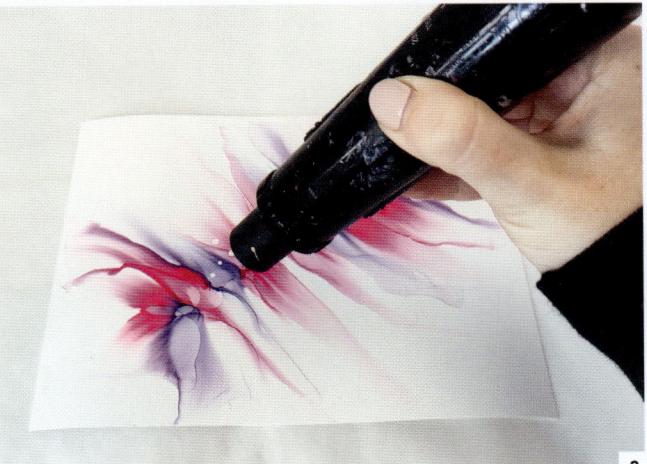

3

Creating golden ripples

In this exercise, you'll use a heat tool to create ripples, color blends, and golden edges. Each time, you'll reactivate the inks and experiment with different ways to control the inks. Keep in mind we're just practicing here, so focus more on how the inks react and behave than on the result.

Materials

- Alcohol ink in three colors
- Gold alcohol ink and isopropyl alcohol mix in a needle tip bottle at a 50/50 ratio
- 91% or 99% isopropyl alcohol in a needle tip bottle
- Synthetic paper or glazed ceramic tile
- Small brush
- Heat tool
- Paper towels
- Painter's tape
- Safety supplies

Step 1

Clean the synthetic paper with isopropyl alcohol and a paper towel and make sure it's dry before proceeding. Ensure the paper is flat or secure it with painter's tape. Begin by applying ink colors to the background. Add one drop of ink at a time and use your brush to distribute the ink and dry it with a heat tool before changing colors. Cover the background with the three ink colors. Don't worry about its appearance; it won't be visible in the end.

Step 2

Add five to ten drops of isopropyl alcohol and use the heat tool from different directions around the wet ink to observe how the inks react (2a). Alter between moving the tool left to right, up and down, or in circular motions around the wet ink to get a feel for how the ink flows. When you slowly move the heat tool from different directions around the wet ink, the outer edges will start drying. When the wet ink hits the dry ink, ripples will start to appear (2a). Keep going until all the isopropyl alcohol has dried (2b). Use a paper towel to lift excess ink building up toward the center or edges of the paper. Experiment with the tips from "How to Use the Heat Tool" on page 32 to refine your control over the heat tool. Repeat this process a few times to explore different effects. Also try layering isopropyl alcohol over multiple colors at once and watch how beautifully they blend. Experiment with different amounts of isopropyl alcohol and vary the shapes in which you apply it, reactivating both large and small areas.

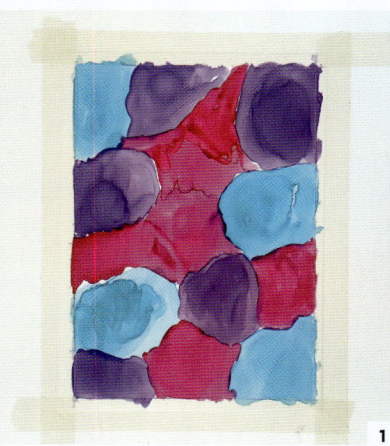
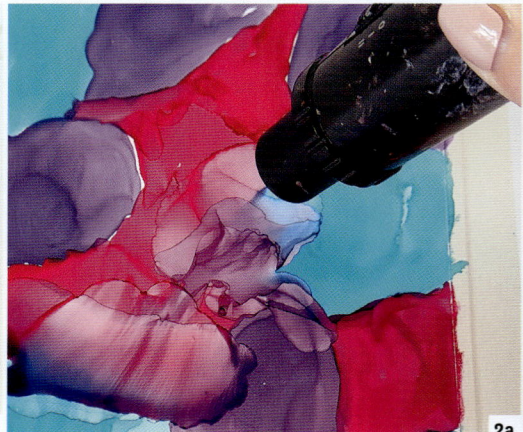
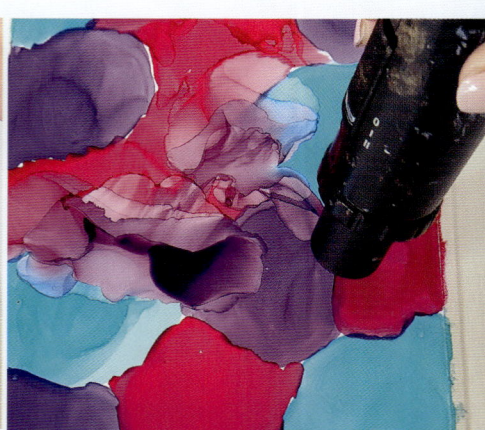

1   2a   2b

Step 3

To create golden edges, prepare a gold alcohol ink mix by adding isopropyl alcohol and gold alcohol ink at a 50/50 ratio in a needle tip bottle (or cup with pipette). Repeat the process from step 2, but add one or two drops of the gold alcohol ink mix after applying the isopropyl alcohol. The gold alcohol ink will start sticking to the dried edges, creating beautiful golden ripples. Repeat this a couple of times.

Step 4

Keep repeating steps 2 and 3 until you have reactivated all the inks on the background. Note you can also reactivate the inks for a third or fourth time. If you're having trouble, review the "Heat Tool Troubleshooting Tips" on page 35 for more tips on common issues.

on page 35

tip

Heat tool ripples technique

Need to see the ripples technique in action? Scan the QR for a video of this technique.

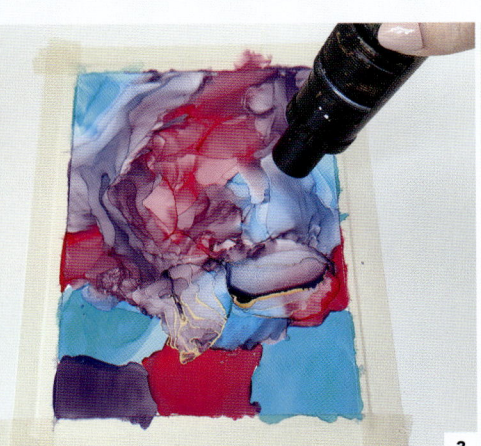

3

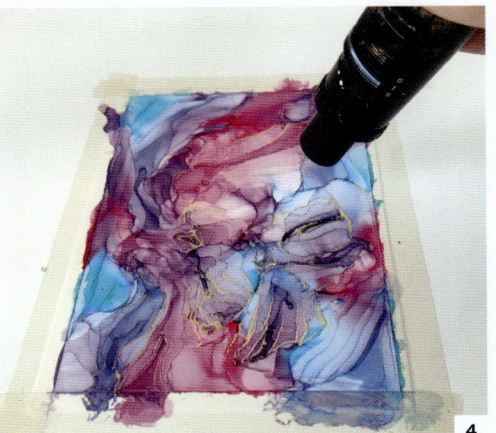

4

working with a brush and other tools

While heat tools and ink air blowers are popular for manipulating alcohol inks, a brush is great for various techniques, such as applying the inks, adding finer details to flowers, lifting the ink, adding texture, and my favorite: splattering! Besides brushes, silicone tip tools and a palette knife are great to have in your tool kit (2.18).

Best Uses for Brushes

Applying inks: Brushes are very practical to use to apply inks directly on the surface in a controlled way. In the Flower Projects, we'll often use this to create the base of the flower and then reactivate the inks to create the flower petals using a heat tool or ink air blower.

Adding details: A brush is great to use for finer details in the center of the flower like the stamens (2.19), as well as for the branches, stems, and leaves.

Guide the ink flow: Pointed edges or specific shapes are difficult to achieve with an ink air blower and heat tool. A brush can be used within this process to guide the inks in the desired shape before or after using a manipulation tool.

Lift ink: You can lighten ink with a brush loaded with just isopropyl alcohol by moving it back and forth over an ink background. This can be used not only to create textures but also to draw in details, such as flower petals.

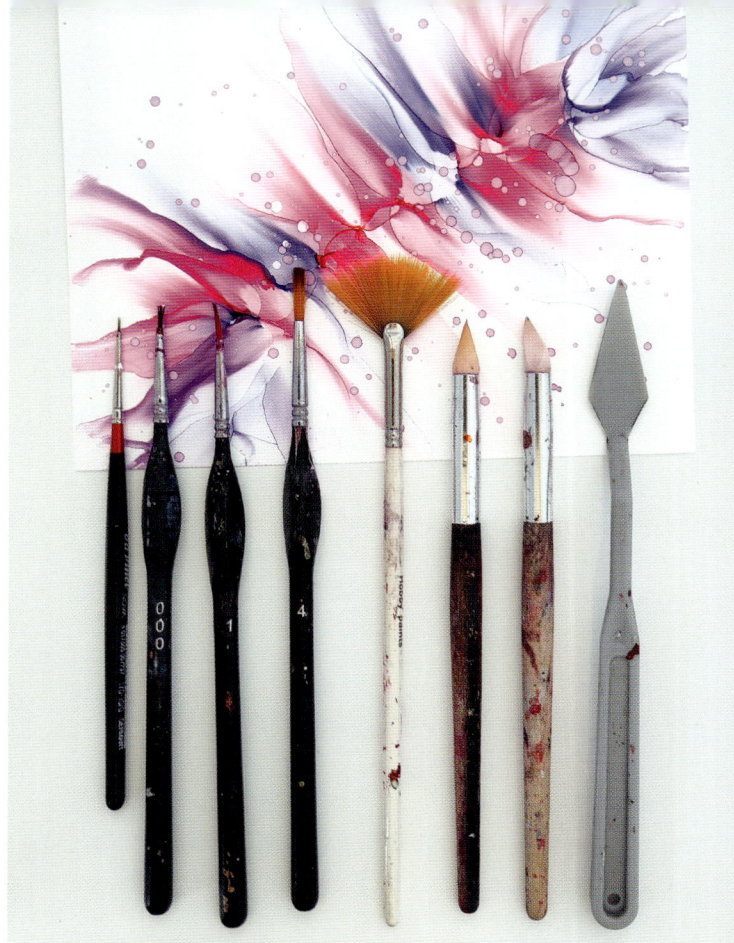

2.18 FROM LEFT TO RIGHT: Miniature synthetic brush, round synthetic brushes (size 00, 1 mm, 4 mm), fan brush, silicone tip tools, and plastic palette knife

Dabbing and splattering: Dabbing the brush on an ink background with isopropyl alcohol or ink is a great way to add texture or to create abstract florals. Splattering ink by tapping a brush against your finger or another brush or tool is my favorite way to finish an artwork (2.20) and give a playful look to the Flower Projects. Splattering can also be used to create the illusion of a field or tree with flowers, as we'll explore in the Flower Projects.

How to Use a Brush

While using a brush might seem quite straightforward, alcohol ink reacts differently than watercolors or acrylics. Here are some general guidelines:

Use only a little ink or isopropyl alcohol: Alcohol inks spread out quickly after applying them, so it's best to use just a little alcohol or ink to paint smaller details like

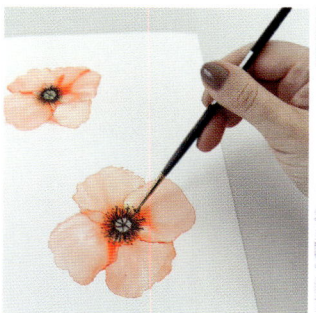

2.19 Adding details

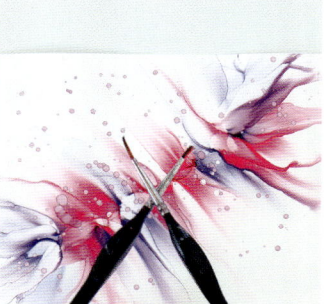

2.20 Splattering inks

a stem or stamen. It's useful to dab the brush on a paper towel before applying it to the surface.

Choose the right brush size: The fine brushes (000 and 00) are best for adding small details like stamens (the thinner, the better); the smaller brushes (0 to 2.0 mm) are good for adding stems, dabbing, and for splattering; the larger brushes (3.0 and 4.0 mm) are good for filling in areas and making bold strokes, such as creating bigger leaves; and fan brushes are used for spreading inks across the paper.

Control the speed: Move quickly to prevent the inks from spreading out too much; move slowly to intentionally create bigger strokes.

Cleaning: Clean your brushes with isopropyl alcohol. When working on a piece, I often use one brush per color and clean them after use.

Working with Other Tools

Silicone tip tool: A silicone tip tool does not spread or lift ink like a brush will, which makes it a very practical tool to manipulate the inks. It's great for guiding movement and can also be used to add finer details and textures without absorbing or spreading the ink too much.

Palette knife: A plastic palette knife is fun to use for creating all kinds of floral shapes like flower petals and leaves as well as creating finer details and texture in a flower center.

Silicone wedges or old credit cards: Instead of a palette knife, you can use a catalyst wedge (a shaped, flexible silicone tool), silicone spatula used for baking (dedicated solely for non-food use), a wide silicone brush used for resin or nail art, or even an old credit card to create floral shapes and textures.

Using brushes to lift, splatter, and add details

To get comfortable with brushes and alcohol inks, try these exercises on an ink background (perhaps from the previous warm-up exercise):

1. **Lifting Ink:** Apply isopropyl alcohol with a clean brush and lift ink by dabbing or moving back and forth.
2. **Splattering:** Flick clear alcohol or ink from a brush to create organic droplets and textures. Make sure you protect the surroundings!
3. **Add details:** Use a fine brush to create delicate lines and shapes.

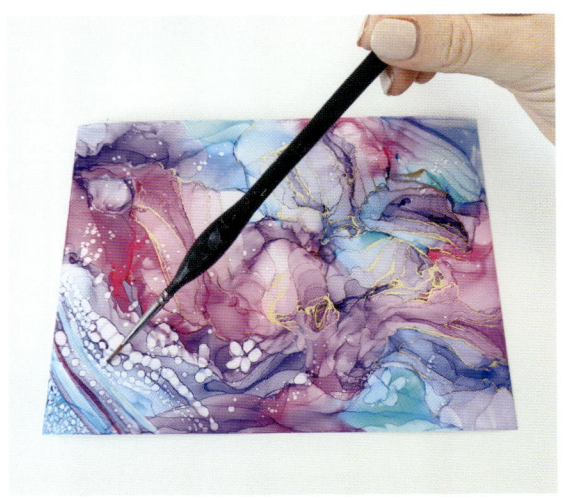

sealing alcohol inks

Alcohol inks need sealing with varnish to fix the inks to the surface and protect them from color fading and moisture. Because alcohol inks are not lightfast, the artwork also needs to be UV protected.

How to Seal Alcohol Inks

While there are multiple ways to seal alcohol inks, the most common and suitable one is using a spray varnish. Follow the steps below but always read the instructions of the specific varnish you're using and test it before use.

Materials

- Artwork to varnish
- Varnish spray suitable for alcohol ink (See recommendations in Tools and Materials on page 17)
- UV-protective spray (if varnish does not have UV protection)
- Cardboard box to cover the artwork
- Table protection such as large sheets of paper or plastic sheets
- Water mister to reduce dust in the room

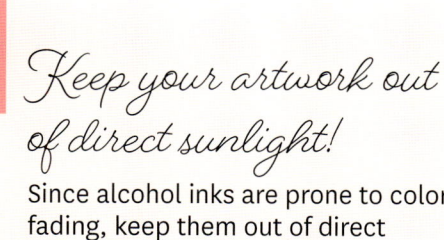

tip

Keep your artwork out of direct sunlight!

Since alcohol inks are prone to color fading, keep them out of direct sunlight to protect the colors in your artwork.

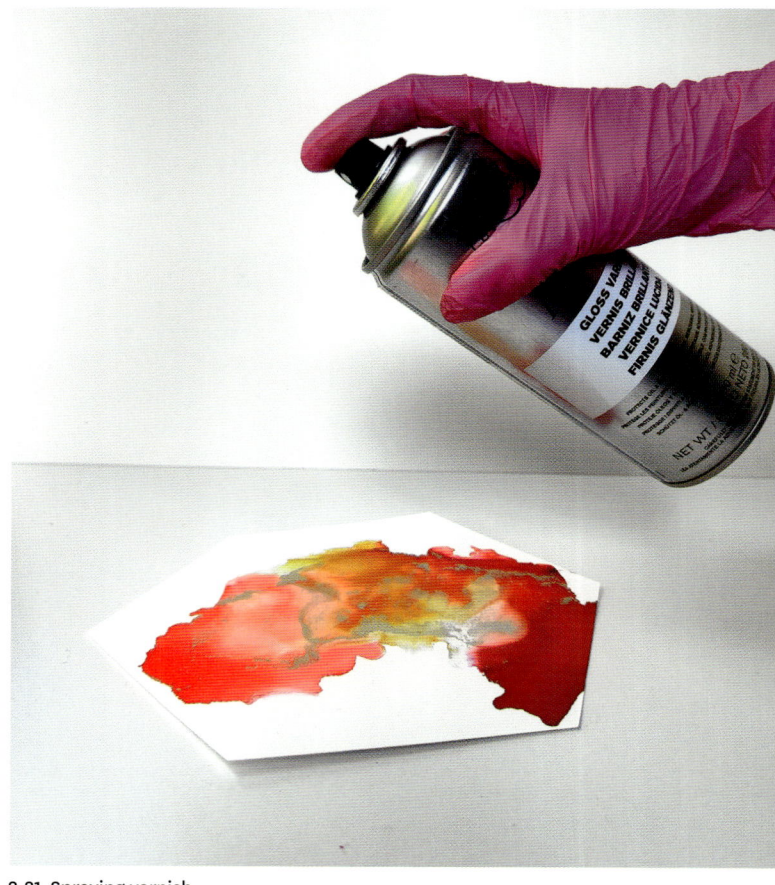

2.21 Spraying varnish

Step 1: Prepare the artwork.

Wait at least 24 hours after finishing your alcohol ink artwork to ensure the inks are fully dry before varnishing.

Step 2: Prepare the workspace.

For best results, apply varnish in a room with moderate temperature and humidity (50 to 80°F [10 to 27°C]). Work in a room that can be ventilated (with an open window or mechanical ventilation). Protect the table with large paper or plastic sheets. Find a cardboard box large enough to cover the artwork. Remove dust from the artwork using a microfiber cloth, fan brush, or canned air. Place the artwork inside the box, ensuring there's enough space to spray evenly. After varnishing, you will close the box lids to protect the artwork from dust. Alternatively, you can cut off the top flaps of the box, place the artwork on the table, and use the box as a protective cover.

Step 3: Reduce dust in the room.

To reduce dust in the room (besides cleaning), use a water mister and spray a fine water mist in the room so dust particles floating around the air will drop to the floor (make sure your artworks are protected by the cardboard box). Allow the room to settle for a few minutes.

Step 4: Shake the varnish.

Meanwhile, thoroughly shake your varnish spray for 2 to 3 minutes. Check the instructions on your varnish for exact timing.

Step 5: Start spraying.

Open the lids of the box or remove it. Hold the varnish spray about 12 inches (30 cm) away from the artwork. Spray lightly from left to right in one continuous motion from a diagonal angle at your artwork (2.21). Move from the top to the bottom of the artwork. Thin, even layers provide the best coverage, so only go over your artwork once. Close the lids or cover the artwork with the box to prevent dust particles ending up in the box.

Step 6: Ventilate the room properly.

I only ventilate the room after spraying, to prevent the air stream bringing in new dust particles. After varnishing, make sure to ventilate the room properly by opening one or multiple windows and if you have one, use an air purifier.

Step 7: Wait for the varnish to dry.

Refer to the instructions on your varnish for drying time. Most sprays take about 2 hours to dry before you can apply a new layer, but some may take up to 24 hours.

Test your varnish first

Before varnishing, test the varnish spray on a small, test piece with similar ink colors to check how it reacts with the inks. Some varnishes can cause alcohol inks to reactivate or change colors slightly; sometimes this is also due to the specific ink color or brand. For example, bright yellow, orange, and red tones tend to react with varnishes. Also note that varnishes can react differently when using another surface than synthetic paper.

Step 8: Repeat the process.

To achieve full coverage, repeat steps 3 to 7 two more times to get three even, thin coats of varnish. If you have a separate UV-protective spray, you'll also need to repeat steps 3 to 7 to apply one to three coats of the UV-protective spray. How many coats depends on the type of UV spray you're using. Some need several layers, while others only need one final coat.

Step 9: Await final drying time.

Let the varnish dry fully according to the varnish's instructions. Typically, this is around 24 hours for a complete cure. After that, you can frame your artwork or safely store it by protecting it with glassine paper and storing it in a safe space. Avoid stacking artworks directly on top of each other without any protection as they may stick to each other.

tips for working with alcohol inks

Alcohol inks are an exciting and challenging medium to work with because of their unique fluid and unpredictable nature. Their spontaneity is what creates stunning effects, but it also requires a different approach than more controlled art forms. While the Flower Projects in this book will include many specific tips, these general guidelines will help you embrace the process, develop your technique, and fully enjoy your creative journey with alcohol inks.

1. Less is more. The most practical tip when it comes to working with alcohol inks is *less ink is more*! When starting out, it can be addictive to keep adding new inks to the surface every time, but the more ink on the surface, the more it becomes a sticky mud. Instead, use more isopropyl alcohol in the process to reactivate the inks on the surface and create ink flow (2.22). Start with less ink, and you can always add more in the process if needed. Alcohol inks are very saturated, and while those bottles seem small, they can last for a very long time. Usually, just one or two drops of ink are enough to create an entire flower (e.g., a rose).

2. Go with the ink flow. Inks have a mind of their own and can never be perfectly controlled, making them a great way to let go of perfectionism. The key is to embrace their unpredictability rather than force control. In the beginning, it's tempting to move too fast or overwork the inks with a heat tool or blower. Instead, slow down and observe how they react. This will help you understand their behavior and manipulate them more intentionally. While techniques vary, some of the most beautiful effects happen when you let the inks flow naturally, creating unexpected patterns and textures. Guiding the inks, rather than controlling them, leads to the best results.

3. Materials and conditions matter. Many factors influence how alcohol inks behave, including the type of ink, tools, and surface used. For example, always clean the surface of your synthetic paper with isopropyl alcohol and a paper towel to prevent any dust from sullying the alcohol inks. While materials matter, the effects are usually still achievable, but it just may take slight adjustments. If an ink stains and won't reactivate, try a different ink. If a heat tool is too strong, move it further away, and if it warps the paper, switch to a lower- heat option. Throughout this book, you'll find additional tips to troubleshoot these challenges. Environmental conditions also play a role. Humidity and temperature can affect ink flow: High humidity may cause moisture buildup and tiny water droplets as the ink dries. This is especially problematic when using heat tool techniques. If you experience this, using air conditioning or a dehumidifier can help.

4. Practice and experiment! The key to learning any new medium is practice and experimentation, and this is especially true for alcohol inks. Since they can't be perfectly controlled, every result will be different, and your flowers will look different from mine. This can sometimes feel frustrating (trust me, I've been there), but give yourself time to practice and don't aim for perfection. Experimentation is also essential for developing your own way of working with alcohol inks. It helps you understand how the inks flow and react to different manipulation tools and which techniques feel natural to you. The more you play with your inks, the better you'll understand their behavior, and over time, manipulating them will become more intuitive. As you progress through the Flower Projects in this book, notice which techniques

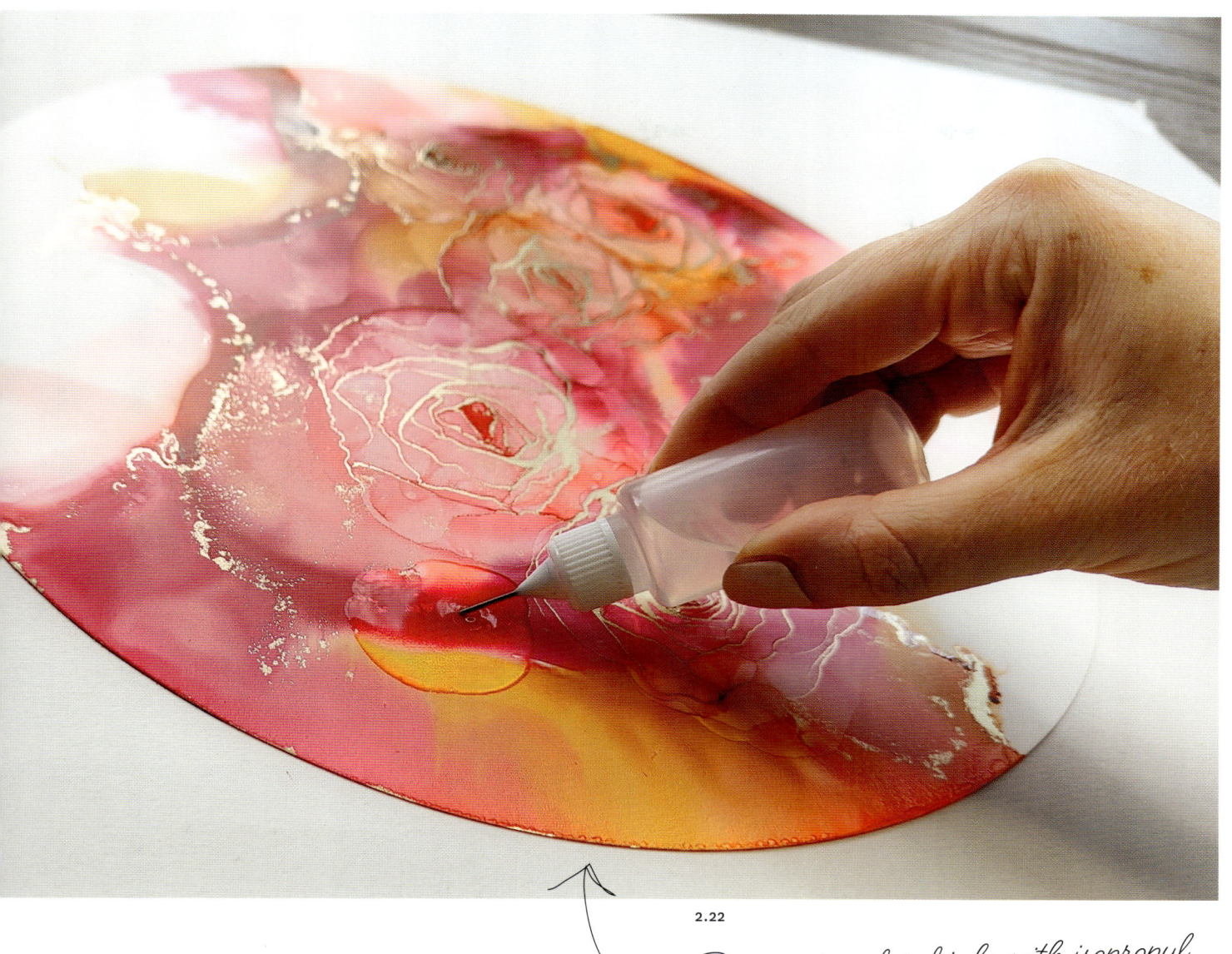

2.22

Reactivating dried inks with isopropyl alcohol gives beautiful effects.

you're drawn to and make them your own. The more you practice, the more comfortable and confident you'll become.

5. Dare to fail and enjoy the process. The fear of making mistakes or failing can restrict the creative process. However, failing helps in understanding what works and what doesn't and is just as much part of the process. The failed pieces are often the ones we learn most from, so dare to fail! The good news is, while they are unpredictable, alcohol inks are also very forgiving. Since they can be reactivated, you can keep working over an area as many times as needed. On nonstaining synthetic paper, you can even wipe it clean and start fresh. The real challenge is knowing when to stop! As Bob Ross famously said, "We don't make mistakes, just happy little accidents." So, embrace the unpredictability, trust the process, and most importantly, enjoy creating.

tips for floral compositions

Composition is the way different elements are arranged in an artwork. For floral art, this refers to arranging all the floral elements in an aesthetically pleasing way that guides the viewers' eyes and creates interest. Just like a florist arranges a bouquet of flowers, we arrange the flowers in our artwork. These five guidelines will help to create a beautiful floral composition that draws the viewer in. Once you've reviewed them, sketch different flower compositions or look at floral art you enjoy and see if you can apply the guidelines and recognize which ones have been used.

1. Create one focal point. Start with one central flower close to the center of the artwork. This serves as the focal point in the artwork, and the other floral elements can be arranged around the central flower. This is usually the attention-grabbing flower, with smaller flowers supporting the composition around it. Because of its fluidity, alcohol ink flowers often turn out larger than expected, so although I'll sometimes sketch a composition beforehand, I often prefer starting with just one central flower. Then, I can envision how other elements can be added to create a visually appealing arrangement of flowers. Creating a single flower composition can also be very powerful as there is a clear focal point, usually the center of the flower.

2. Asymmetry and the rule of odd numbers. When building a composition, asymmetry can add interest to an artwork and creates more visual balance than symmetry. As humans, we often have the tendency to create a symmetrical arrangement. However, asymmetrical arrangements are much closer to nature. You can create asymmetry by combining different, unequal floral elements on both sides of the composition. An easy way to do this is using the rule of odd numbers. Through creating a composition of three or five flowers, it's easier to achieve asymmetry than using an equal number. Furthermore, composing the flowers at different heights and varying the shape and size (see next guideline) creates a more natural, asymmetric look.

3. Vary shapes and sizes. Creating a mix of different shapes and sizes keeps an artwork visually interesting. For a floral composition, this can be done by creating a mix of flowers: front- and side-facing flowers, buds, and varying the shape and size of the flower petals. Adding stems and leaves in different shapes and sizes will also create variation in an artwork. Even when using similar flowers (e.g., roses), varying the size can make the composition more interesting. Moreover,

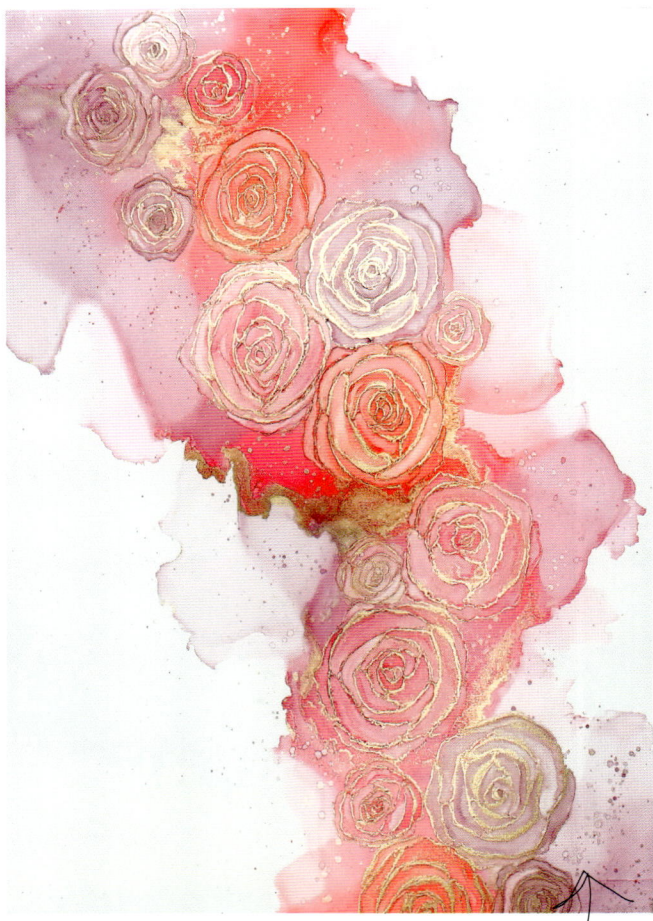

2.23

I arranged roses along a diagonal line to create visual interest and guide the viewer's eyes.

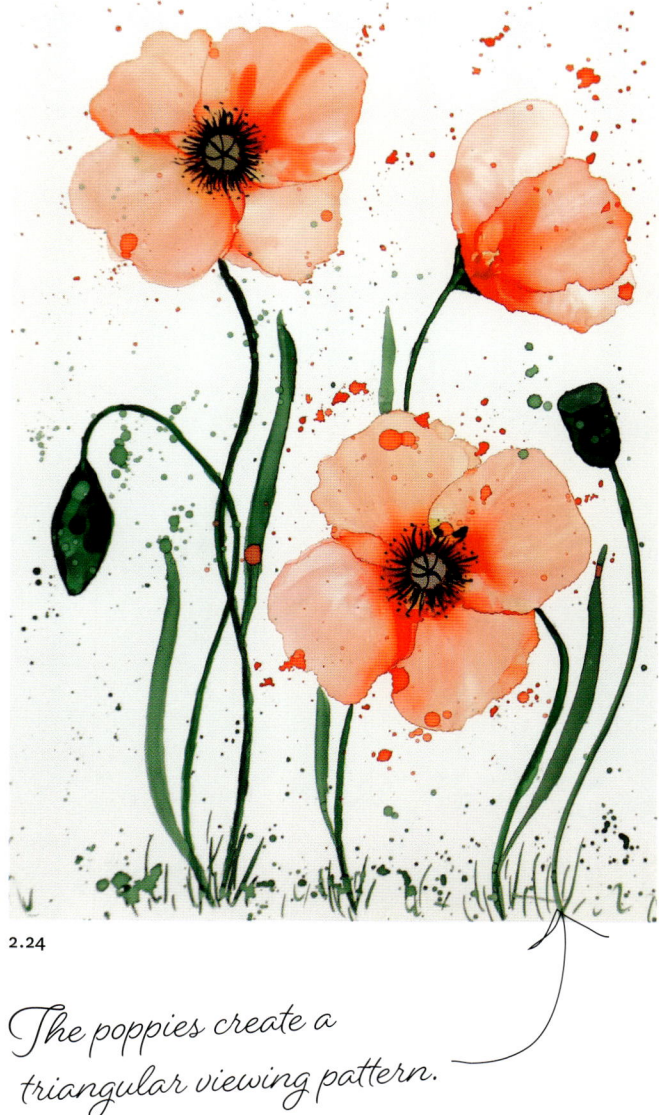

2.24

The poppies create a triangular viewing pattern.

4. Guide the viewers' eyes. To draw the viewer in, it helps to arrange the flowers in such a way that their eyes are guided through the entire arrangement of flowers. All the guidelines outlined above can be used to create a viewing pattern. The focal point in the artwork is what attracts attention and is the starting point. Then, by arranging the flowers around that, creating asymmetrical balance and varying the shapes and sizes, the viewers' eyes will be guided through the artwork. Two common viewing patterns are a triangle shape, which works well for a composition of three flowers, or a zigzag, S-shape, or diagonal pattern. The poppies create a triangle viewing pattern through the painting (following the three red poppies, 2.24), while the roses create a diagonal viewing pattern by the way the roses are arranged along a diagonal line (2.23).

5. Use negative space. Negative space refers to the unoccupied areas around and between the flowers. This can be the white of the paper or a soft background as we sometimes also use in the Flower Projects. A composition is attractive when it is visually balanced, and negative space can help with that. If there's very little negative space, the artwork may be overcrowded with different flowers competing for attention, making it difficult to guide the viewers' eyes. On the other hand, a floral composition with too much negative space can create underwhelm, creating an unbalanced composition that feels unfinished and will only lead the viewers' eyes through a small part of the artwork. The trick is to find a midway to create a visually balanced composition that leaves enough space between the flowers to calmly guide the viewers' eyes.

arranging the flowers in a certain pattern can add a new shape to the artwork. For example, I like to create flowers along a diagonal line with negative space on both sides (2.23). The variation is not created through varying the shapes of the flowers, but in the way they are arranged together. This will also help in creating a viewing pattern (see next guideline).

These are guidelines, not strict rules to follow. Stay open to surprise and experimentation, as following strict rules can limit creativity. See them as puzzle pieces that can help in creating a visually attractive composition when you're stuck, or you feel your artwork is missing something.

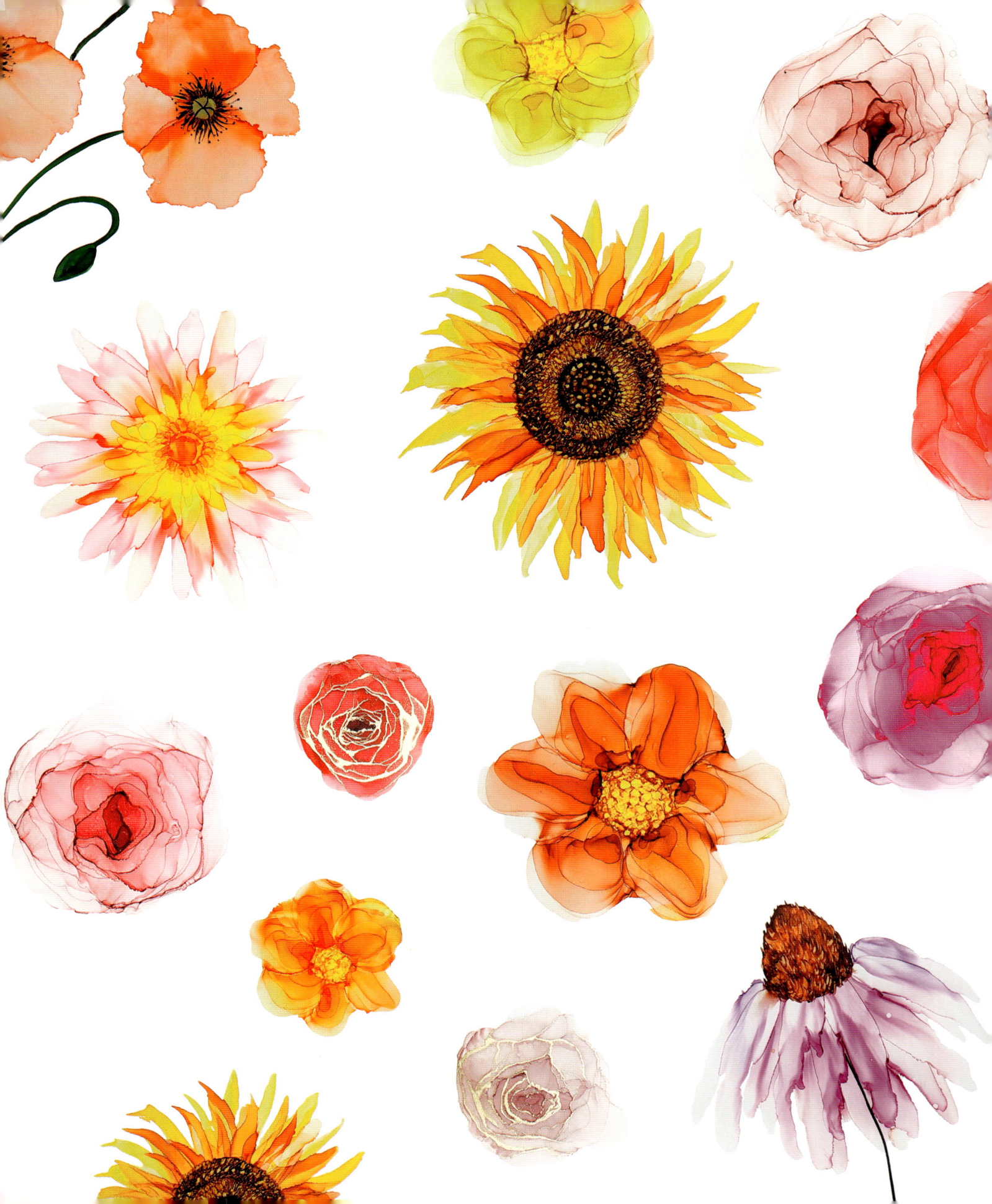

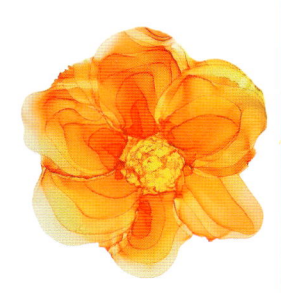

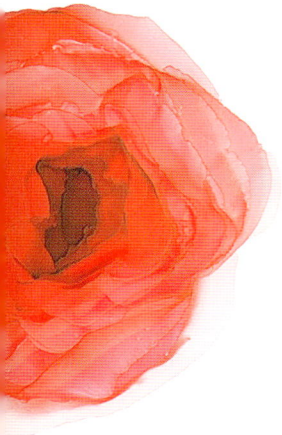

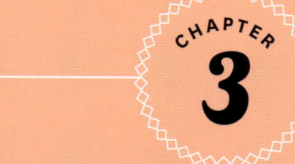

flower projects

Now that you're set up with your materials and have played around with your inks, it's time to dive into the most exciting part—creating flowers! From vivid poppies and playful lavender to bright sunflowers and classic roses, each project will introduce you to unique techniques and tools for bringing these blooms to life with alcohol inks. The difficulty levels vary throughout, so expect some pieces to take a bit more practice. But that's the beauty of alcohol ink: Each flower will be uniquely yours. Embrace the unpredictability, unleash your creativity, and most of all, enjoy the process!

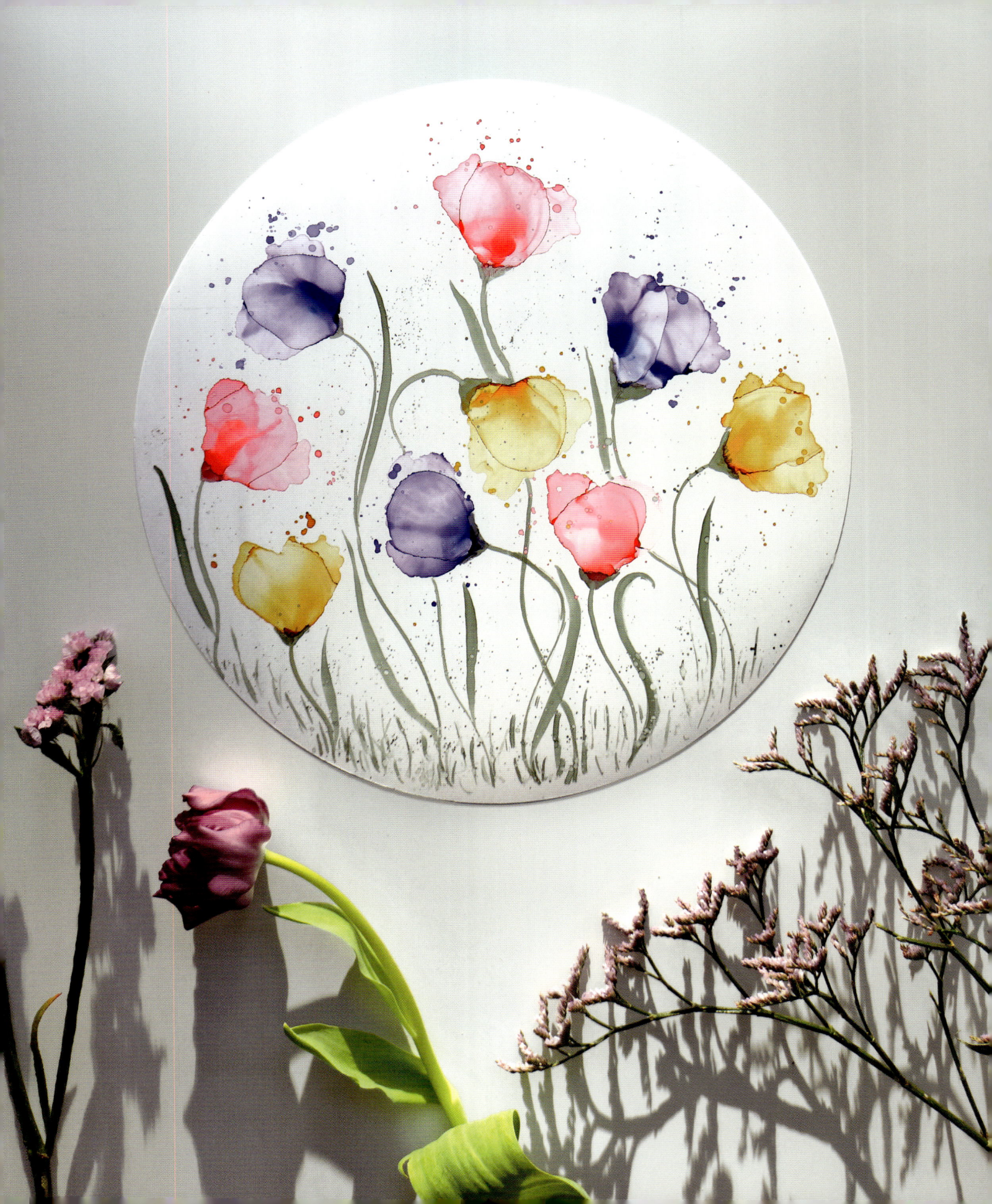

wildflowers

These whimsical wildflowers are great for beginners. Since they're imaginary, they don't need to resemble any specific flower. At first, they may just look like blobs of ink, but when we add the stems and leaves, the blobs of ink turn into flowers!

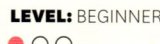

materials

- Alcohol inks in pink, purple, yellow, and green
- 91% or 99% isopropyl alcohol in a needle tip bottle
- Round synthetic paper 10 or 12 inches (25.5 to 30 cm)
- Glazed ceramic tile for practicing (optional)
- Ink air blower
- Heat tool to speed up drying process (optional)

- Set of miniature round synthetic brushes, 000 to 4.0 mm
- Silicone tip tool (optional)
- Paint palette or parchment paper
- Paper towels
- Cup with isopropyl alcohol to clean brushes (optional)
- Safety supplies

Step 1

Add a few drops of the pink, purple, and yellow ink to your paint palette or parchment paper. Use a small brush to paint small triangular shapes to form the base of the wildflower petals. Adjust the angles of the triangles to vary the direction the flowers face. Distribute the colors evenly across the surface (I created three triangular shapes of each color) and use one brush for each color (or clean with isopropyl alcohol in between). Leave enough space between flowers and from the edges to prevent overlapping. Use a heat tool to dry the ink completely before moving to the next step.

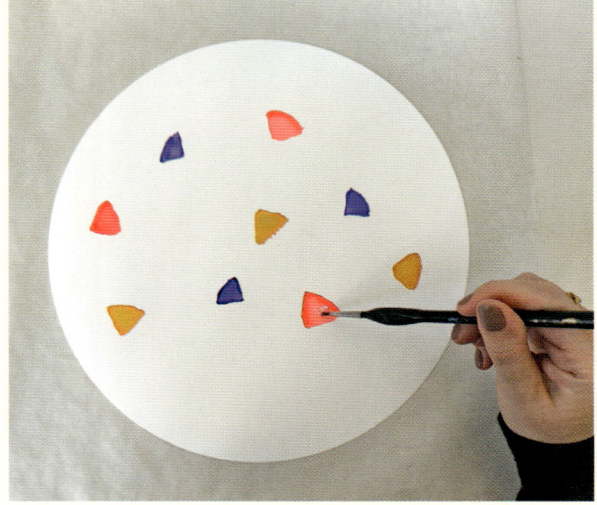

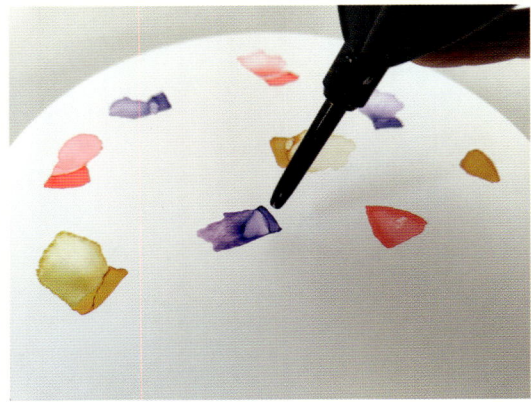

Step 2

To create the petals, add two drops of isopropyl alcohol at the edge of a triangle to reactivate the ink, starting on the upper-left side. Wait 2 to 3 seconds for the alcohol to spread, then use an ink air blower at a diagonal to push the ink outward in the direction of the petal. Experiment with the pressure to find the right strength to blow out a nice petal shape. After blowing out the petal, allow the ink to air-dry as it will continue to spread and change shape naturally.

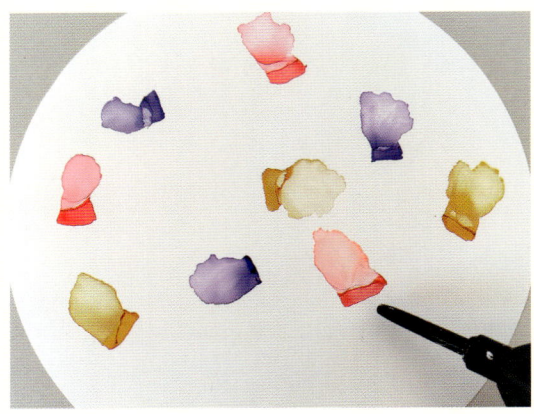

Step 3

Repeat the process for all the triangles, adding a petal to the left side of each triangle. Once all the petals are complete, allow them to dry before moving to step 4. If needed, use a heat tool to speed up the drying process.

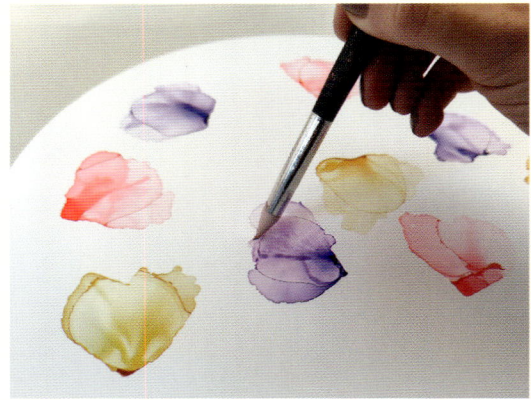

Step 4

Create a second row of petals for each flower using the same technique as in step 2, this time working on the right side of each triangle. A silicone tip tool or a brush can be used after blowing out the petals to adjust the shape if needed. Once completed, ensure all petals are fully dry before moving on to step 5.

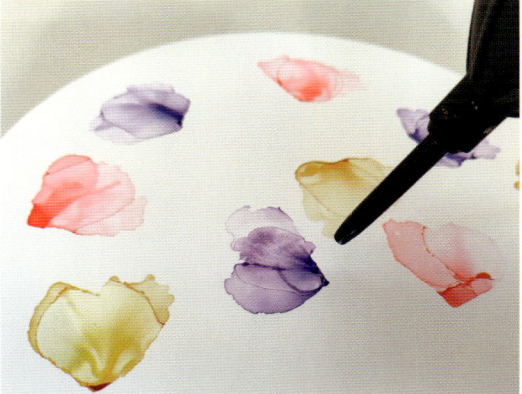

Step 5

Create a third petal in the middle of the first two petals by adding two drops of isopropyl alcohol at the base of the triangle instead of the edge. Each time the ink is reactivated, its color may lose saturation. If the color becomes too light, add a small touch of ink to the triangle with your brush, let it dry, and then create another petal. Finish all the flowers with a third petal. You can repeat this process to add more petals if desired.

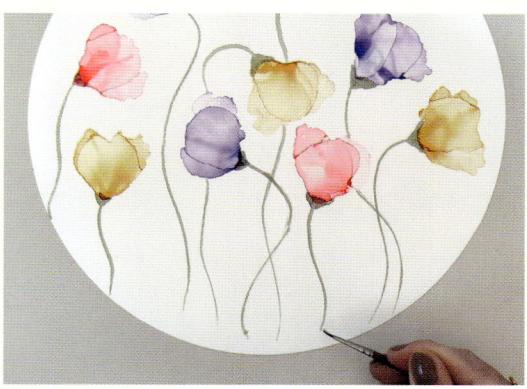

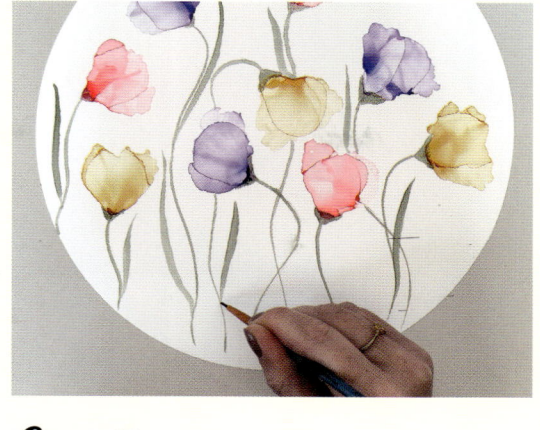

Step 6

Using a small brush, add a stem to each wildflower by applying a few drops of green ink to your palette or parchment paper. For a playful look, use an S-shaped movement to draw the stems. Lightly load your brush with ink, then make a quick, light stroke from the base of the flower to the bottom of the paper. Be mindful of stems that pass behind other flowers and avoid drawing over them. You can add a bud at the base of the flower by creating a small triangle shape to bring the petals together.

Step 7

Using a small brush, add long, narrow leaves to the stems. Pick up some green ink with your brush, then softly touch the paper with the tip of your brush. Press down lightly for a broader stroke, then lift your brush to create a narrow leaf attached to the stem. If necessary, thin down the green ink with a little isopropyl alcohol for a softer look. Add more small green strokes at the bottom of the paper to suggest a wildflower field.

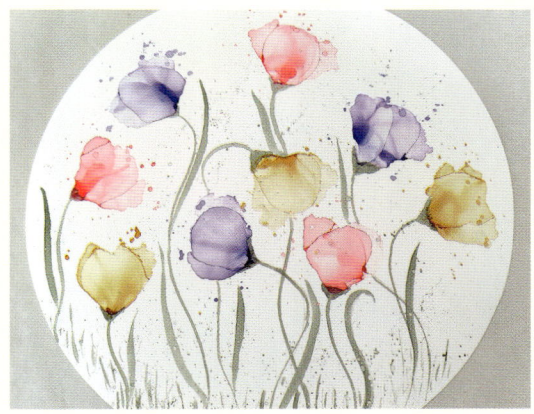

Step 8

As a final touch, I like to add splatters for a playful look. Load a brush with the desired ink color and gently tap it with another brush or tool to create splatters across the surface. Add green splatters where the stems and leaves are and splatters that match the colors of the wildflowers on the outside of the petals. If you want to avoid splatters on your flower petals, cover them with small pieces of paper towel.

 tip

Basic wildflower technique

Need to see how to create a wildflower in action? Scan the QR for a video of this technique.

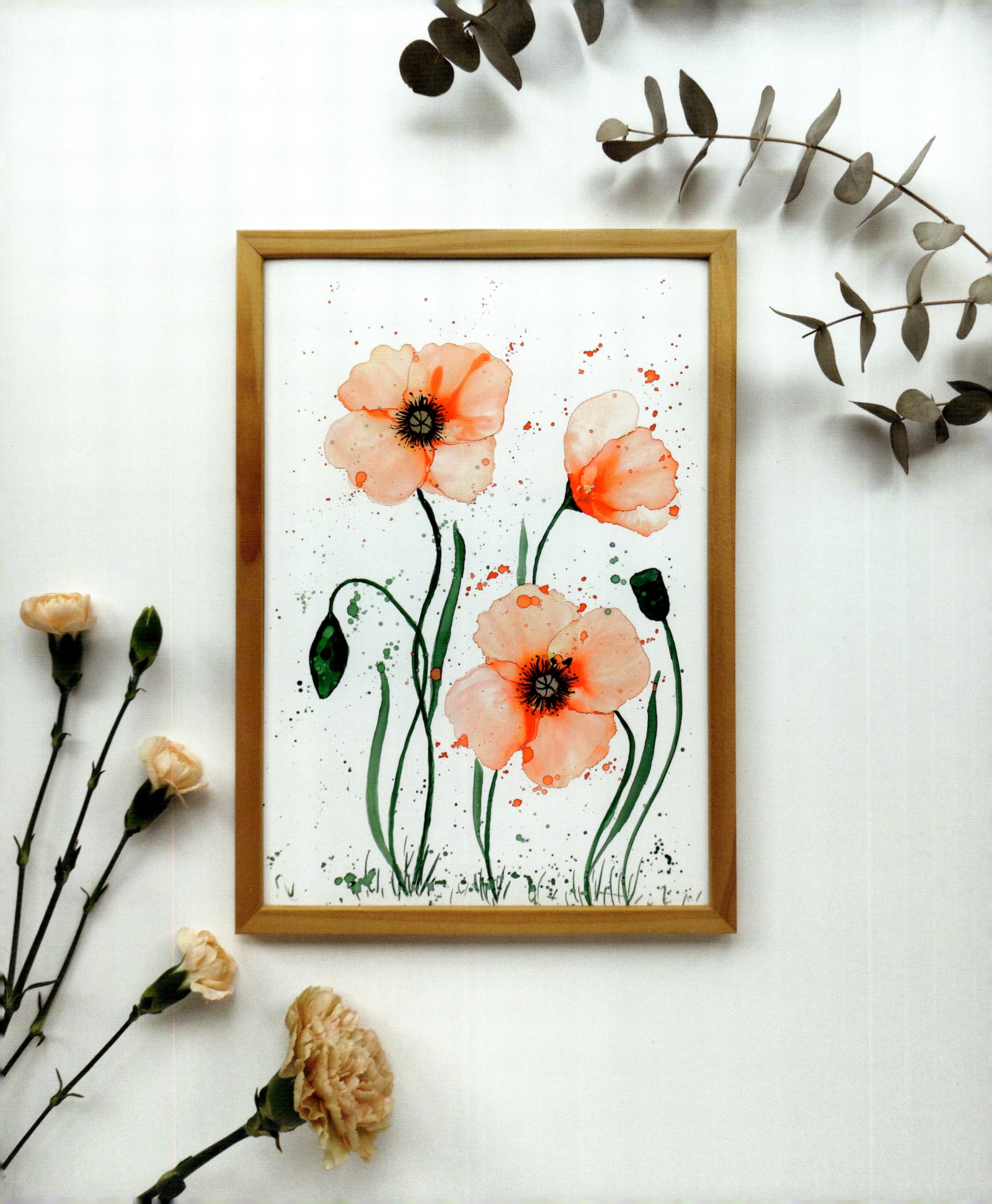

poppies

Poppies are one of my favorite wildflowers because of their bright color, delicate petals, and playful look, which I aimed to capture in this project. Using techniques from the previous Wildflowers project, you'll learn to create a front-facing poppy with more intricate details and complete the composition with side-facing poppies, buds, and seedpods.

LEVEL: BEGINNER
● ○ ○

materials

- Alcohol inks in red, light and dark green, black, and white
- 91% or 99% isopropyl alcohol in a needle tip bottle
- Synthetic paper 8 × 12 inches (20 × 30 cm)
- Glazed ceramic tile for practicing (optional)
- Ink air blower
- Heat tool to speed up drying process (optional)

- Set of miniature round synthetic brushes, 000 to 4.0 mm
- Silicone tip tool (optional)
- Paint palette or parchment paper
- Paper towels
- Cotton swabs
- Safety supplies

Step 1

To create two front-facing poppies, add one drop of red ink on the top-left corner and one drop on the lower-right corner. Use a small brush to spread the ink in a round circle about 1 inch (2.5 cm) in diameter. This will be the center of the poppy. Leave enough space from the edges to fit in the petals of the poppy. Use a heat tool to dry the ink completely before moving to the next step.

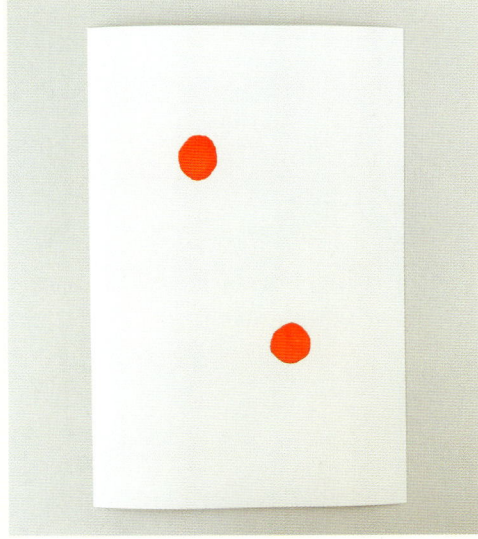

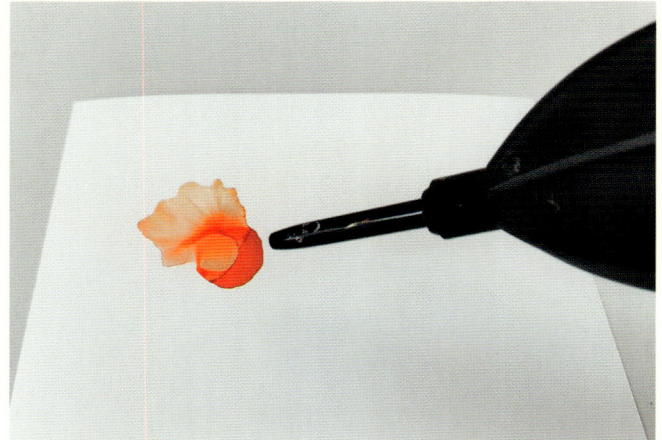
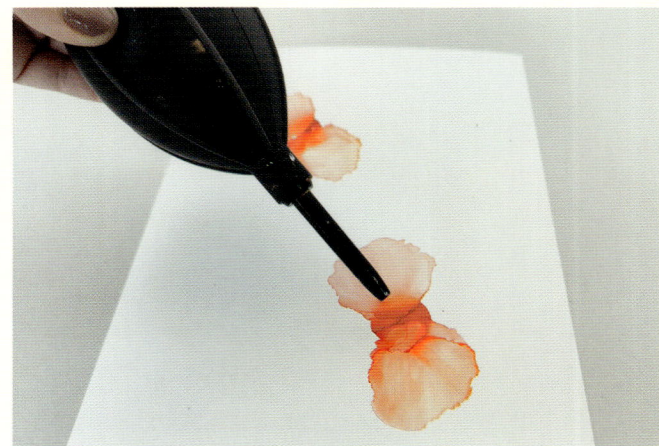

Step 2

Poppies have four wide, overlapping petals. To create the petals, add three drops of isopropyl alcohol at the edge of the circle to reactivate the ink. Start on the top-left diagonal so the petal will face the upper-left corner of your paper. Wait 2 to 3 seconds for the alcohol to spread, then use an ink air blower to push the ink outward in the direction of the petal. Squeeze the blower briefly, with moderate pressure. You may need to give it two squeezes (one on left and one on right) to properly spread the ink. After blowing out the petal, allow the ink to air-dry as it will continue to spread and change shape naturally. Repeat this step for the second circle. If needed, use a heat tool to speed up the drying process, but keep it at a distance to avoid blowing the ink and altering the petal shape.

Step 3

Using the technique from step 2, create a second petal at the opposite side of the first petal (the lower-right side), with the ink air blower facing the lower-right corner. You can turn your paper around to make it easier to position your ink air blower. Repeat this for both flowers. Ensure all petals are fully dry before moving on to step 4.

 tip *Poppy technique*

Need to see how to create a poppy flower in action? Scan the QR for a video of this technique.

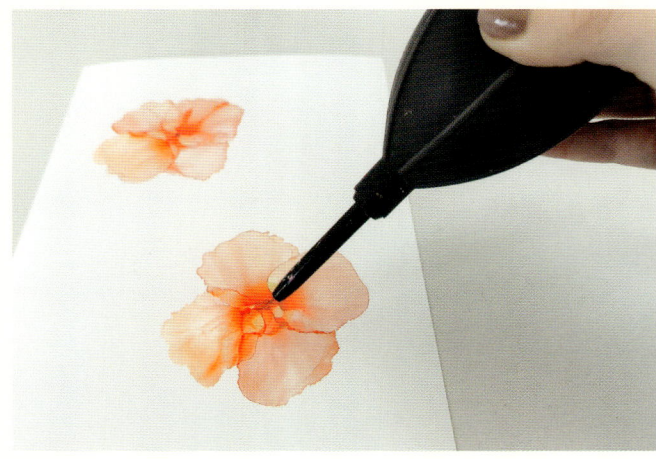

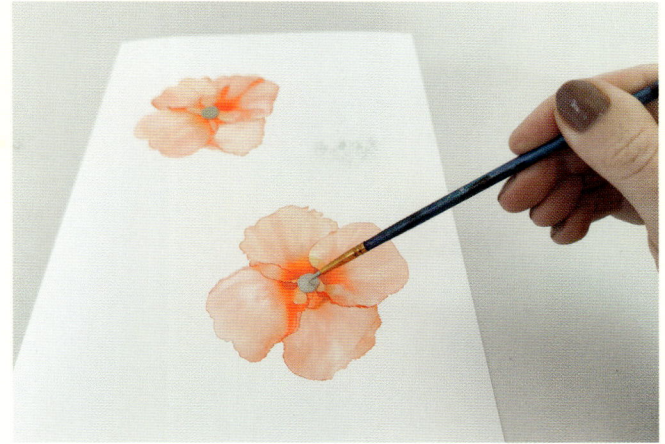

Step 4

Repeat steps 2 and 3 for both flowers to create two additional petals: one facing the top-right corner and one facing the bottom-left corner, each time waiting until the inks of the petal have dried before adding another one. If the color of the petal becomes too light, add a small touch of ink to the circle with your brush at the place where you will blow out the petal, let it dry, and then redo the petal. If a petal turns out too big, you can carefully remove the outside of the petal with a paper towel and isopropyl alcohol and redo the petal the same way. If a petal turns out too small, you can redo the petal by simply going over the previous petal a second time.

Step 5

To create the center of the poppy, remove the red ink from the center using a paper towel or a cotton swab—you want a small circle about ⅓ inch (8 mm). Mix a couple of drops of white ink with one drop of light green ink (or less if you have a darker green color) on your paint palette or parchment paper to create a light green, opaque color. Use a fine brush to draw a small circle with the soft green mixture where you have just removed the red ink. Use a heat tool to dry the ink. Repeat this step for both flowers.

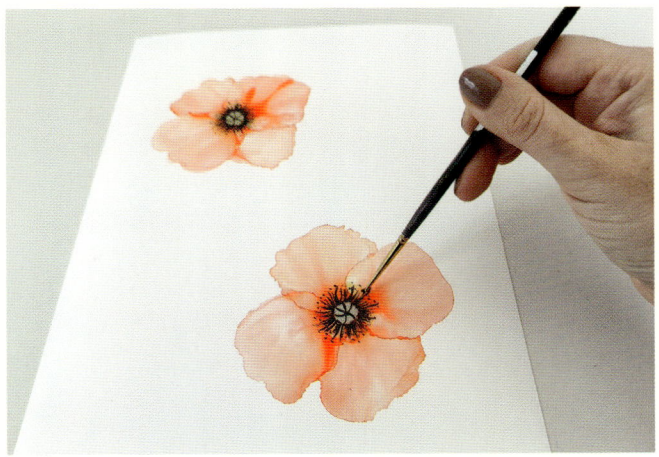

Step 6

Add one or two drops of black ink to your paint palette. Use a fine brush or a silicone tip tool to pick up a small amount of black ink (be careful not to apply too much ink). To finish the center, add six diagonal lines on top of the green circle. To draw the stamens, paint the stamens from the edge of the green circle to the outside using small, light brushstrokes. To finish the stamens, add small dots of black ink on the outside of the brushstrokes.

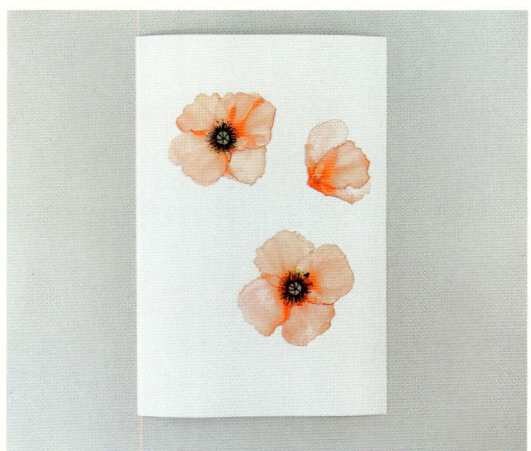

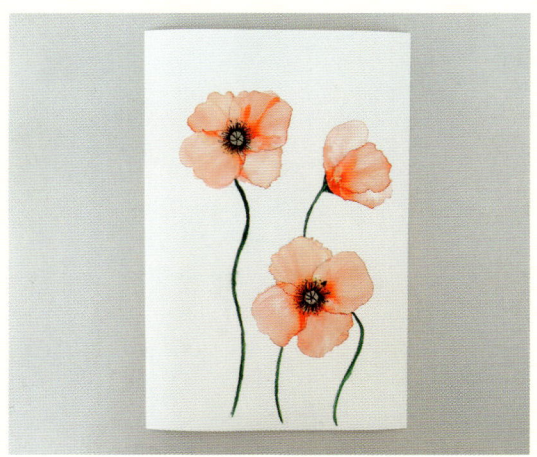

Step 7

To finish the composition, add one side-facing poppy in the top-right corner. Use the same red ink to draw a triangle with your small brush for the base of the poppy. Referring to the technique explained in the Wildflower Project (see pages 49 to 51), create three petals by adding two drops of isopropyl alcohol at the edge of the triangle, wait for 2 to 3 seconds, and blow out the petal using your ink air blower. Each time wait for the petal to dry before moving on to the next one.

Step 8

Using a small brush, add a stem to each poppy flower by applying a few drops of dark green ink to your palette. Lightly load your brush with ink, then make a quick, light stroke from the base of the flower to the bottom of the paper in an S-shape. Be mindful of stems that pass behind other flowers to avoid drawing over them. You can also add a bud at the flower's base by creating a small triangle shape to bring the petals together.

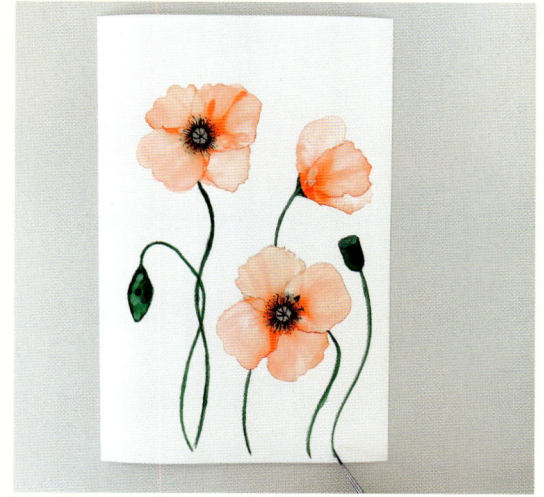

Step 9

To fill up the rest of the composition, add a poppy bud (an unopened poppy) and a seedpod (a poppy that has lost its petals). Use a small brush to pick up some dark green ink from your paint palette (add a few drops of isopropyl alcohol to reactivate the green ink if it has started to dry on your palette). Paint an oval shape on the center-left using light brushstrokes, next to the front-facing poppy. On the right side, add a seedpod by painting half an oval shape. After drying, add a small, narrow circle on top of the oval shape to create the top of the seedpod. Add stems to the poppy bud and seedpod.

Don't worry if your composition turned out different than mine. Use your own creativity to build your own composition combining the front and side-facing poppies and the poppy buds and seedpods.

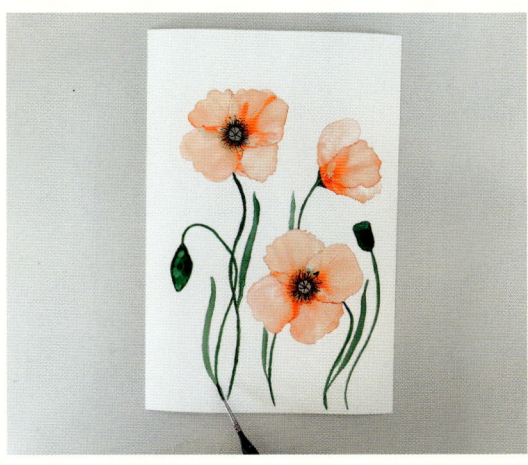

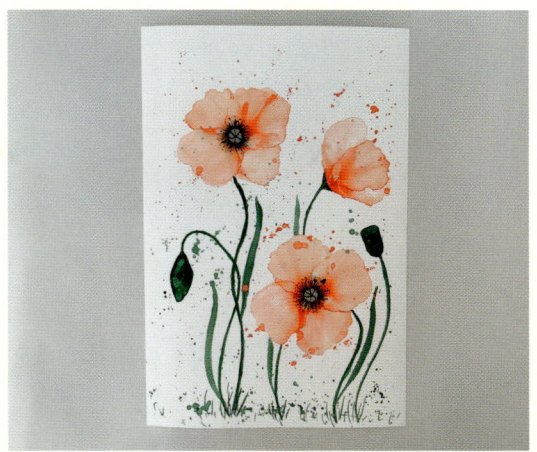

Step 10

Use a small brush to add long, narrow leaves to the stems. Pick up some dark green ink, then softly touch the paper with the tip of your brush. Press down lightly for a broader stroke, then lift your brush to create a narrow leaf attached to the stem. If necessary, thin down the green ink with a little isopropyl alcohol for a softer look. Add more small green strokes at the bottom of the paper to suggest grass.

Step 11

As a final touch, I like to add splatters for a playful look. Load a brush with the desired ink color and gently tap the brush with another brush or tool to create splatters across the surface. Add green splatters where the stems and leaves are and splatters that match the red color of the poppies on the outside of the petals. If you want to avoid splatters on your flower petals, cover them with small pieces of paper towel.

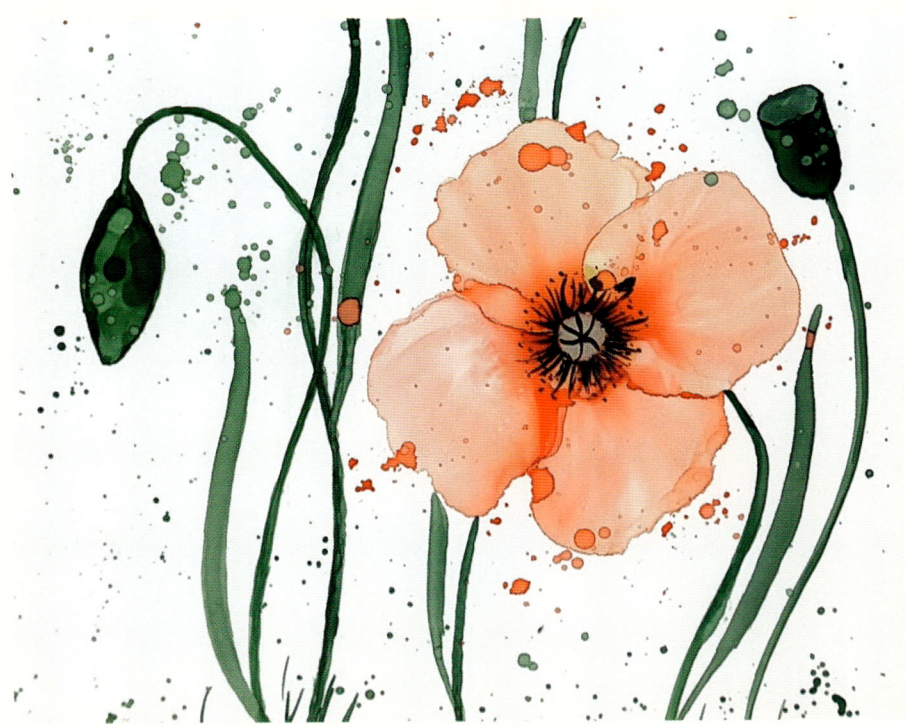

I like to add splatters for a playful look!

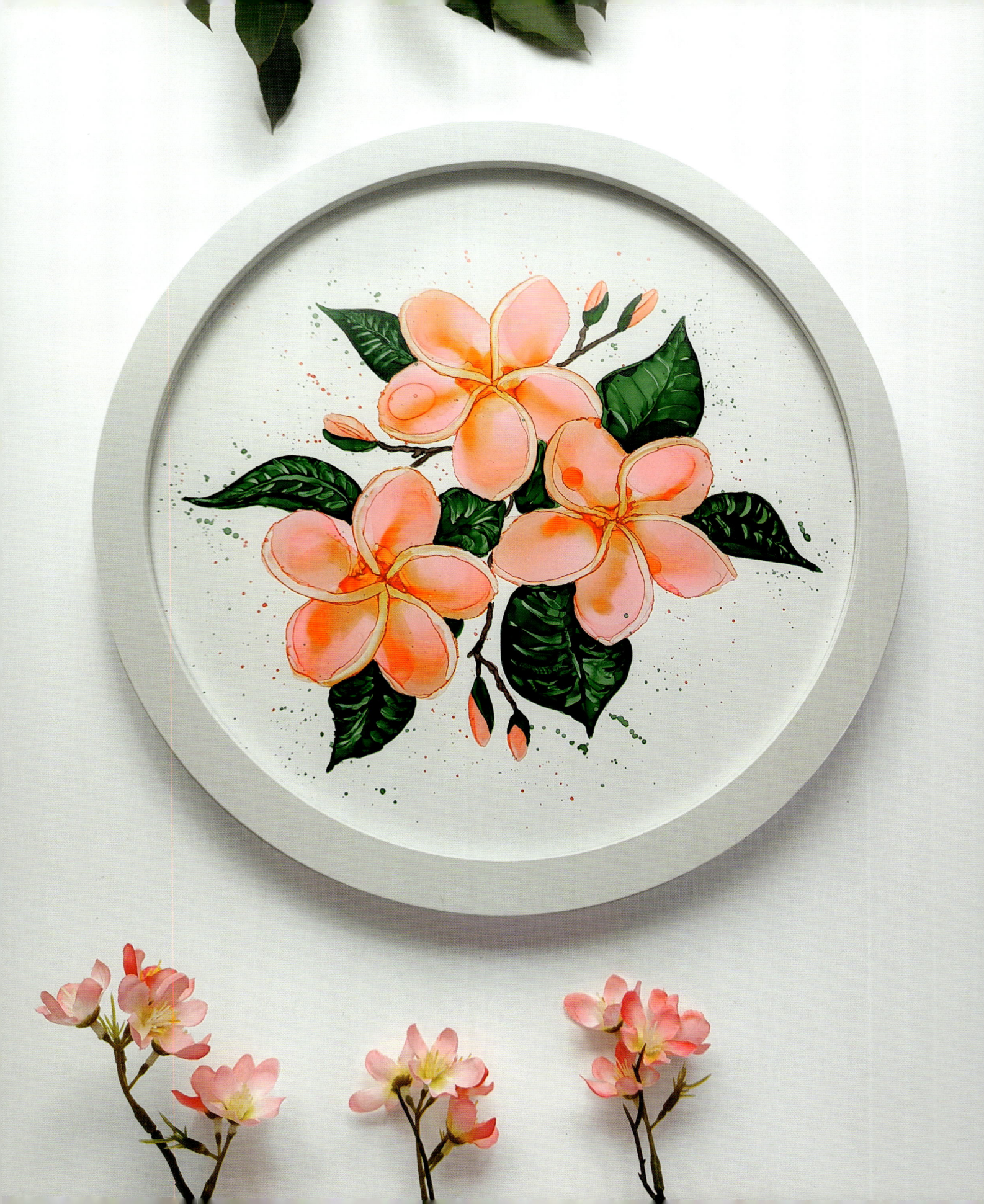

plumeria

The plumeria, also called the frangipani, is the ultimate exotic flower and symbol of Hawaii. In this Flower Project, we'll build upon the technique from the Wildflowers and Poppies and take it one step further by creating multicolored petals and adding shape and detail to the petals.

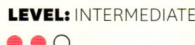

materials

- Alcohol inks in yellow orange, bright pink, dark (jungle) green, and brown
- 91% or 99% isopropyl alcohol in a needle tip bottle
- Extra needle tip bottle or cup and pipette
- Synthetic paper round or square 12 × 12 inches (30 × 30 cm)
- Glazed ceramic tile for practicing (optional)
- Ink air blower

- Heat tool to speed up drying process (optional)
- Set of miniature round synthetic brushes, 000 to 4.0 mm
- Silicone tip tool (optional)
- Paint palette or parchment paper
- Paper towels
- Safety supplies

Step 1

To create the center of the three plumeria flowers, add three drops of the yellow-orange ink to your palette (you can also mix a bright yellow with orange). Use a small brush with the yellow-orange ink and create three circles about 1 inch (2.5 cm) in diameter. These will be the centers of the plumeria. Leave enough space between the circles (about 4 inches [10 cm]) and edges. Use a heat tool to dry the circles. Load a bit more ink onto your brush and draw out five evenly distributed brushstrokes from each circle, to indicate where the petals are going to be. Dry it with your heat tool.

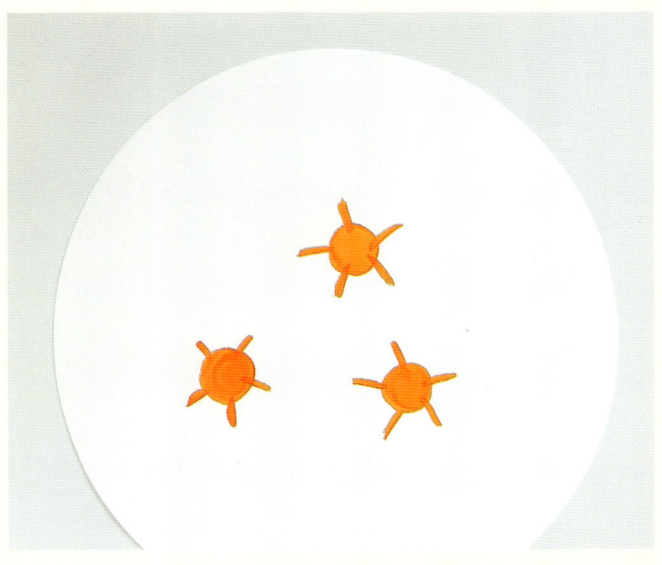

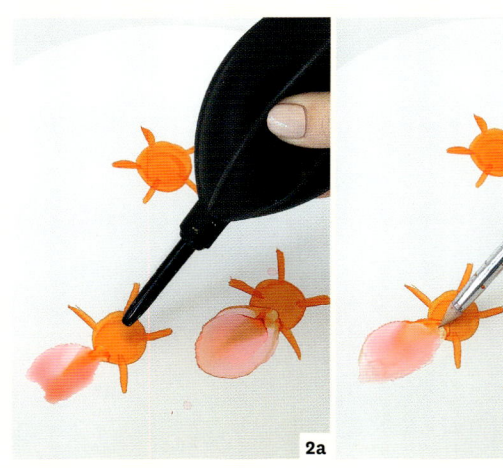

2a 2b

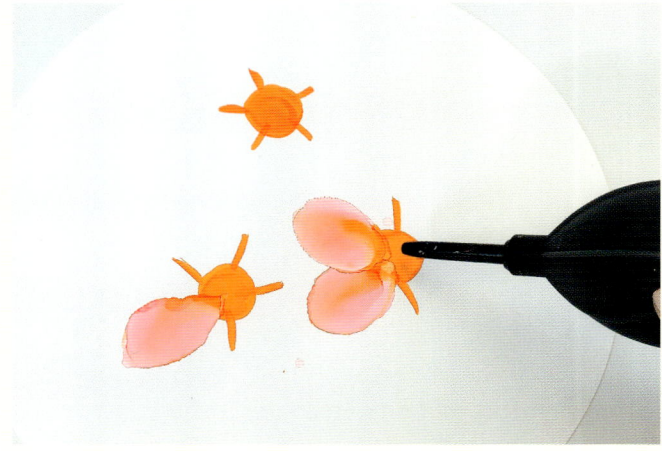

Step 2

To create the petals, first prepare a pink ink mix by adding pink ink and isopropyl alcohol in a needle tip bottle or plastic cup at about a 50/50 ratio. Then, add two drops of the pink ink mix with the needle tip bottle or pipette at the edge of the yellow-orange circle to reactivate the ink. Wait 2 to 3 seconds for the alcohol to spread, then use an ink air blower to push the ink outward in the direction of the petal (2a). Squeeze the blower with moderate pressure. Give it another 2 to 3 seconds to spread out. Then, come in with a silicone tip tool or small brush and help move the ink in the desired shape by creating a round pointed edge on the outside and toward the inside (2b). If needed, come in with your ink air blower again to help the orange blend into the pink a little more. Then, leave it alone to air-dry or use a heat tool to speed up the drying process but keep it at a distance. Repeat this process for the other two circles. If your petals are not saturated enough, add more pink ink to the mix.

Step 3

Using the technique from step 2, create a second petal next to the previous one (indicated by the yellow-orange brushstroke). Turn your paper around to make it easier to face the right direction with your ink air blower. Repeat this for all flowers. Ensure all petals are fully dry before creating a new one. Keep going until you have a full round of five petals, each time adding a new petal next to the previous one. It's important to follow this order to create the iconic pinwheel shape of the plumeria. If there's not enough of the yellow-orange ink left in the center, add a small touch to the circle with your brush. If a petal turns out too big, remove the outer edge with a paper towel and isopropyl alcohol and then redo the petal shape. If a petal turns out too small, you can redo the petal by simply going over the previous petal a second time.

tip

Plumeria technique

Need to see how to create a plumeria flower in action? Scan the QR for a video of this technique.

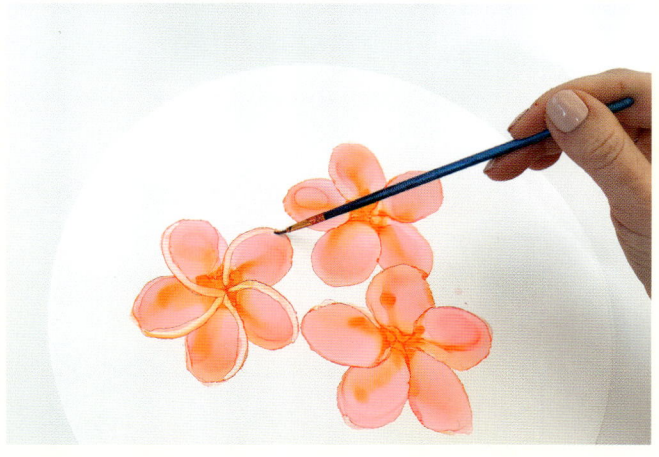

Step 4

To create the fold in the petals, load a fine brush with a small amount of isopropyl alcohol or the pink ink mix and create a small brushstroke along the edge of the left or right side of each petal. Be careful not to apply too much isopropyl alcohol as it will quickly spread. If needed, first dab your brush on a paper towel before using it on the petal shape. Softly move back and forth to create the fold. This will give the plumeria its iconic look.

Step 5

Next, you'll add leaves. Add dark green ink to your palette and lightly load your large brush with it. Paint a wide, pointed oval shape on the outside of the plumeria petals. Carefully fill in the shape and be extra careful around the edges of the petal shapes to avoid the green ink spreading over them. While still a bit wet, come in with a silicone tip tool or a small brush and add small brushstrokes to give texture to the leaves. Add several leaves on the outside and fill the space between the plumeria flowers as well. Fill any empty spots with some plumeria buds by painting small oval shapes with the pink ink with a small brush and an overlapping green leaf. Add a crooked stem with a small brush loaded with brown ink.

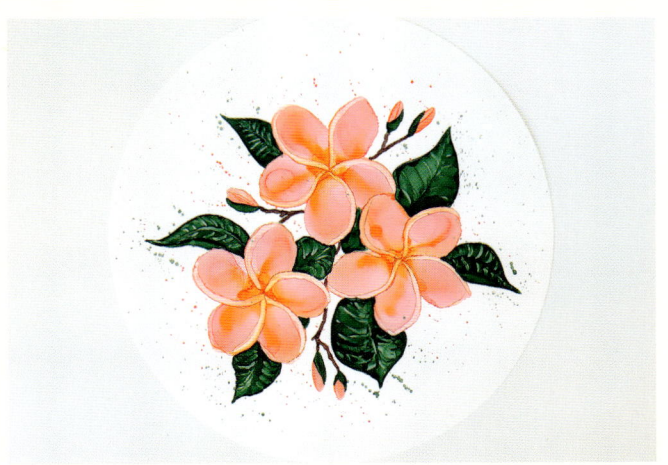

Step 6

To finish the artwork, add splatters using the yellow-orange and pink ink on the outside of the composition. Load a brush with the desired ink color and gently tap it with another brush or tool to create splatters around the composition until you're satisfied with the overall look. If you want to avoid splatters on the flowers and leaves, cover them with small pieces of paper towel.

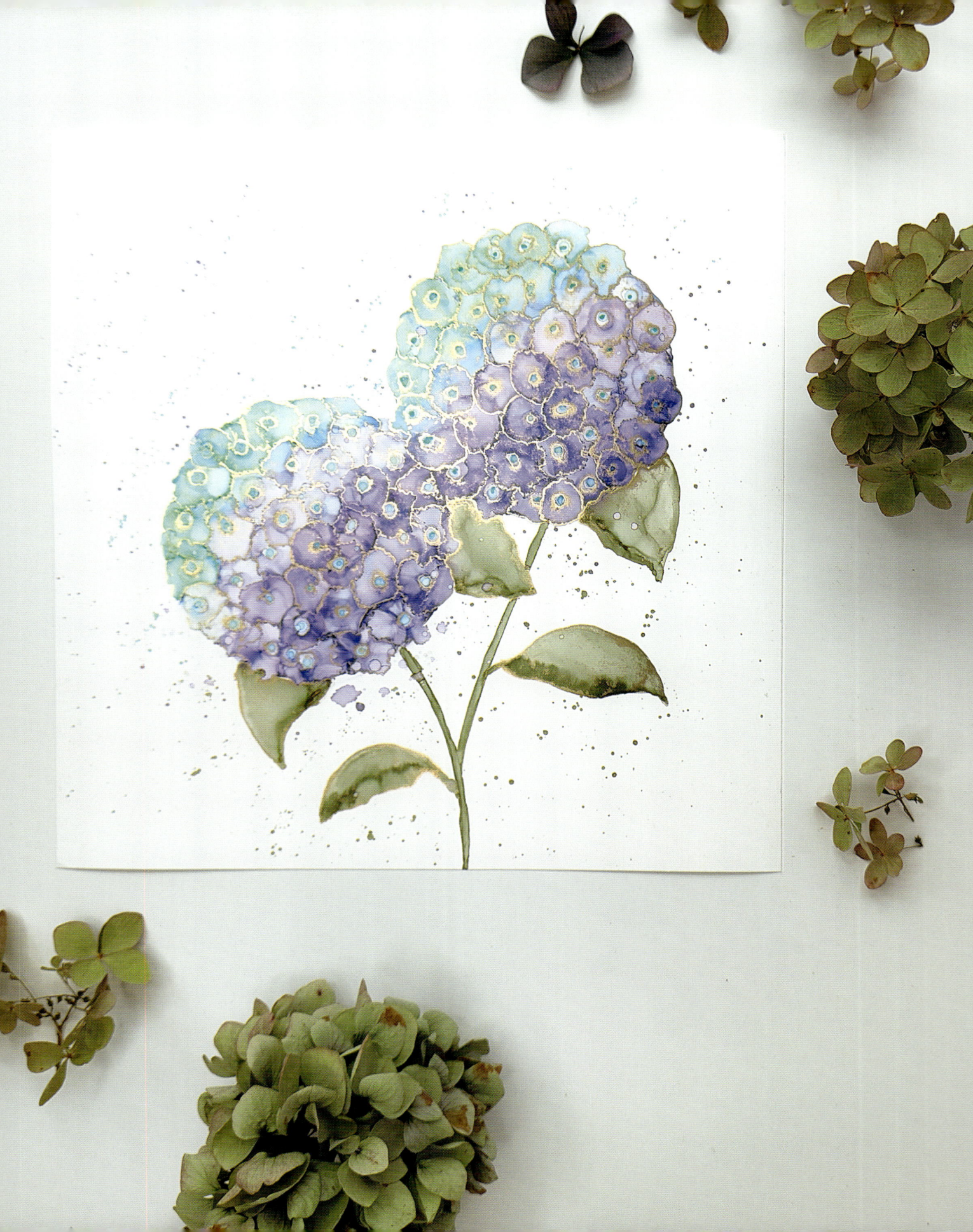

hydrangea flowers

Hydrangea flowers grow in large, beautiful clusters made up of many small pastel blossoms, giving them a soft, dreamy appearance. In this project, you'll practice a technique to create an abstract version of these flowers. Each tiny bloom may seem simple, but together they form a beautiful bulb of hydrangea flowers, imitating that dreamy look!

 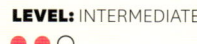

materials

- Alcohol inks in light blue, lilac, purple, and green
- Gold alcohol ink and isopropyl alcohol mix in a needle tip bottle at a 50/50 ratio
- Synthetic paper 12 × 12 inches (30 × 30 cm) square or round
- Glazed ceramic tile for practicing (optional)
- Ink air blower

- Heat tool to speed up drying process (optional)
- Set of miniature round synthetic brushes, 000 to 4.0 mm
- Silicone tip tool (optional)
- Paint palette or parchment paper
- Cup with isopropyl alcohol to clean brushes
- Paper towels
- Safety supplies

Step 1

Add a few drops of your blue, lilac, and purple alcohol ink to your paint palette. Hydrangea flowers are usually pastel colored, so thin down the color with isopropyl alcohol to make it lighter if needed. Load a large brush with a bit of the blue ink to draw out the outline of two circles of about 4 inches (10 cm). Optionally, use a round object to trace a circle around. This is where the hydrangea bulbs are going to be. Fill each circle with blue, lilac, and purple ink by creating three roughly even strokes working from blue to lilac to purple to create a gradient in the hydrangea flowers. Clean your brush with isopropyl alcohol in between colors (or change brushes) and work while the inks are still wet to let the previous color blend into to the next color a bit. Allow to dry or use a heat tool to speed up the drying process.

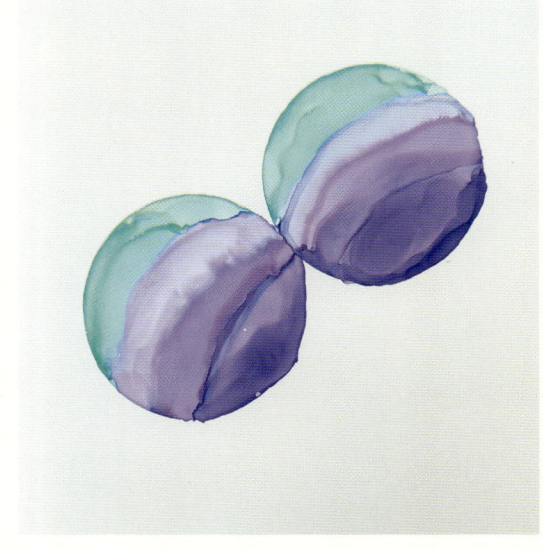

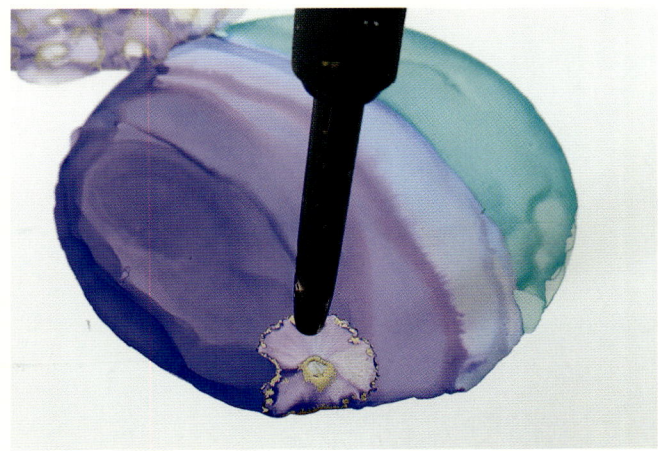

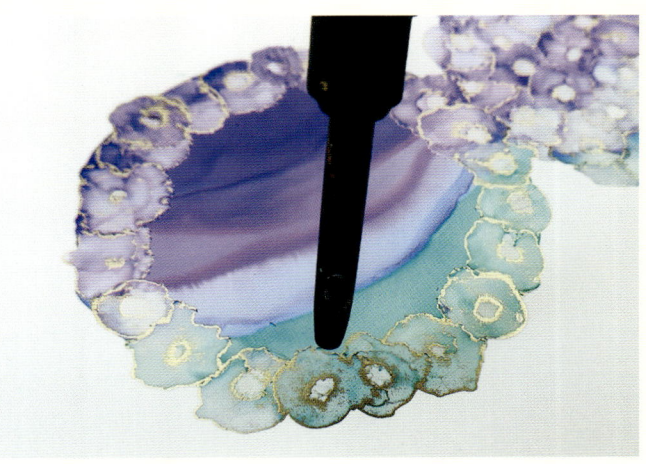

Step 2

To create the flowers, add one drop of the gold ink mix at the edge of the circle. You can also choose to leave out the gold and work with isopropyl alcohol only. Wait 1 or 2 seconds for the alcohol to spread. Then, use your ink air blower and very lightly squeeze it at the center of the ink puddle at a close distance from the paper to softly push the inks outward. Squeeze softly multiple times until you see a small, dry dot in the center. Experiment with the pressure to find the right strength. Keep squeezing the ink air blower lightly so the center remains dry each time the inks try to push back in (you may need to do this five to ten times). The gold ink will start sticking to the dot in the center and the outside edges to form the outline of the hydrangea flower. Keep going until the flower has dried or alternatively use a heat tool to speed up the drying process. If there's too much gold in the flower, add more isopropyl alcohol to your gold ink mix; if there's too little, add more gold to your mix. Always shake the gold ink mix in between so the gold doesn't sink to the bottom.

Step 3

Using the technique from step 2, create flowers along the entire edge of the circles. Add each new flower alongside the previous one, partly overlapping. Make sure each flower is dry before continuing with the next one. To speed up the process, you can alternate adding flowers between the two circles. Every flower is going to look different, so don't get preoccupied with the shape of each individual flower as it's about the overall appearance. Keep going until you have a ring of flowers for both circles.

tip

Hydrangea technique

Need to see how to create a hydrangea flower in action?
Scan the QR for a video of this technique.

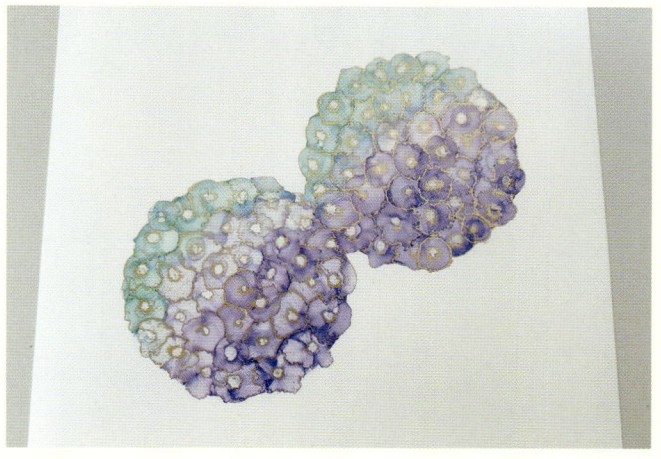

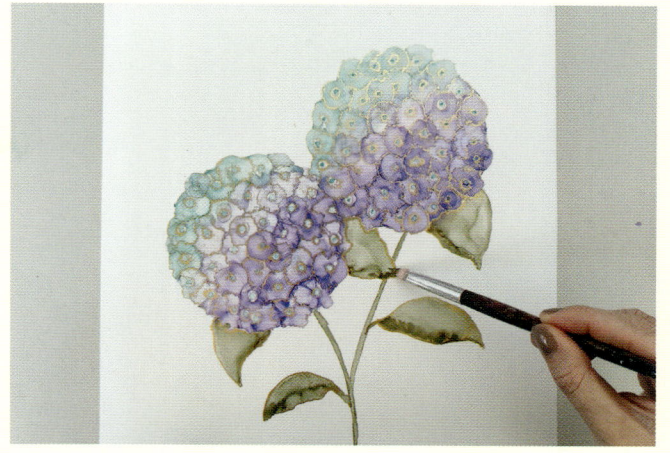

Step 4

Continue by creating a second ring of flowers within the previous ring. Keep adding a new ring of flowers until you have reached the center of both circles. Toward the center it becomes more difficult to fit the flowers in. You can use a silicone tip tool or brush to help spread the gold ink mix in a circle to fit it in between or move over the other flowers. If some flowers turned out too large or need redoing, you can use a paper towel with isopropyl alcohol to remove a flower, add new ink to the circle with your brush, let it dry, and then redo the flower or simply create a new one on top. Repeat this until you are satisfied with the overall look of the hydrangea bulbs.

Step 5

To finish the hydrangea flowers, use a fine brush loaded with a small amount of the blue ink and add a tiny dot of ink in each flower to represent the center. Add a few drops of green ink to your palette and use a small brush to add a stem to each hydrangea bulb, bringing the two stems together at the bottom. Use a large brush to paint the broad, oval-shaped leaves with pointed tips, focusing on the leaves that emerge from the base of the hydrangea bulbs and some along the stems. To add gold to the leaves, add one or two drops of the gold ink mix and use a fine brush to spread it into the leaf shape, then fill them in with green ink using your small brush and the gold will spread toward the edges. If needed, thin down the green with isopropyl alcohol. Be careful not to add too much ink as it will spread quickly.

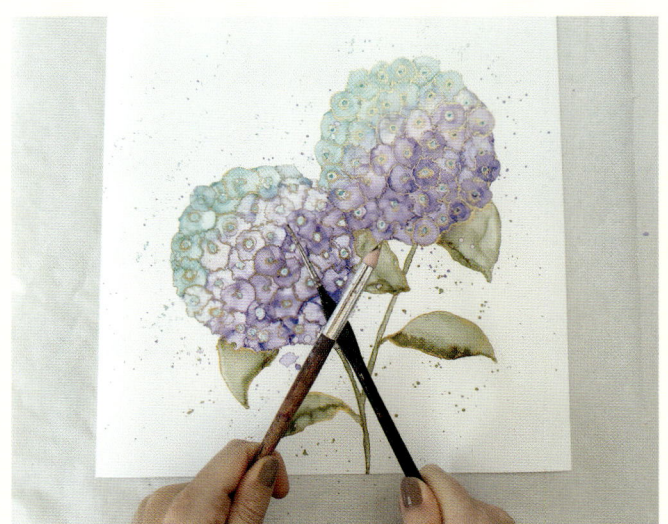

Step 6

For the final touch, I like to add splatters in the same colors as the hydrangea flowers. Load a brush with the desired ink color and gently tap it with another brush or tool to create splatters across the surface. Add green splatters where the stems and leaves are and splatters that match the color of the hydrangea flowers on the outside of the bulbs. If you want to avoid splatters on your flowers, cover them with small pieces of paper towel.

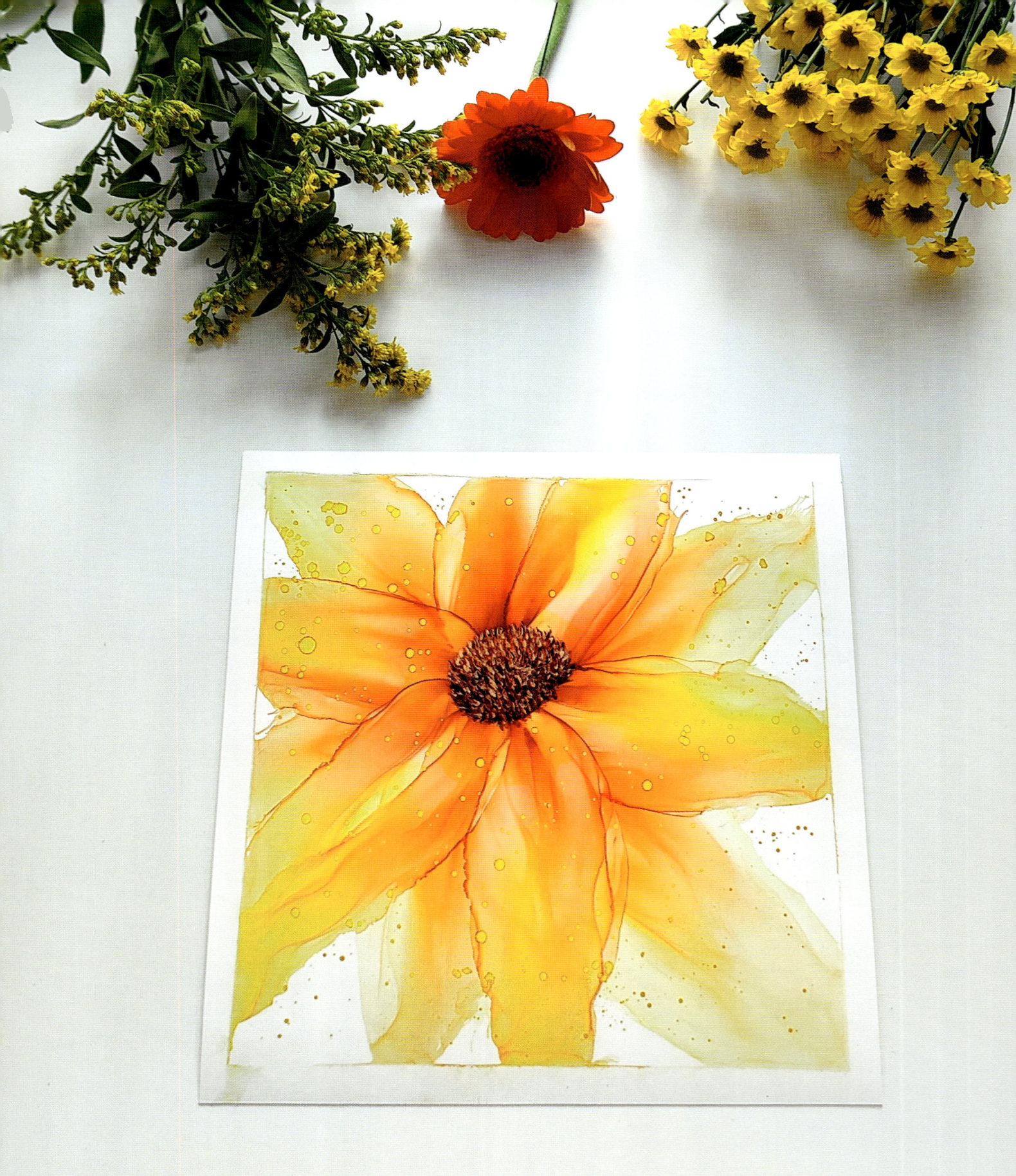

big bloom

The Big Bloom project is a great technique to create a big, zoomed-in flower with the petals spreading out over the edges, with a beautifully detailed center that draws the viewer in. Be patient, as the flower only really comes alive when adding the detailed center.

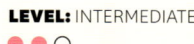

materials

- Alcohol inks in yellow, orange, brown orange (sienna), and white (or a white acrylic paint marker
- 91% or 99% isopropyl alcohol in a needle tip bottle
- Synthetic paper round or square 10 × 10 inches (20 × 20 cm)
- Glazed ceramic tile for practicing (optional)
- Ink air blower
- Heat tool

- Set of miniature round synthetic brushes, 000 to 4.0 mm
- Silicone tip tool (optional)
- Paint palette or parchment paper
- Painter's tape
- Craft knife, ruler, and cutting mat (for trimming edges if needed)
- Paper towels
- Safety supplies

Step 1

Apply painter's tape to the edges of your synthetic paper and adhere it carefully. This will help keep your edges clean as the ink will be moving over the edge of the paper. Make sure the surface underneath your paper is protected. To create the base of the bloom, paint a circle slightly off-center to the upper-left corner. Add three drops of the orange-brown ink to your paper and use a small brush to shape it into a circle about 1½ inch (4 cm) in diameter. Use your heat tool to dry it. Next, apply a few drops of yellow and orange ink on your palette. Use a brush to draw a yellow circle around the brown circle and dry it with your heat tool. For color variation, add some orange stripes into the yellow circle using a small brush. Dry it before continuing to step 2.

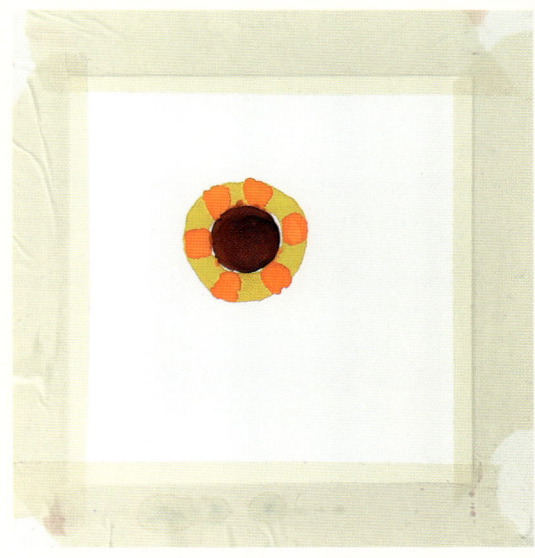

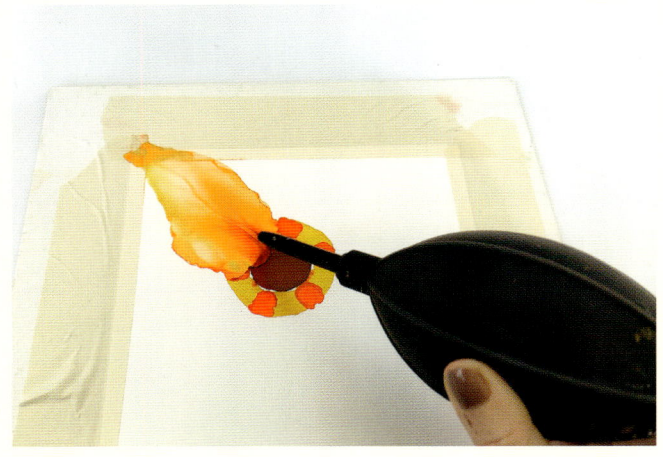

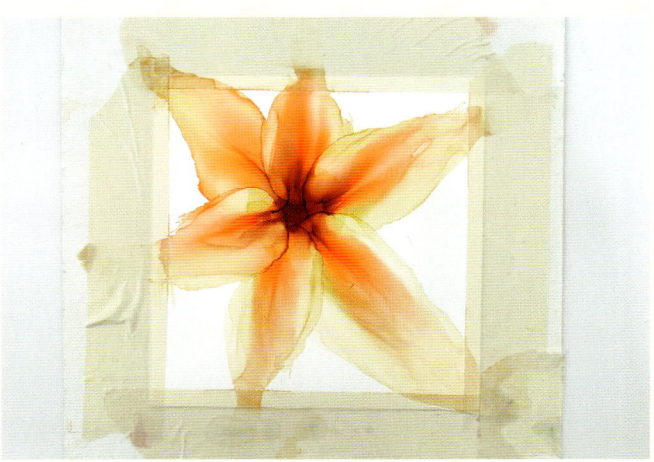

Step 2

To create the first petal, add ten to fifteen drops of iso-propyl alcohol on the yellow outer circle, making sure it slightly overlaps the brown circle. Quickly use your ink air blower to blow the ink outward to start forming the petal. Angle the blower diagonally and push from the center toward the edge of the paper. Apply enough pressure to move the ink without splattering. Keep squeezing the ink air blower until the ink starts drying from the inside out. Push the inks over the edge of the paper so the petal looks like it's "falling off" the paper. Sometimes, it helps to also blow the ink from the sides (left and right) to shape the petal nicely. It takes a bit of practice to get it right. Continue until the petal is completely dry. Remove any wet ink that has spilled over your paper using a paper towel.

Step 3

Repeat the process from step 2 to create a full bloom, each time creating a new petal next to the previous one, partly overlapping it. This will take five or six rounds. Don't worry about the messy edges; you can trim them later or remove the tape to hide them. If the petal doesn't move over the edges, use more isopropyl alcohol and go over the petal again. If you have trouble getting a nice petal shape, you can use a silicone tip tool or brush to help spread the ink in the right shape.

tips

Ink staining tip

Note that some inks may stain the paper and are not easily reactivated. Use a nonstaining ink for this technique (test this out on scrap paper first). Ranger Ink works well for this technique.

Big bloom technique

Need to see how to create the big bloom petals in action? Scan the QR for a video of this technique.

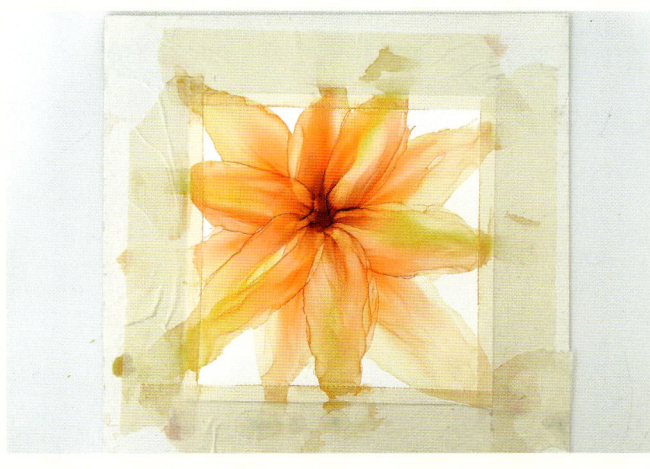

Step 4

After finishing the first round, decide whether you'd like to add more petals at the empty spots. If so, repeat steps 2 and 3 to create another layer of petals. If the petals need more saturation, add more of the brown-orange ink toward the center. Each time, layer a new petal between two other petals. You do not need to add another five or six petals, but see where you may need to fill up some empty spots until you're satisfied with the flower. For the composition, I always like to keep some empty spots toward the edges.

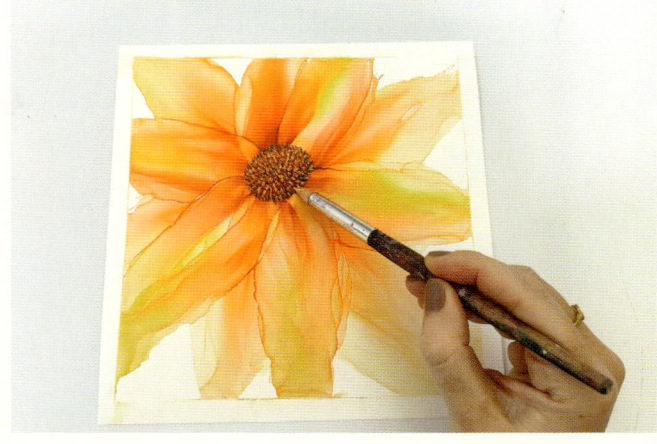

Step 5

To create the center of the bloom, start by applying one or two drops of the orange-brown ink in the center in a circular or oval shape and dry it with your heat tool. Add a couple of drops of white ink to your paint palette. Use a silicone tip tool or a small brush to add dots or tiny brushstrokes to the center, leaving empty spots between them. Dry the layer with a heat tool and repeat the process using the orange-brown ink in the empty spots. To create depth, apply lighter colors at the top and darker shades at the bottom. You can also incorporate yellow or orange to create more variation in the colors. For better coverage, you can also use a white acrylic paint marker instead of white ink, which may need multiple layers to get an opaque look. Continue layering until you are satisfied with the result.

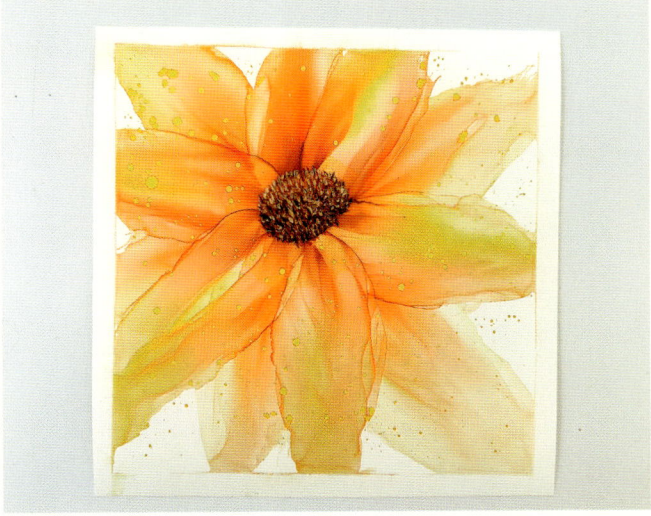

Step 6

To complete the bloom, add splatters to the petals. Load a brush with the desired ink color and gently tap it with another brush or tool to create splatters around the petals until you're satisfied with the overall look. Remove the painter's tape. The clean white edges can be left as they are or trimmed using a craft knife and ruler. Trimming is also useful if inks have leaked under the painter's tape and the edges are messy.

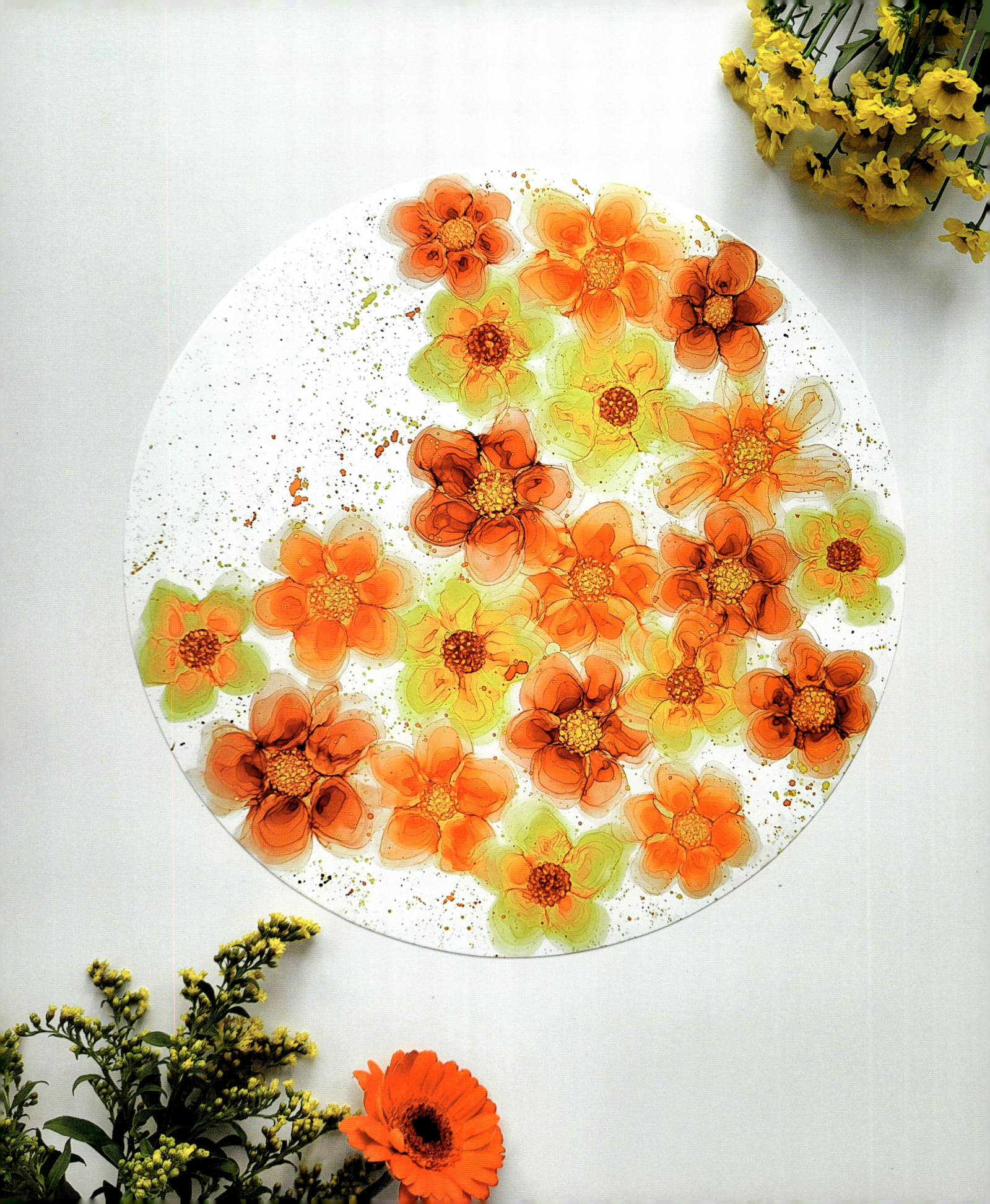

small blooms

These small blooms with fluffy rounded petals are the perfect way to start practicing with a heat tool and a good warm-up for the advanced roses technique. This project will help you learn how to control the inks with your heat tool and experiment with varying the size and shapes of the petals. These small blooms look easier than they are to create, but with practice, you'll get there!

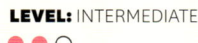

materials

- Alcohol inks in yellow, orange, and brown orange (sienna)
- 91% or 99% isopropyl alcohol in a needle tip bottle
- Synthetic paper round or square 12 × 12 inches (30 × 30 cm)
- Glazed ceramic tile for practicing (optional)
- Heat tool

- Set of miniature round synthetic brushes, 000 to 4.0 mm
- Silicone tip tool (optional)
- Paint palette or parchment paper
- Cup with isopropyl alcohol to clean brushes
- Paper towels
- Safety supplies

Step 1

To create the base of the flowers, add yellow, orange, and brown-orange ink to your paint palette. Load a small brush with the yellow ink and draw three small circles ½ inch (13 mm) in diameter in the center of your paper. Keep enough distance between the circles for the flower petals to fit in (about 2 inches [5 cm]). Dry them with your heat tool. Use your brush to draw another ring of ink of about ½ inch (13 mm) wide around each circle with one of each of the three colors. Clean your brush with isopropyl alcohol in between or use different brushes for each color. You can add a tiny bit of orange to the yellow ring so the outside color is just a little darker than the yellow center. Dry the circles with your heat tool before continuing to step 2.

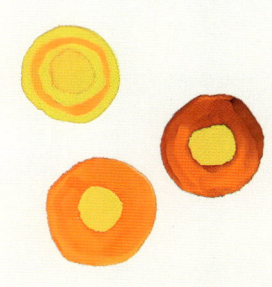

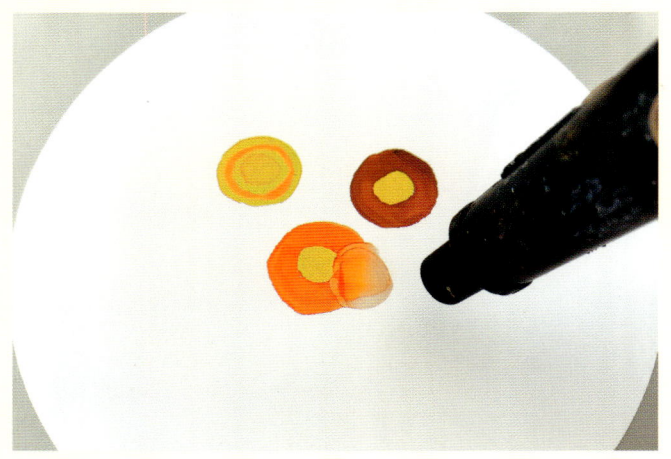
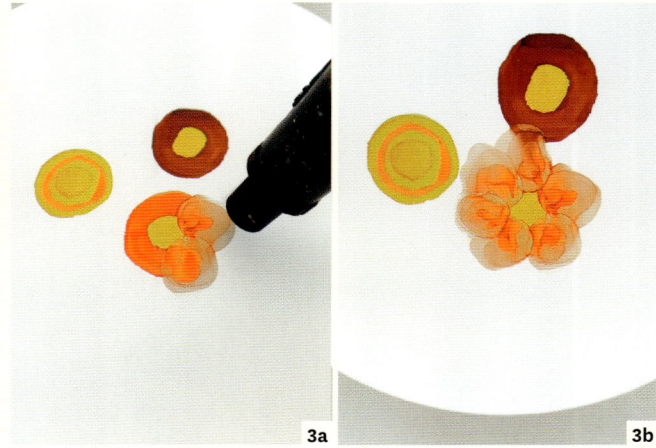

Step 2

To create the round petals, add four drops of isopropyl alcohol with a needle tip bottle at the edge of the outer circle to reactivate the ink. The alcohol should cover the outside circle, but not the inside. Let it spread for 2 to 3 seconds and then use your heat tool and slowly start moving in a round motion around the wet ink puddle. Depending on the strength of your heat tool, keep it 1 to 3 inches (3 to 7.5 cm) away from the ink. Use a medium-hot (not cold) setting on your heat tool. Position the heat tool along the side of the wet area (not directly above it). Move slowly enough to dry the outer rings of the ink and keep moving inward until all the ink is dry. If there's too much ink left toward the center, use a paper towel to lift some of the ink before fully drying it.

Step 3

Create a second petal right next to the previous one using the technique from step 2 (3a). If you have trouble forming a nice petal shape, you can use a silicone tip tool or brush to help spread the ink in the right shape after applying the alcohol and before coming in with your heat tool. It may take some time to get this technique under control, so don't expect to get perfect results right away. Layer a new petal next to the previous one, until you have a full bloom (3b). This will take five to six rounds.

Advanced tip

If you feel comfortable with the technique and you'd like an extra challenge, use a gold alcohol ink mix instead of clear alcohol and experiment with adding golden edges to the blooms.

Small blooms technique

Need to see how to create the small blooms in action? Scan the QR for a video of this technique.

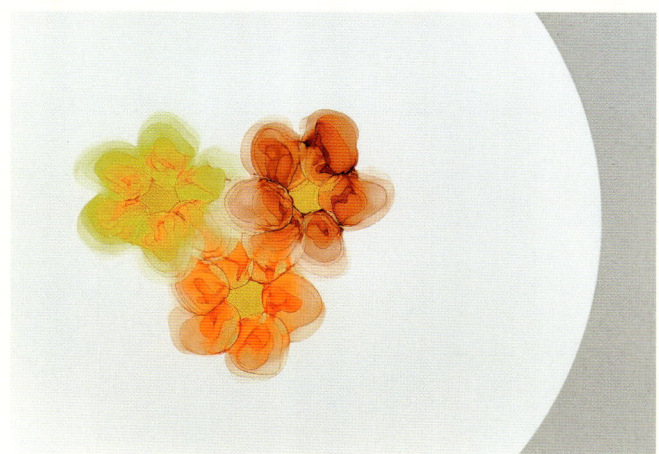

Step 4

Repeat steps 2 and 3 to finish the other two flowers. Don't worry if the petals partly overlap another flower's petals. If you need to redo a petal because it turned out too large, use a paper towel with isopropyl alcohol to gently remove it. Reapply the same color with a brush, dry it, and then blow out the petal again using the technique from step 2. If the petal is too small, you can simply move over it a second time. Don't be too critical in the beginning—you'll probably need to create multiple flowers to get the technique down.

Step 5

Finish the composition by repeating steps 1 to 4 and fill your paper with small blooms in various sizes. Once you're comfortable with this technique, you can practice using different methods and assorted petal sizes. Instead of moving in a round manner, try moving side to side for a different pattern in the petal. You can also vary the size of each bloom by adding more or less of the isopropyl alcohol for each petal. By using your brush or silicone tip tool, you can also alter the shape by choosing a longer, narrower petal or a pointed petal. This project is all about experimenting with your heat tool, so I encourage you to try different things and see what you like best. Keep going until you're satisfied with the overall composition.

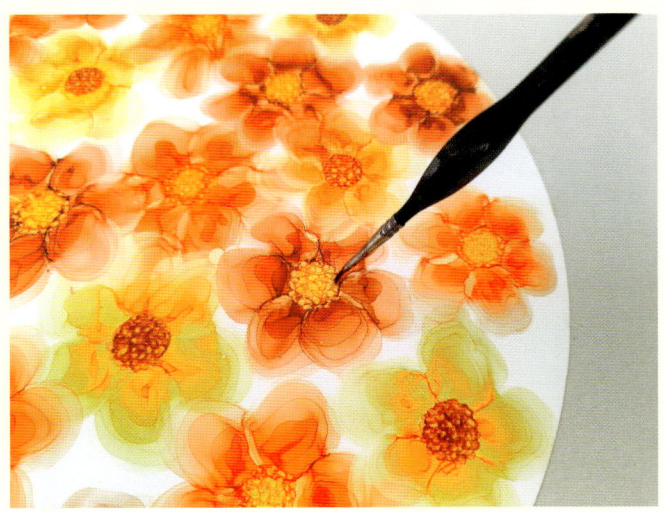

Step 6

To finish the center of the blooms, load a small brush with a small amount of yellow ink and dab it in the yellow center of the blooms to create small dots. You can also add a bit of orange or brown orange to the center to create more depth. You can go over it as many times as you like and dry the layers in between. As always, I like to finish the composition with some splatters across the composition. Load your brush with the desired ink colors and gently tap it with another brush or tool to create splatters around the blooms until you're satisfied with the overall look (don't overdo it!).

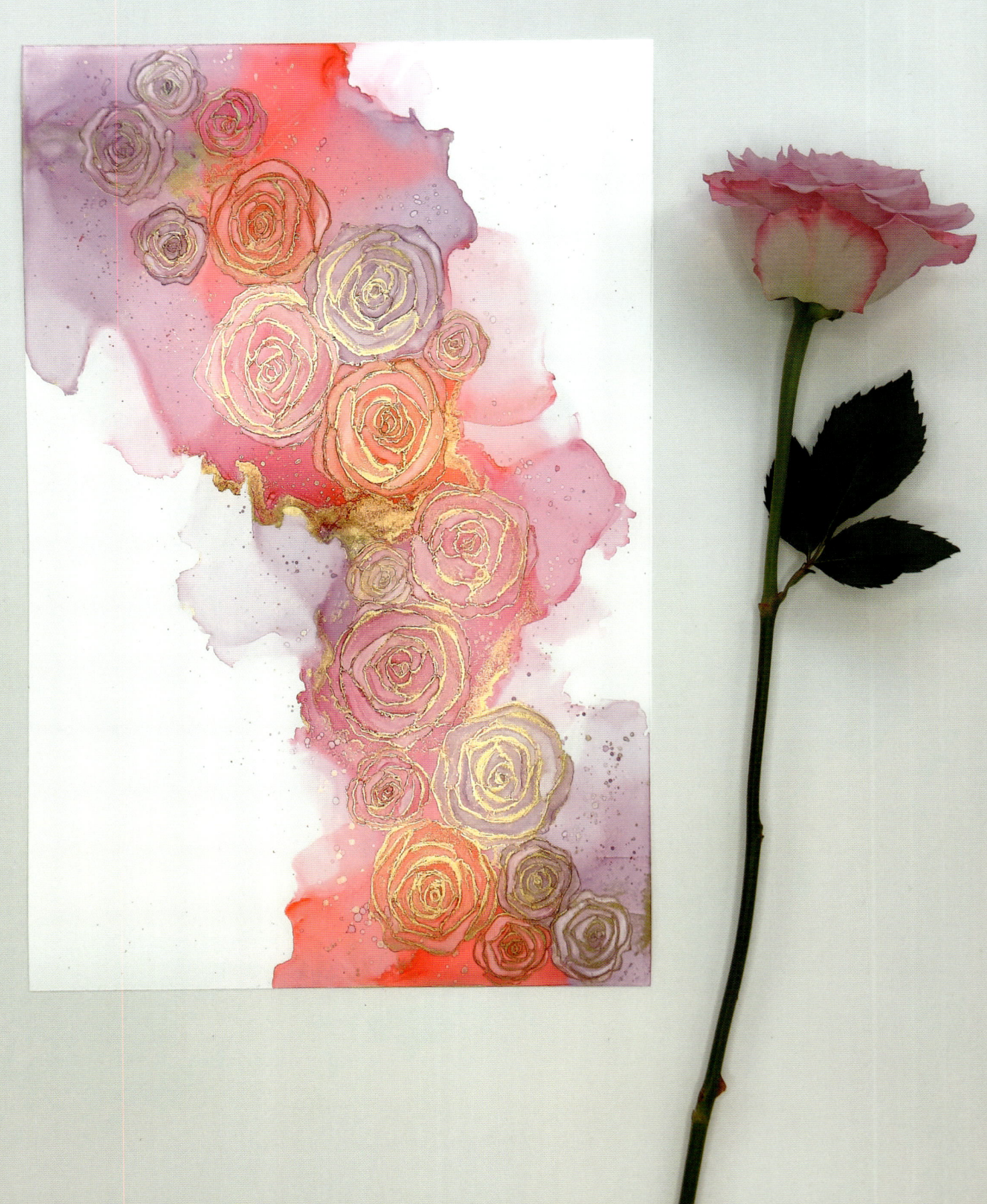

roses *(beginner version)*

This beginner version of my roses is a great alternative to the more advanced heat tool technique. By using a brush, we can imitate the roses technique in a more beginner-friendly way and still get pretty results! We'll first work on a fast and intuitive ink air blower technique to create a playful background and then work with a more detailed and precise brush technique to draw the roses on top. This composition combines fun free-flowing abstract art with detailed floral art on top.

LEVEL: BEGINNER
● ○ ○

materials

- Alcohol inks in three shades of pink
- Gold alcohol ink and isopropyl alcohol mix in a needle tip bottle at a 50/50 ratio
- Synthetic paper 10 × 12 inches (20 × 30 cm)
- Glazed ceramic tile for practicing (optional)
- Ink air blower

- Heat tool to speed up drying process (optional)
- Set of miniature round synthetic brushes, 000 to 4.0 mm
- Paint palette or cup
- Paper towels
- Safety supplies

Step 1

Before creating the roses, you need an ink background on which to draw the roses. Create a background composition by layering your inks in a diagonal line over the paper. Refer to the steps in "Warm-Up Exercise 2: Creating an Abstract Ink Background" and video on page 30. Alternatively, you can draw the rose shapes with a small brush, by drawing circles in a diagonal line and varying the ink colors and sizes of the circles to simplify the process.

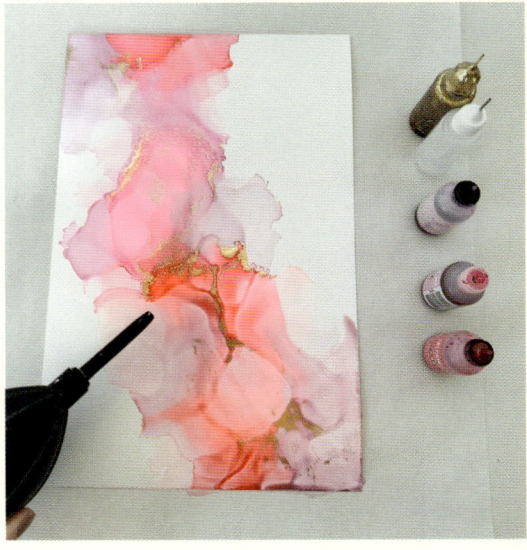

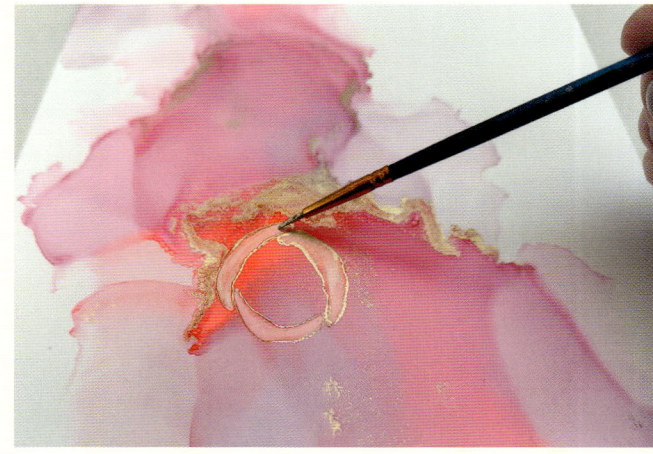

Troubleshooting and additional tips

Consider the following situations:

- **How much of the gold alcohol ink mix you need:** If the shape gets too big and the ink spreads fast, use less. If it dries too quickly to draw out the C-shape, use more of the gold ink mix.

- **The ratio of the gold alcohol ink mix:** If there's too much metallic in the petals, add more isopropyl alcohol to your gold ink mix. If there's too little metallic, add more gold in your mix.

- **The type and size of the brush:** Some brushes are easier to work with than others (I prefer synthetic brushes) and the size also matters. If your brush is too big, the petals may also become too big and vice versa.

Rose beginner technique

Need to see how to create a rose in action? Scan the QR for a video of this technique.

Step 2

Let's start creating the first rose in the center of the paper. First, apply your gold ink mix on your paint palette or in a small cup. To make the petal more saturated, you can add two or three ink drops of the background color in the mix. Then, to create the petals on the outside of the rose, use your small brush to draw three slightly overlapping C-shapes, which together will form a circle of about 2 inches (5 cm) in diameter. To do so, lightly load your brush with the gold ink mix, draw the first C-shape, and softly move back and forth with your brush within the shape. The ink underneath will get reactivated, and the gold ink will start moving to the edge of the shape, creating the golden edges of the petal. You may need to move over a petal shape multiple times. If it's already dried, reload your brush and then go over it again. Once you're satisfied with the petal shape, make sure it's dry before moving to the next. Use a heat tool to speed up the drying process. Create a second and third C-shape, which will form the outside petals of the rose. Make sure you stir the gold ink mix in between using your brush so the metallics don't sink all the way to the bottom. Refer to "Troubleshooting and Additional Tips" at left if needed.

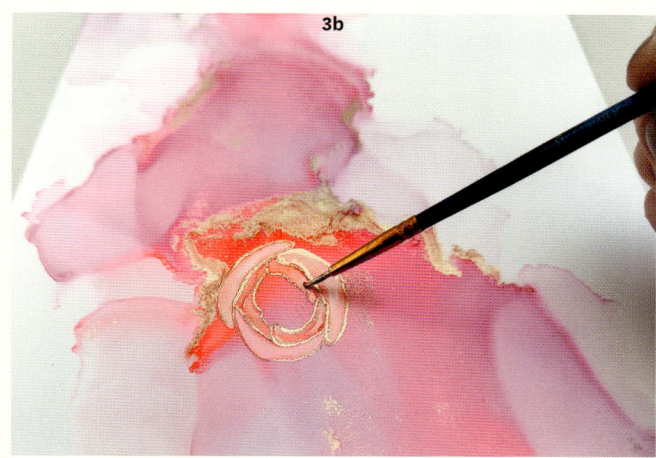

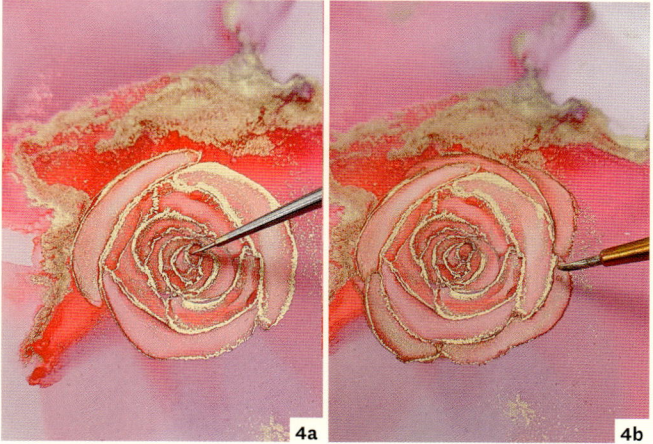

Step 3

Continue by creating a new ring of C-shapes within the previous ring created in step 2 using the same technique. Outline the petal shapes in the middle of two petals from the outside ring for a natural look (this doesn't need to be very exact). You will need less of the ink mix because the petals will become smaller. Be careful not to move over the previous petals but make them touch each other so there's no room in between the petals.

Step 4

Keep adding a new ring of C-shapes until you have reached the center (4a). For each ring, the petals will become smaller and narrower, so you may need to work with a small brush, apply less of the gold ink mix, and need fewer petals. To tie the rose together, I like to add some narrow, ruffled petals to the outside for a more natural look (4b). If petals turn out too large or need redoing, you can move over them by creating new petals on top. Alternatively, you can use a paper towel with isopropyl alcohol to remove one or more petals, add new ink in the color of the background with your brush, let it dry, and then redo the petal(s). Repeat this until you are satisfied with the overall look of the rose. But as I always like to say: Don't be too critical! It's the overall look that counts.

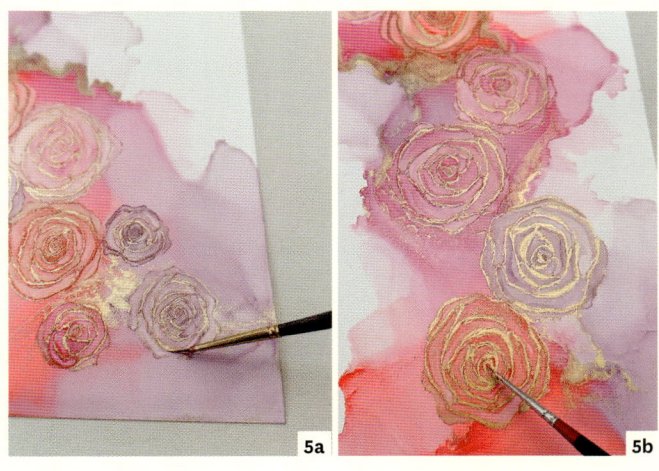

Step 5

Repeat steps 2 to 5 to create a composition of roses along the diagonal line of your paper (5a). I like to work with bigger and smaller roses by varying the size of the petals. It's best to work from the first, central rose in the middle and position a rose next to it. Vary the position of the roses so there's not one straight line but a zigzag pattern in the roses to create a nice composition (5b). To finish off the artwork, you can add golden splatters on the outside of the roses. Load a brush with the gold ink mix and gently tap it with another brush or tool to create splatters around the petals until you're satisfied with the overall look. If you want to avoid splatters on your roses, cover them with small pieces of paper towel.

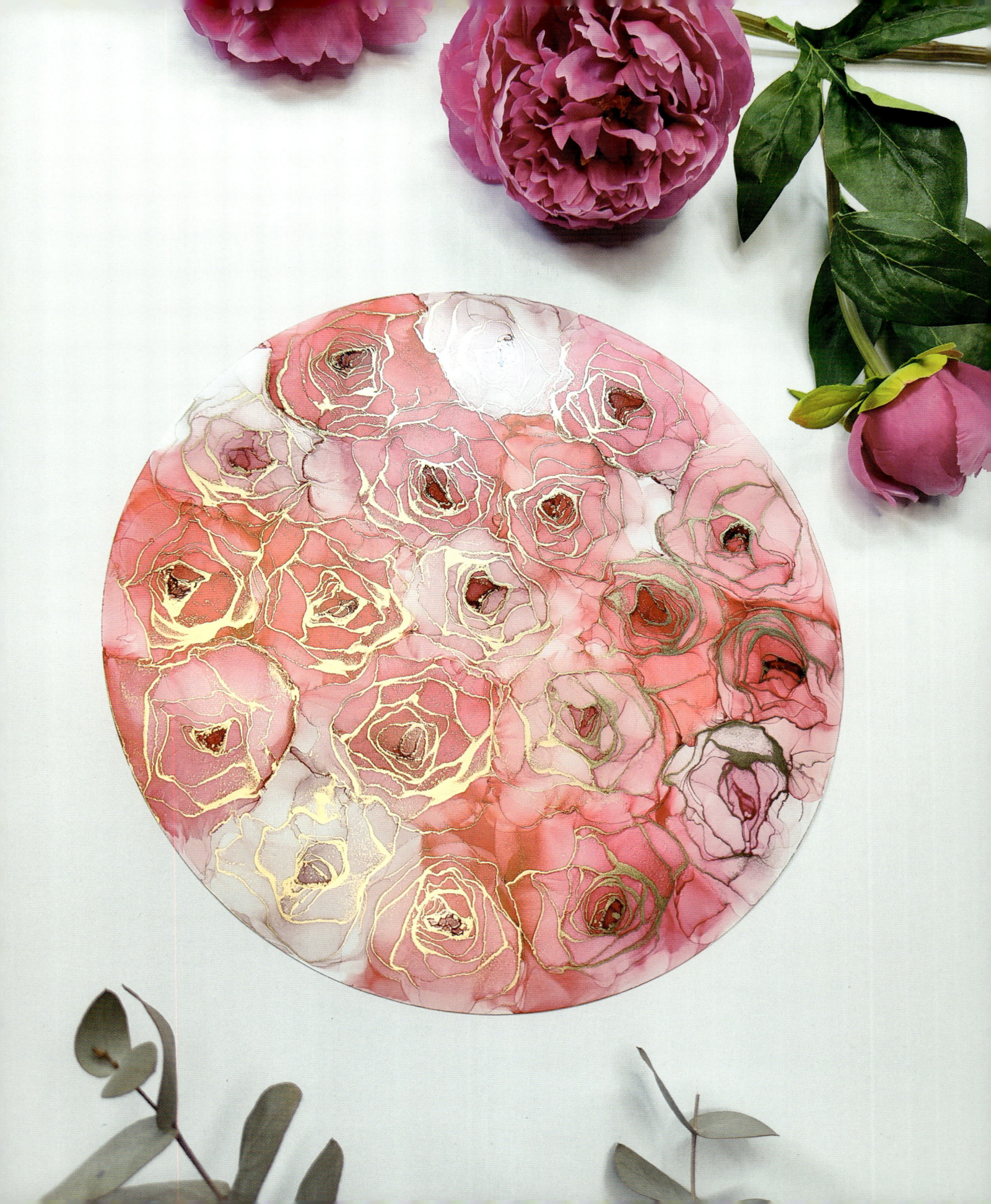

bouquet of roses

Roses are one of the most popular flowers to create with alcohol inks—and they're also my signature flower (and my second name!). They can be more challenging than some of the other flowers we've made so far, as they require a lot of control. Before attempting the golden-edged Roses or this Bouquet of Roses composition, make sure you've practiced the basics of creating a rose first! If you have any trouble, refer to the "Heat Tool Trouble-shooting Tips" on page 35.

LEVEL: ADVANCED

materials

- Alcohol inks in bright and soft pink and deep red
- Gold alcohol ink and isopropyl alcohol mix in a needle tip bottle at a 50/50 ratio
- 91% or 99% isopropyl alcohol in a needle tip bottle
- Round synthetic paper 10 or 12 inches (25.5 to 30 cm)
- Glazed ceramic tile for practicing (optional)

- Ink air blower (optional)
- Heat tool
- Set of miniature round synthetic brushes, 000 to 4.0 mm
- Silicone tip tool (optional)
- Varnish for protecting work
- Paper towels
- Safety supplies

Part 1: Basics of Creating a Rose

Step 1

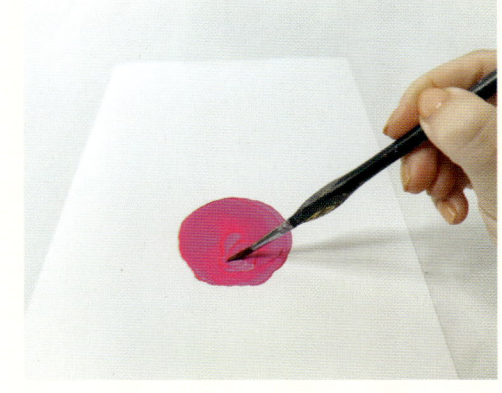

Start by creating the base for your rose. I'm using a bright pink color here. Bright saturated colors are usually easier to work with. Add one or two drops of alcohol ink onto your synthetic paper and use a large brush to spread the ink in a round shape about 2 to 3 inches (5 to 8 cm) wide. If needed, add a few drops of isopropyl alcohol to help the inks spread more easily. Use a heat tool to dry the ink.

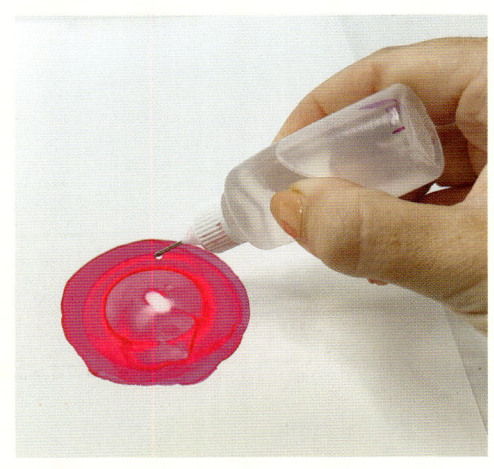

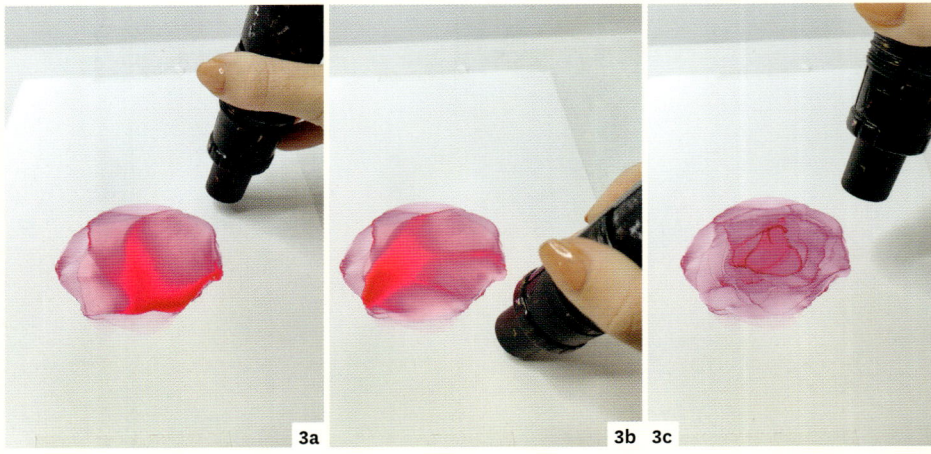

3a **3b** **3c**

Step 2

Reactivate the round shape by applying isopropyl alcohol until it's completely wet. You can use a silicone tip tool or brush to help spread it. Use plenty of isopropyl alcohol to create enough flow for the inks to move around—most people tend to use too little, so don't be afraid to apply more than you think you need.

Step 3

Move your heat tool slowly around the wet ink puddle. Depending on the strength of your heat tool, keep it 1 to 3 inches (3 to 7.5 cm) away from the ink. Position the heat tool along the side of the wet area (not directly above it). Move slowly enough to dry the outer rings of the ink (3a), which will form the rose petals.

Vary your movement by pausing for 2 to 3 seconds in each position before moving to another spot (3b). If you see ink flowing too much to one side, move the heat tool there to bring the inks back. This step is especially tricky at the beginning. Keep moving toward the center until all the ink is dry (3c).

tips

Warping

Because of the temperature of the heat tool, the synthetic paper may warp a little. This happens to me too, and it will usually flatten out in a few minutes. If your paper is extremely warped and does not flatten out, your heat tool is too hot to use for this technique. Check my recommendations for heat tools in Tools and Materials on page 16.

Basic rose technique

Need to see how to create a rose in action? Scan the QR for a video of this technique.

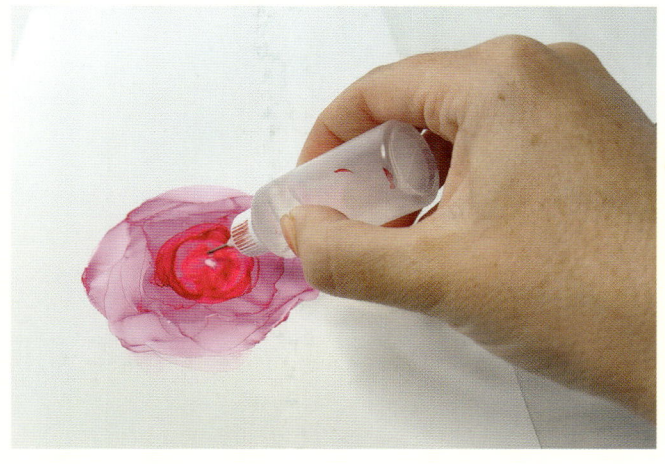

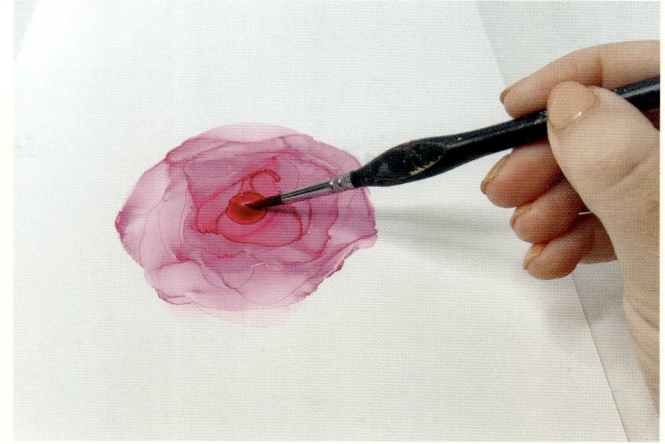

Step 4

While it's possible to create a single rose in one go, when you're starting out, you probably haven't achieved enough detail toward the center of the rose yet. If this is the case, reactivate the rose center with isopropyl alcohol where the petal shapes end. Using the same technique, slowly move your heat tool around the center until it's dry. Keep reactivating the center of the rose until you have enough detail toward the center. The smaller the area you need to reactivate, the less isopropyl alcohol you'll need.

Step 5

Each time you reactivate the ink, the color will lose a degree of saturation. If it becomes too light, add a touch more ink to the center with your brush, dry it, and then reactivate it with isopropyl alcohol.

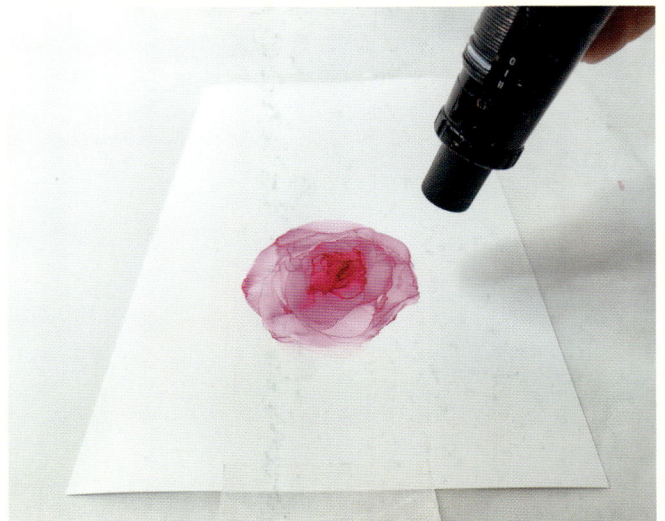

Step 6

Continue working toward the center of your rose. Once you're comfortable with this technique, try to create the rose in one go, which yields the most beautiful results but also requires the most control. This "one go" technique is what we'll also use to create roses with golden edges, so practice before moving on to that step!

Part 2: Creating a Rose with Golden Edges

Did you manage to turn your blob of ink into something resembling a rose? Great job! Let's try the golden edged roses next.

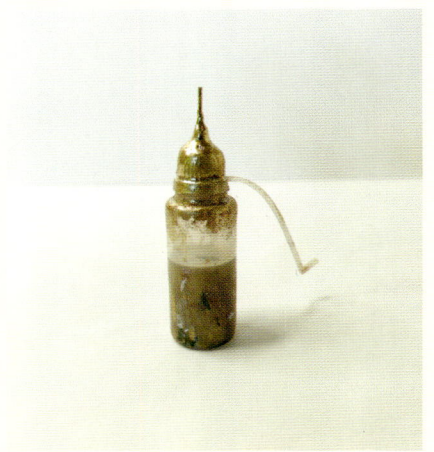

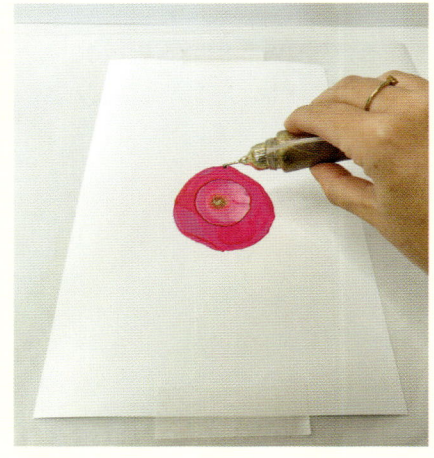

Step 1

For the golden-edged roses, follow the same steps as in part 1, but add gold alcohol ink to create the shimmering golden edges. Check my recommendations for gold alcohol inks in Tools and Materials on page 12. Prepare a 50/50 mix of gold alcohol ink and isopropyl alcohol in a needle tip bottle. The exact ratio may vary depending on the brand of gold alcohol ink you use—if there's too much gold, increase the isopropyl alcohol; if there's too little, add more gold ink or a few extra drops as you go. Always shake the gold ink mix before use.

Step 2

Create the base of the rose by adding one or two drops of the bright pink alcohol ink (don't add the gold yet!) onto your synthetic paper and use a large brush to spread the ink in a round shape about 2 to 3 inches (5 to 7.5 cm) wide. Use a heat tool to dry the ink.

Step 3

Reactivate the round shape with isopropyl alcohol and the golden ink mix. To get the best flow, start by adding a few drops of isopropyl alcohol, then add the gold ink mix, and finish with more isopropyl alcohol on top. I usually add about three drops of the gold ink mix, but adjust as needed based on your gold ink and rose size. **Do not add the gold ink mix first, as it will more easily sink and stick to the paper.** Ensure the entire shape is fully wet with isopropyl alcohol.

 Golden-edge rose technique

Using the gold ink mixture can be tricky. Scan the QR for a video of this technique.

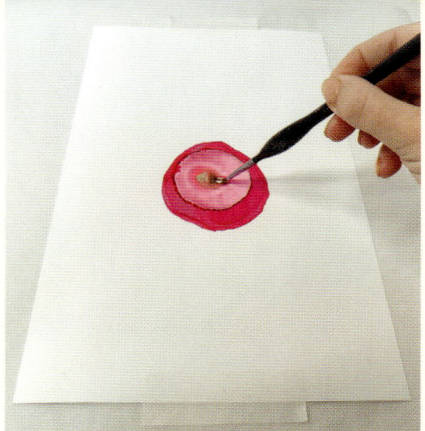

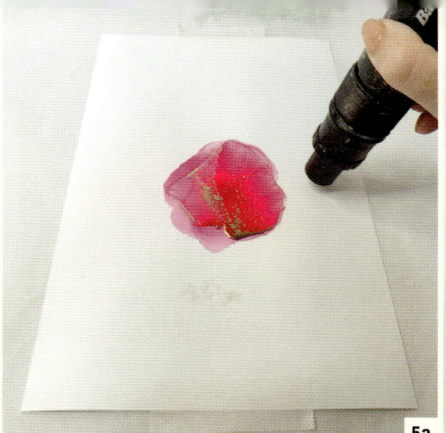

5a

5b

Step 4

If the gold sticks to the bottom and does not float, use a brush to loosen up the gold ink so it will float in your ink mix. Make sure you have enough isopropyl alcohol for a good flow.

Step 5

Move your heat tool slowly around the round shape (5a). The gold ink will begin sticking to the dried edges, forming the golden edges of the petals (5b). Continue moving toward the center until all the inks have dried.

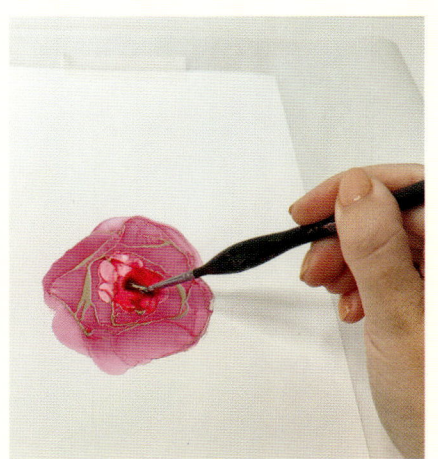

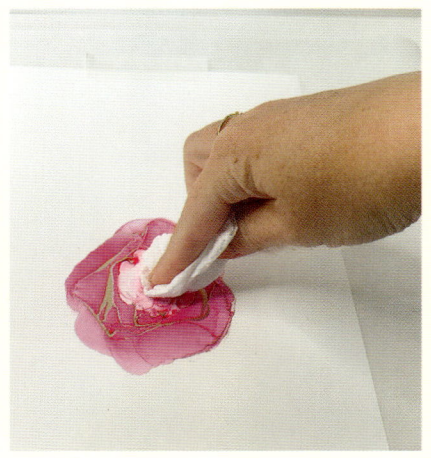

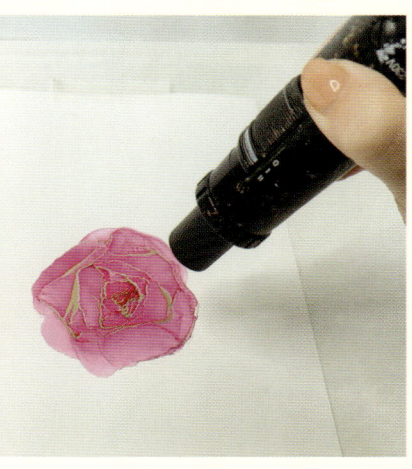

Step 6

This technique is best done in one go, as the gold ink can be difficult to reactivate. However, it *is* possible to reactivate the center by using isopropyl alcohol and loosening the gold ink with a brush. You may need to add another drop of the gold ink mix in this step.

Step 7

Alternatively, use a paper towel with some isopropyl alcohol to remove the center, especially if you notice a sticky buildup there. After removing the ink in the center, use your brush to add the same color ink and dry it with your heat tool. From here, follow step 6 and add one or two drops of the gold ink mix.

Step 8

Continue moving your heat tool until you reach the center of your rose. If you end up with too much isopropyl alcohol or gold ink mix in the center, use a paper towel to lift some of it up and finish the center. Repeat steps 6 and 7 if needed.

Part 3: Creating a Bouquet of Roses

Now that you've mastered the basics, let's create a composition of roses! A bouquet of roses is one of my favorite designs. To create the illusion of a bouquet, it's best to work on round synthetic paper. If you don't have any, you can trace and cut your own from square paper using scissors or a craft knife. Alternatively, start on a square paper and cut out the round shape afterward. Choose three or four ink colors for your composition, ideally analogous ones (colors close to each other on the color wheel), and choose light and dark shades to add contrast. My go-to palette includes light and dark shades of pink, with a rich burgundy red.

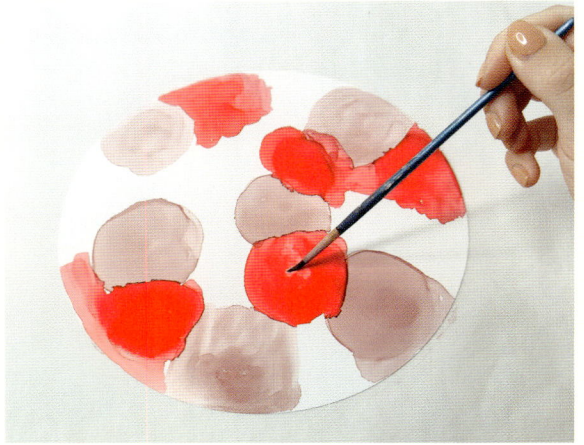

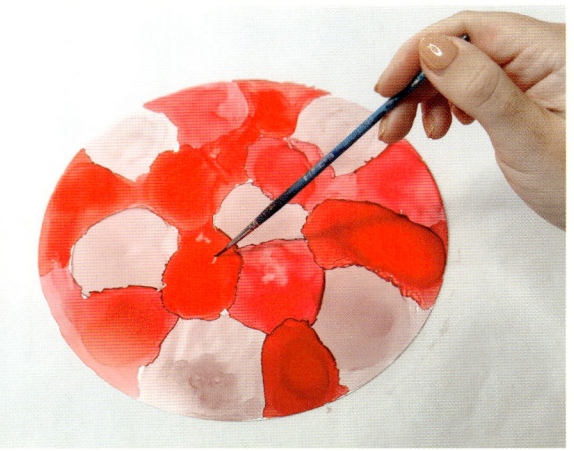

Step 1

Begin by filling the background with your ink colors. Add one or two drops of ink at a time, followed by a few drops of isopropyl alcohol to spread the color. Use a brush, ink air blower, or heat tool to spread and dry the ink before switching colors.

Step 2

Cover the background with an even mix of colors. Don't worry about its appearance; since we'll be adding roses on top, the background won't show in the final piece.

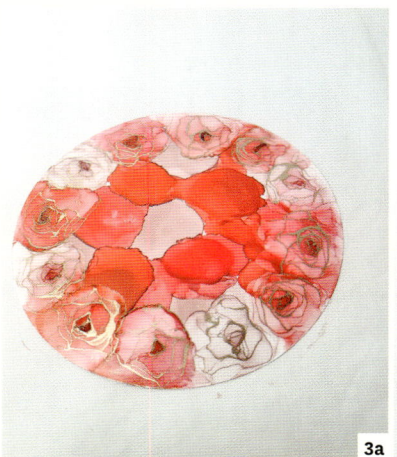

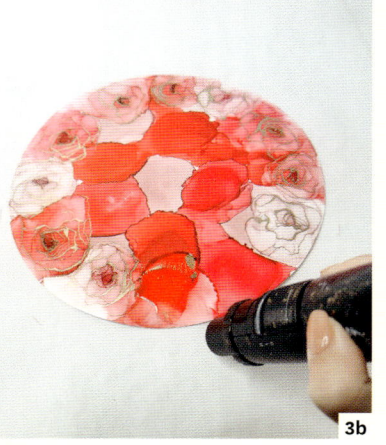

Step 3

Now, let's add the roses! Decide if you'd like to include gold and refer to part 1 or part 2 for the technique. I recommend starting with a ring of roses around the edge of the paper and working your way inward (3a). For roses on the paper's edge, use the heat tool to gently push the ink back from the edge (3b). This can be a tricky process that may need some extra attention.

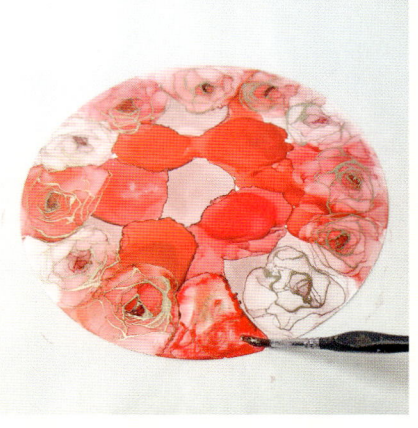

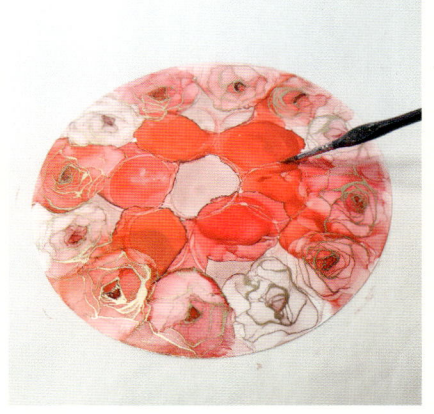

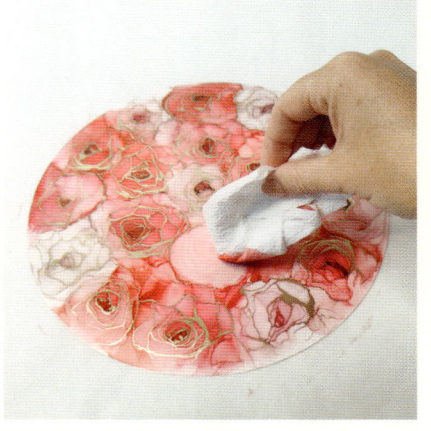

Step 4

Use a silicone tip tool or brush to spread isopropyl alcohol where each rose will go, making sure the background is fully covered with roses. Don't worry about perfect color separation; overlapping colors will create beautiful effects.

Step 5

Once the outer ring is complete, continue adding roses toward the center. Treat it like a puzzle to fit in each rose. You can plan the composition by lightly sketching rose shapes with a bit of ink or isopropyl alcohol, but remember that they will most likely not turn out exactly as planned, so allow for some freedom.

Step 6

Instead of focusing on perfection, fill the entire paper with roses first, then decide if any roses need redoing. If so, simply remove them with a paper towel, add new ink, dry it, and create a new rose on top.

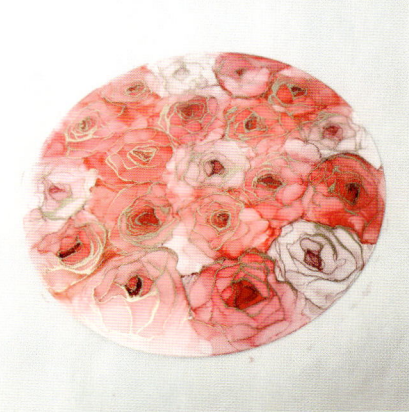

Step 7

Once you're satisfied with the composition, let it dry for 24 hours (avoid stacking anything on top, as it may remain tacky). Finally, seal with varnish as outlined on page 40.

 tip

Use your scrap paper or "failed" pieces

I like to say, "If all else fails, create roses." Sometimes I have failed pieces that are collecting dust, and since alcohol inks can be reactivated, you can use failed pieces to create roses on top. Simply reactivate the inks and create roses on top of your failed piece. You may even discover interesting color palettes by creating roses on top of your old artworks.

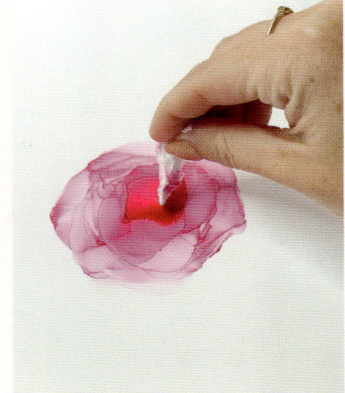

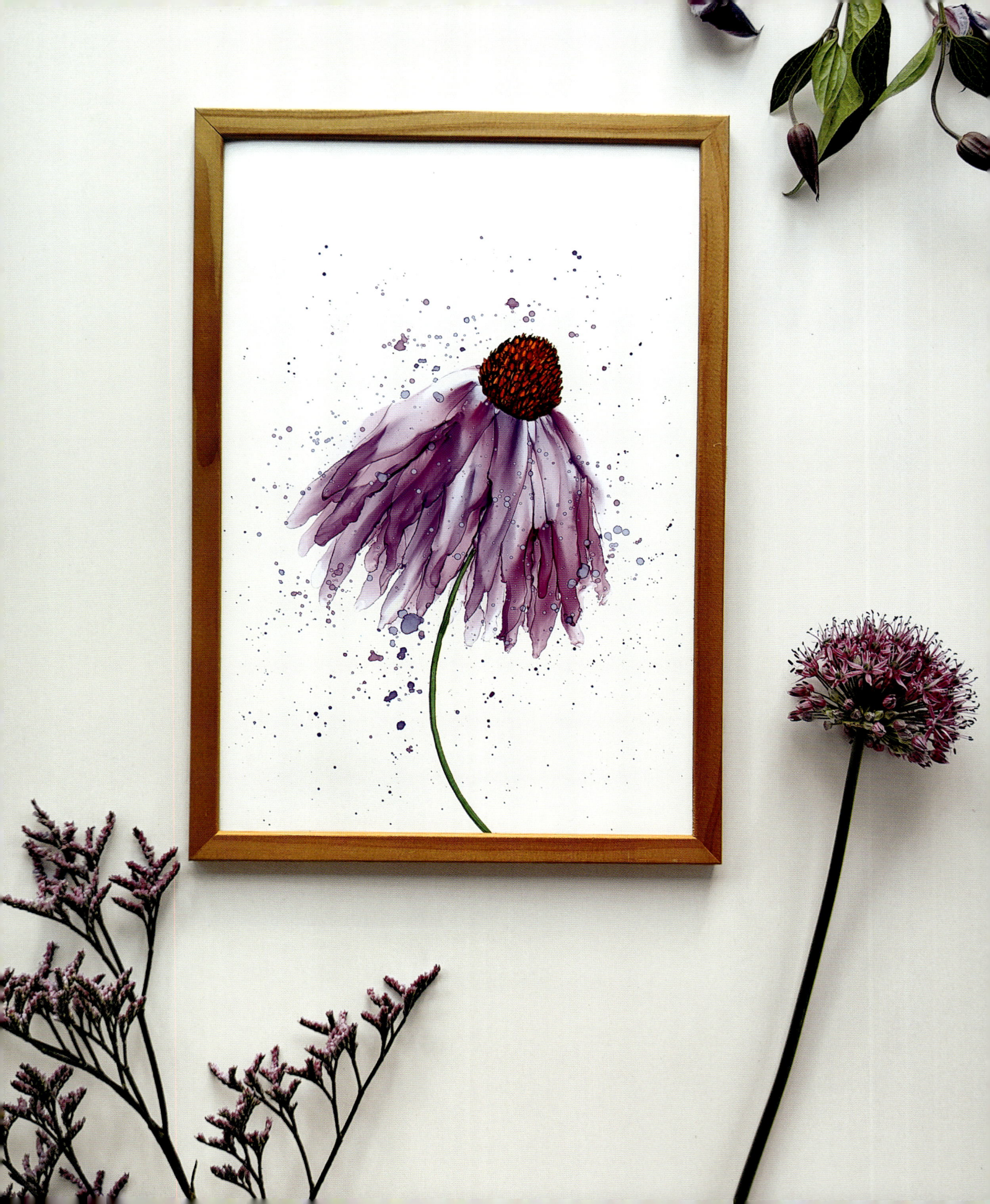

echinacea *(coneflower)*

The coneflower is a very popular flower to create with alcohol inks, and I had to include it in this book. In this Flower Project, you'll create your own version of the Echinacea (coneflower) with a mix of purple shades (or your own choice of colors). By creating multiple layers of petals, you'll see the colors blend together in magical ways.

materials

- Alcohol inks in lilac, plum, and violet (or several shades of purple), brown orange (sienna), orange, and green
- 91% or 99% isopropyl alcohol in a needle tip bottle
- Synthetic paper 10 × 12 inches (20 × 30 cm)
- Glazed ceramic tile for practicing (optional)
- Heat tool

- Set of miniature round synthetic brushes, 000 to 4.0 mm
- Silicone tip tool (optional)
- Paint palette or parchment paper
- Cotton swabs
- Paper towels
- Safety supplies

Step 1

Begin by outlining the cone of the flower to indicate where the petals will emerge. Place a few drops of lilac ink on your palette, then lightly dab your small brush in it to sketch the outline of the flower's cone on the upper mid-right section of your paper. The shape of the coneflower resembles a badminton shuttlecock. At the base of the cone, where the petals start, create a stroke of lilac ink about ½ inch (1 cm) wide with your brush and dry it with a heat tool.

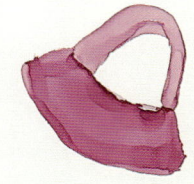

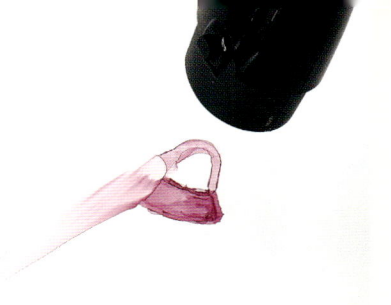
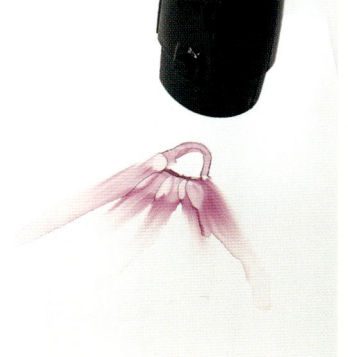
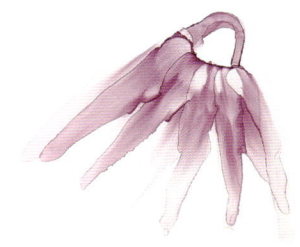

Step 2

To create a long, narrow petal, start on the left side of the cone base and add a small stroke of isopropyl alcohol (no more than two drops) in the direction where the petal is going to be, overlapping the lilac ink. Make sure the stroke of isopropyl alcohol extends beyond the lilac ink to create a nice and even petal shape. Quickly use your heat tool to blow the ink outward from the base of the cone to form the petal. Keep the tool 3 to 4 inches (7.5 to 10 cm) away on the cold or lowest heat setting. Move slowly to dry the petal from the base outward and keep enough distance for slow drying. If excess ink remains at the end (oftentimes a droplet of ink will appear at the end of the petal), lift it with a cotton swab before fully drying it.

Step 3

Create a second petal next to the first one using the technique from step 2. Continue adding new petals next to each other until you have about five. Don't worry about the look of each individual petal. We'll create several layers of petals, so the first few petals will barely be visible in the final result.

Step 4

Repeat steps 1 to 3 by adding more of the lilac ink at the base and each time add a new petal in between two petals. If a petal is too long, use a paper towel to remove the excess and redo it. For shorter petals, just go over them again. Once you're comfortable with the basics of this technique, experiment by shaping petals differently, moving the heat tool from the left, right, or both to create curved shapes. Adjust the amount of alcohol for longer and/or wider petals.

tips

Switching tools

Try this project with an ink air blower or using the air from an air brush tool to create the petals. Each tool will give a different look to the petals, so have fun in experimenting.

Coneflower technique

Need to see how to create the coneflower in action? Scan the QR for a video of this technique.

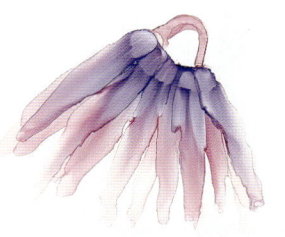

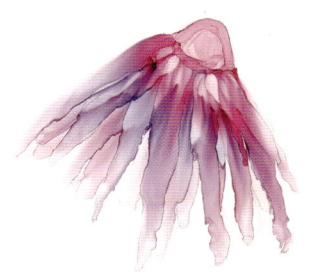

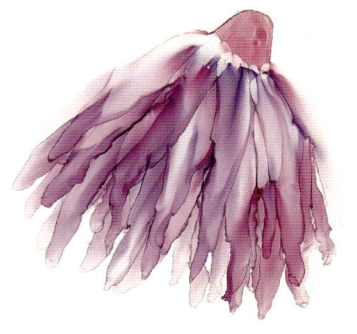

5a   5b   5c

Step 5

Repeat steps 1 to 4, this time applying the violet ink at the base of the cone (5a). The violet will now beautifully blend into the lilac ink color and create multicolored petals. Repeat this process a third time with the plum-colored ink (5b). Use a small brush to fill in the coneflower with lilac ink to get a better idea of where the petals should emerge. Keep repeating steps 1 to 4 with different colors until you are satisfied with the look of the petals (5c). As you can see from the pictures, the more layers, the more voluminous the coneflower will start to look. In this stage, you can use a cotton swab with isopropyl alcohol on it to clean the messy petal ends and make them more rounded if needed.

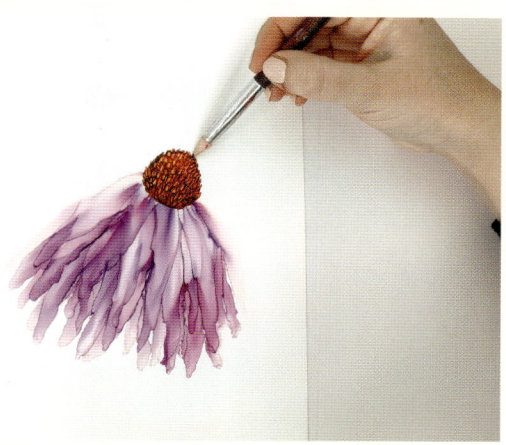

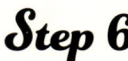

Step 6

To draw the cone of the flower, add a few drops of the orange-brown ink to your palette or parchment paper and lightly dab your small brush into it and fill in the cone with the ink. To create the spiky look of the cone, you can use a silicone tip tool or brush while the ink is still a bit wet but tacky and draw small, pointed brushstrokes starting from the top of the cone toward the base of the cone in a spiral pattern. By applying pressure, the ink will be removed in these places, creating texture in the ink. After drying, you can come in with small, pointed brushstrokes with the orange and orange-brown ink to create lighter toned spikes toward the top and darker ones toward the base of the cone to create more depth.

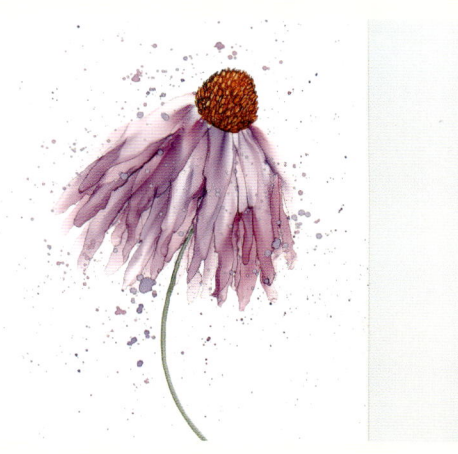

Step 7

Draw a stem by applying one or two drops of the green ink to your palette and use a fine brush loaded with a bit of the green ink to draw a curved stem from in between the petals to the lower center of the paper. Finish the artwork with ink splatters around the petals for a playful touch. Load a brush with the desired ink colors and gently tap it with another brush or tool to create splatters around the coneflower until you're satisfied with the overall look.

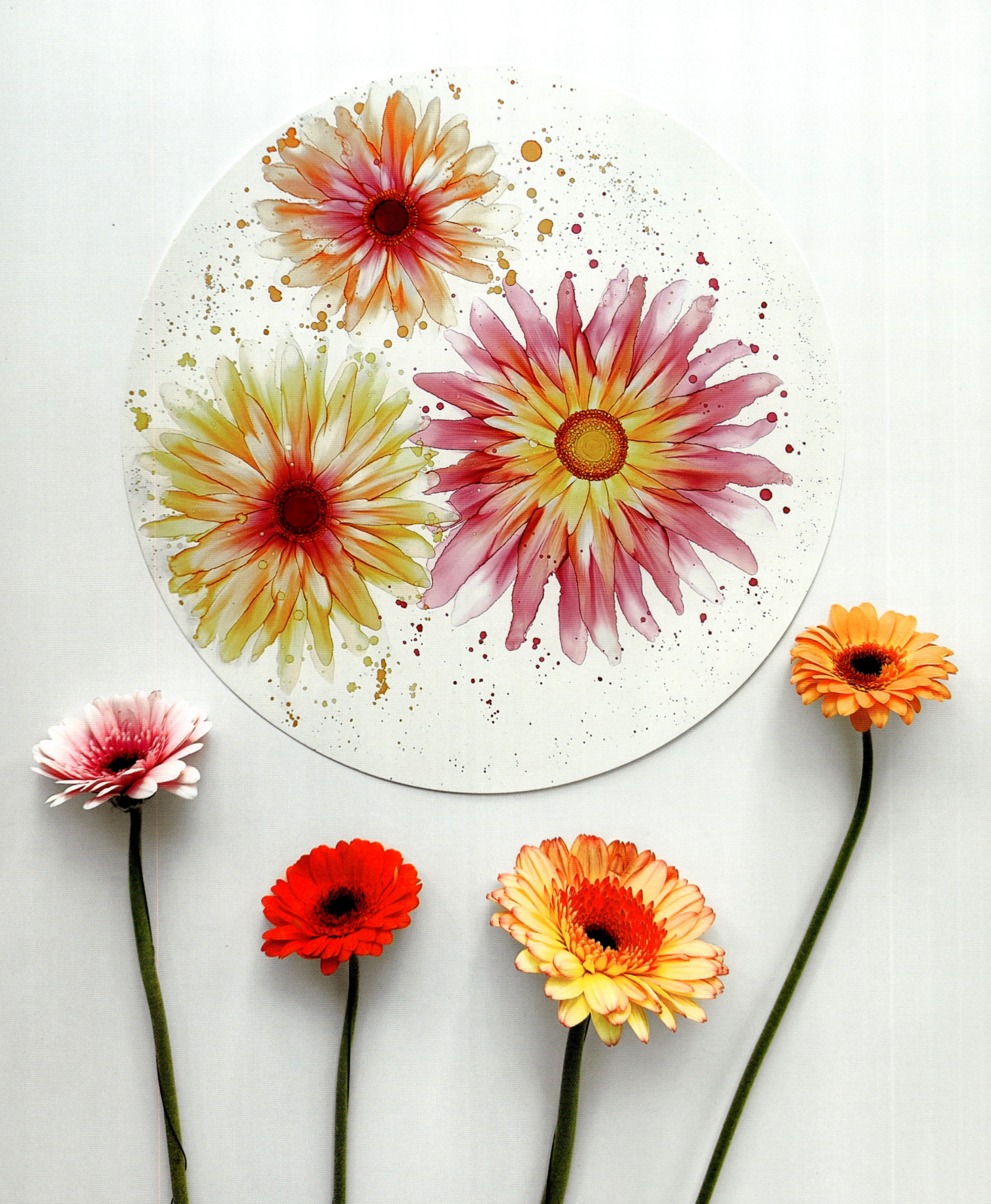

gerbera daisies

The Gerbera is a type of daisy and comes in bold, cheerful colors with a beautifully detailed center. The technique for these daisies builds upon the Coneflower Project, but this time we'll work in a round manner and finish the Gerberas with lots of tiny petals that form a ring around the center of the flower.

LEVEL: ADVANCED
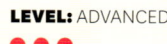

materials

- Alcohol inks in pink, orange, and yellow
- 91% or 99% isopropyl alcohol in a needle tip bottle
- Synthetic paper round or square 12 × 12 inches (30 × 30 cm)
- Glazed ceramic tile for practicing (optional)
- Heat tool

- Set of miniature round synthetic brushes, 000 to 4.0 mm
- Silicone tip tool (optional)
- Paint palette or parchment paper
- Cotton swabs
- Paper towels
- Safety supplies

Step 1

For this technique, it's especially important that the surface of your synthetic paper is very clean; therefore, it's best to use a sheet straight from the packaging. Start by creating the first flower on the center-right of your paper. Add yellow, orange, and pink ink to your paint palette. Using a small brush, apply the yellow ink to create a circle with 1-inch (2.5 cm) diameter, then dry it using your heat tool. Ensure there are at least 3 inches (7.5 cm) from the edges of the paper. Next, use a different brush to draw an orange ring around the yellow circle, approximately ½ inch (13 mm) wide, and dry it with your heat tool. Finally, add a pink ring around the orange circle, also approximately ½ inch (13 mm) wide, and dry it with your heat tool.

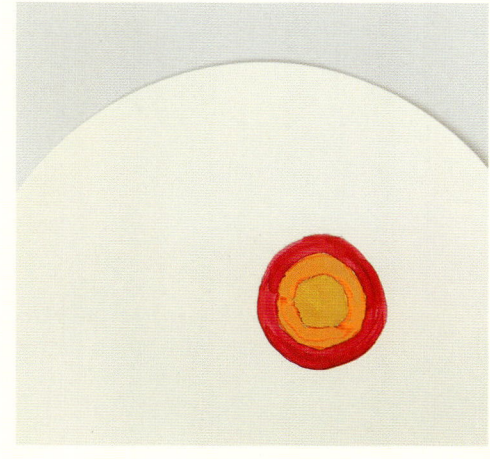

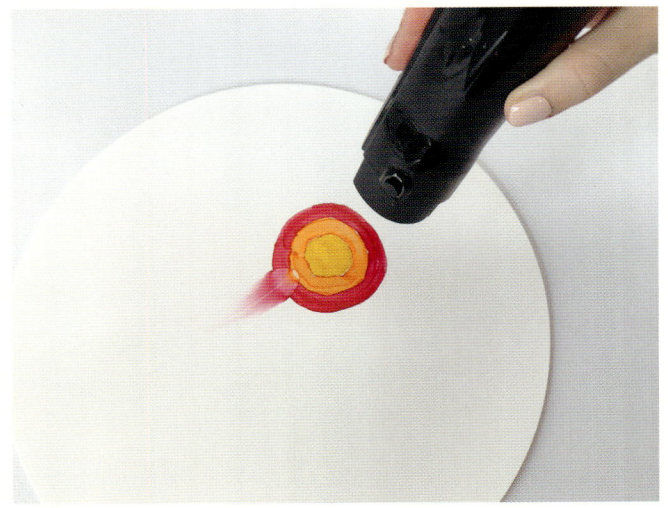

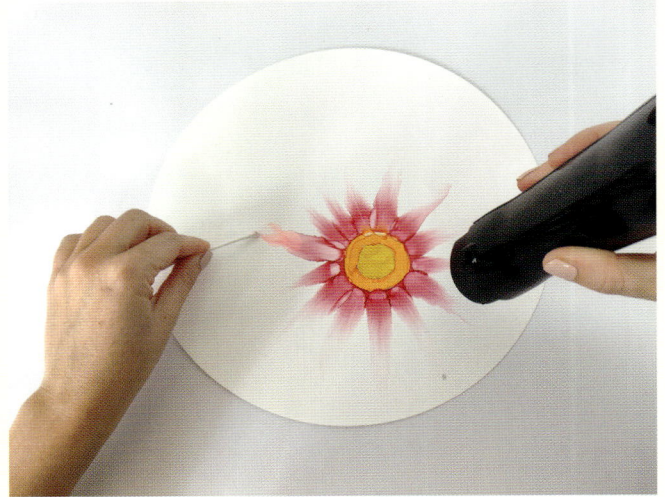

Step 2

To create long, narrow petals, use the same technique as the Echinacea (Coneflower) project (page 87). Apply a small stroke of isopropyl alcohol with a needle tip bottle from the outer pink circle outward to reactivate only the pink ink. Make sure the stroke of isopropyl alcohol extends beyond the outer circle. You only need a small amount of alcohol, so be careful not to add too much. Use your heat tool to blow the ink outward to start forming the petal. Keep the heat tool 3 to 4 inches (7.5 to 10 cm) away, using the cold or the least hot setting. Move slowly to dry the petal from the base outward and keep enough distance to dry the petal gradually. If there's too much ink left toward the end of the petal (sometimes a droplet of ink will appear at the end of the petal), use a cotton swab to lift some of the ink before fully drying it.

Step 3

Create a second petal right next to the previous one using the technique from step 2. Each time, layer a new petal next to the previous one, until you have a full round of about ten petals. If a petal ends up much longer than the others, use a paper towel or cotton swab to remove the end of the petal and go over it another time. If your petal turns out much shorter, you can simply move over it another time. In the beginning, the end of the petals may not be very saturated, but don't worry about the look of each individual petal. We'll create several layers of petals, so the first few petals will barely be visible in the final result.

 tip

Gerbera daisy technique

Need to see how to create the Gerbera daisies in action? Scan the QR for a video of this technique.

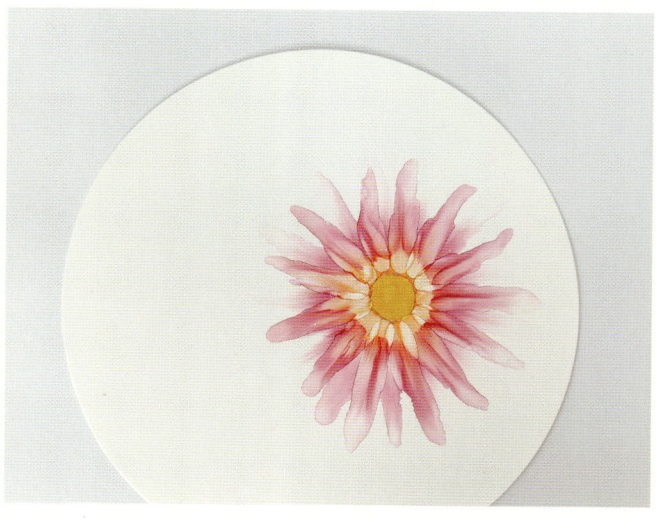

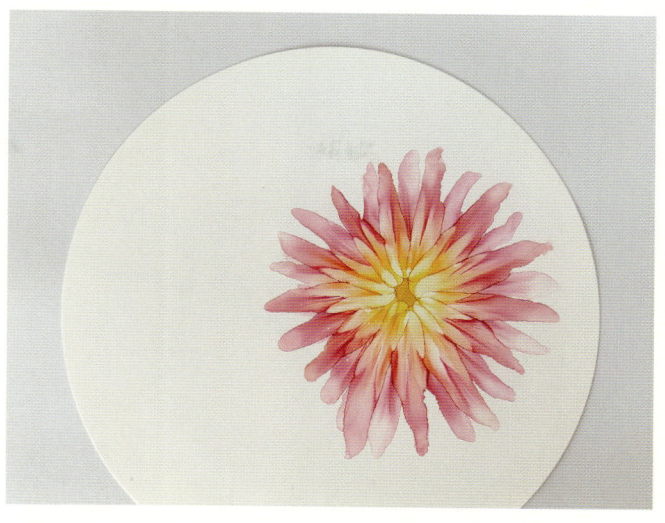

Step 4

Repeat steps 2 and 3 to create another round of petals. This time, use the alcohol to reactivate the ink from the orange circle outward and each time add a new petal in between two others. The orange ink will now blend into the pink ink. To create nice and even petal shapes, ensure that the stroke of isopropyl alcohol extends beyond the orange circle before using the heat tool to blow out the petal.

Step 5

Repeat steps 2 and 3 again. This time, reactivate the ink from the yellow circle outward and add a new circle of petals. Repeat this process until you're satisfied with the look of the petals and there's a nice, full bloom. In this stage, you can use a cotton swab with isopropyl alcohol on it to clean the messy petal ends and make them more rounded if needed.

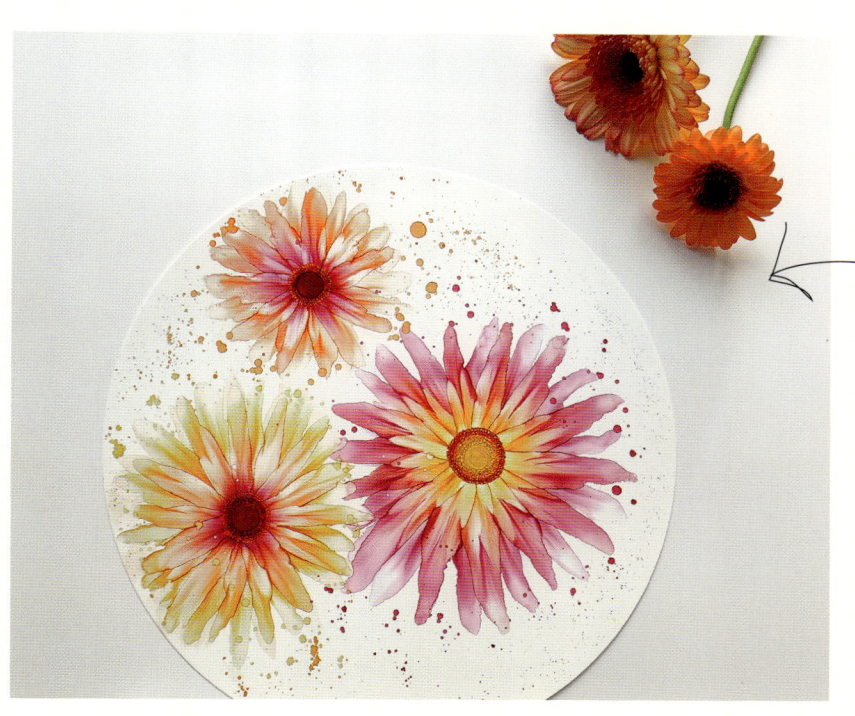

Mix and match different ink colors to create beautiful variations of these daisies.

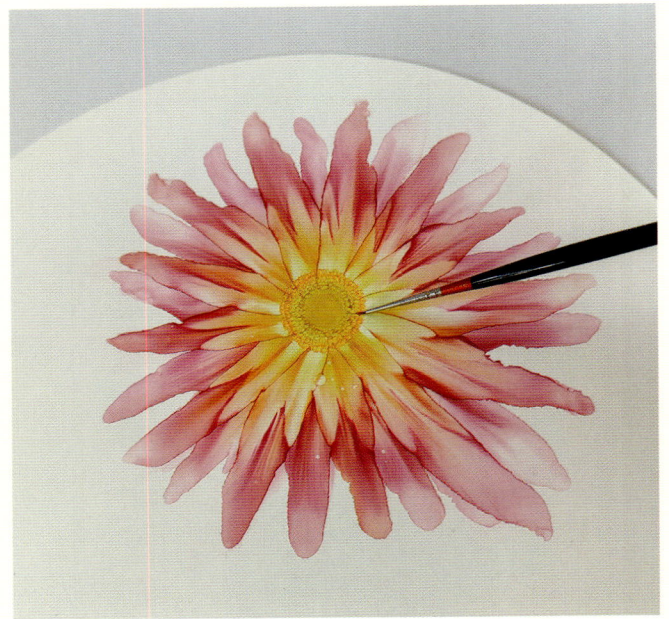

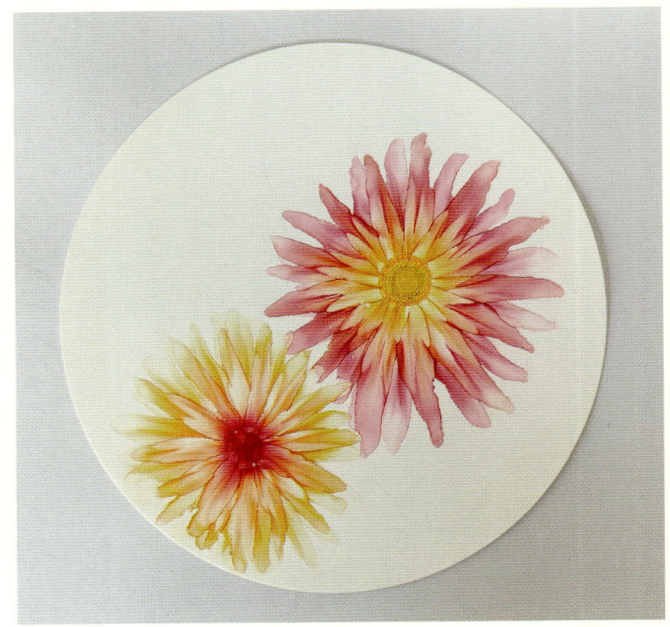

Step 6

To draw the center of the flower, first use your small brush to add more of the yellow ink to the center in a circle of about ½ inch (13 mm) and dry it with your heat tool. Use a fine brush and the yellow ink to create two rings of tiny petals around the yellow circle. Use small dots or short brushstrokes in a circular pattern, working from the inside to the outside. For extra detail, you may need to move over it several times and dry in between until you get a beautifully detailed center. Then, repeat this process with the orange ink and create another two rows of tiny petals outside the yellow ones.

Step 7

Repeat steps 1 to 6 to create a second Gerbera toward the lower left. It's best to create one Gerbera fully before moving to the next, as it is difficult to know exactly where the petals of the flower will end. Since my first flower turned out much larger than anticipated, I chose to add a smaller one next to it. Be careful—it can be quite challenging to add another flower next to the first one, as there's a chance the petals will ruin the first flower by moving over it. You can also keep your composition to one flower to be safe. For the second Gerbera, vary the colors by creating a pink circle with an orange and then yellow outer circle (the reverse from the first flower). To create smaller petals, add less isopropyl alcohol and try and dry the petal even slower. Use the help of a cotton swab to stop the inks from moving over the previous flower too much, or the edges of the paper.

Creating details with alcohol ink markers

Did you know alcohol ink markers are a great tool for adding details to your flowers? Use a similar color of an alcohol ink marker to add the detailing in step 6 or alternatively use an empty, fillable marker and fill it with isopropyl alcohol or a blending solution.

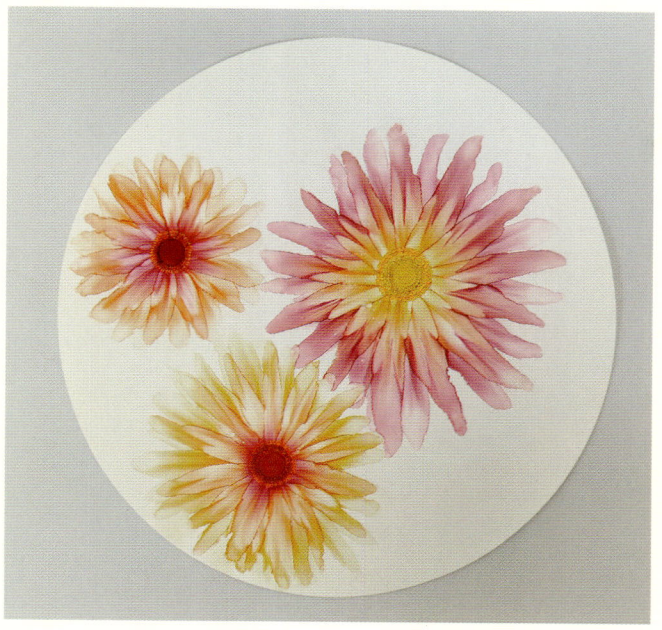

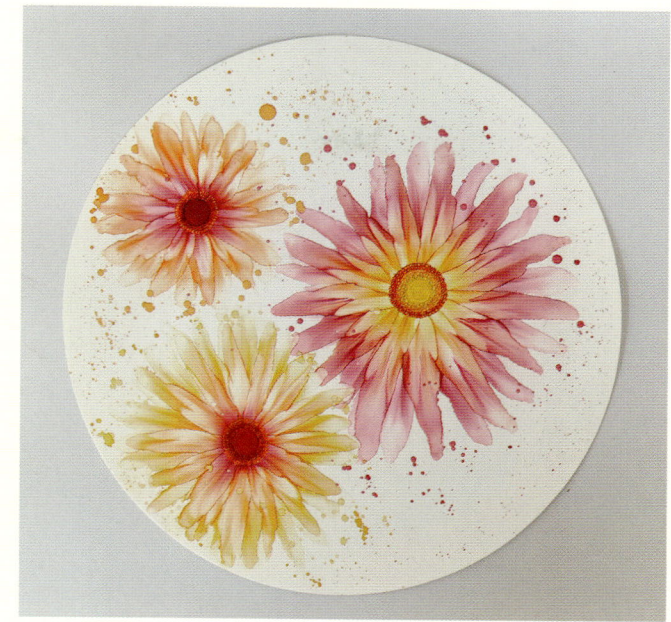

Step 8

If there's still room on your paper, repeat steps 1 to 6 to create a third Gerbera on the upper left. For the third flower, I worked even smaller and used less alcohol to make the Gerbera fit. For the last flower, I chose to work with a pink center and only one orange ring and leave out the yellow to create a smaller flower. To finish off the center of the last two Gerberas, use pink ink with small pink petals and orange petals on the outside.

Step 9

To finish the artwork, add splatters in the same colors as the flower petals on the outside. Load a brush with the desired ink colors and gently tap it with another brush or tool to create splatters around the Gerberas until you're satisfied with the overall look. If you have a lot of negative space left, you can also choose to add stems using S-shaped brushstrokes with green ink in between the petals toward the bottom center of the paper, but I chose to leave them out.

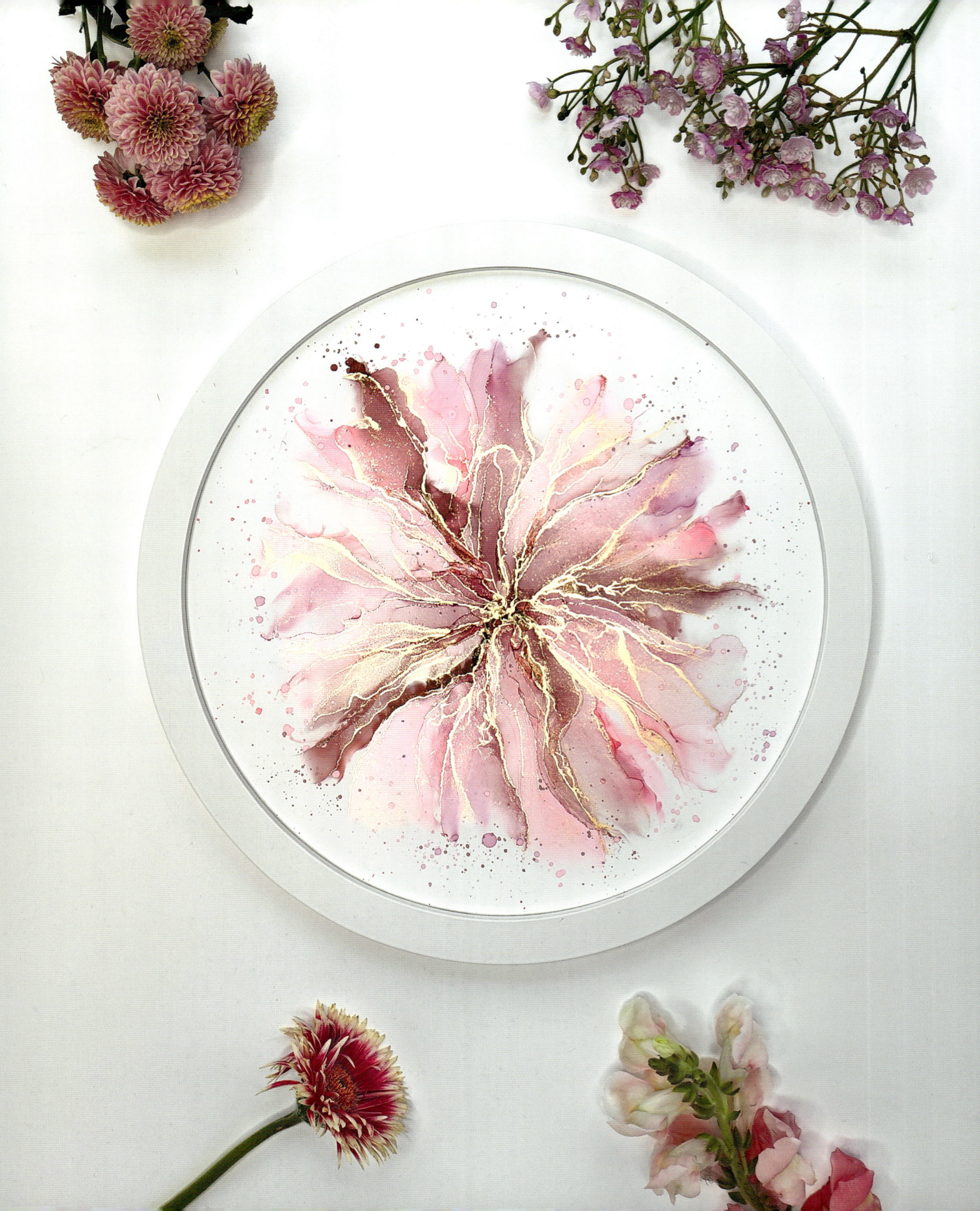

abstract wispy floral

The wispy faded look that can be achieved with alcohol inks is much pursued, but not as easy as it may look! In this project, we'll use a heat tool technique to create an abstract flower with beautiful, wispy petals. The great thing about working on an abstract floral is that it does not need to resemble any specific flower. This project will be easier if you have already practiced with your heat tool in one of the previous projects.

 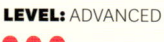

materials

- Alcohol inks in bright pink, lavender, and reddish purple
- Gold alcohol ink and isopropyl alcohol mix in needle tip bottle at a 50/50 ratio
- 91% or 99% isopropyl alcohol in a needle tip bottle
- Synthetic paper round or square 12 × 12 inches (30 × 30 cm)

- Glazed ceramic tile for practicing (optional)
- Heat tool
- Set of miniature round synthetic brushes, 000 to 4.0 mm
- Silicone tip tool (optional)
- Paint palette or parchment paper
- Cotton swabs
- Paper towels
- Safety supplies

Step 1

Add each of the ink colors to your palette. Load your large brush with the reddish purple and make five to six strokes from the center outward, leaving negative space at the edges. Dry them with your heat tool. Repeat this process for each color, creating a variation of brushstrokes around the center with negative space between them. Don't worry about the exact placement of the colors and brushstrokes. Dry each color using your heat tool.

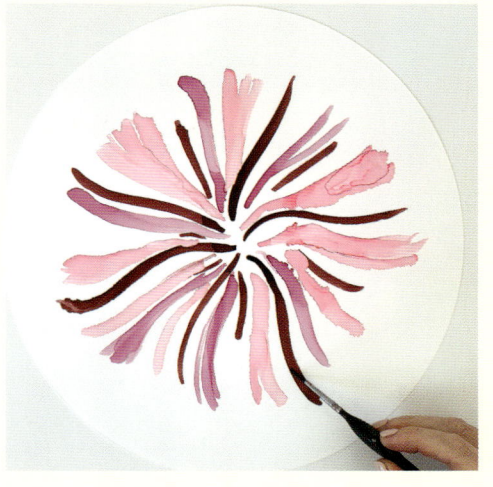

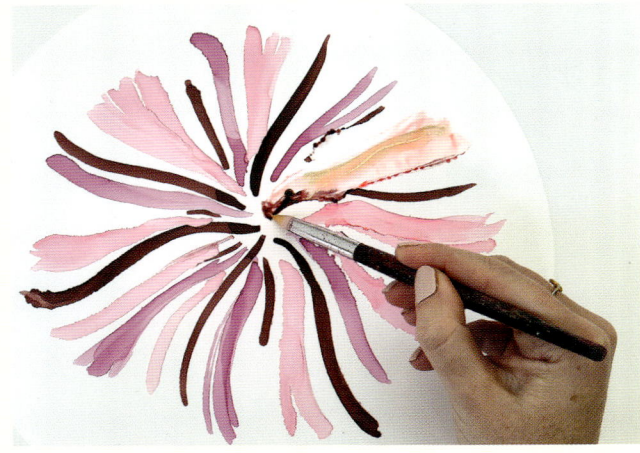
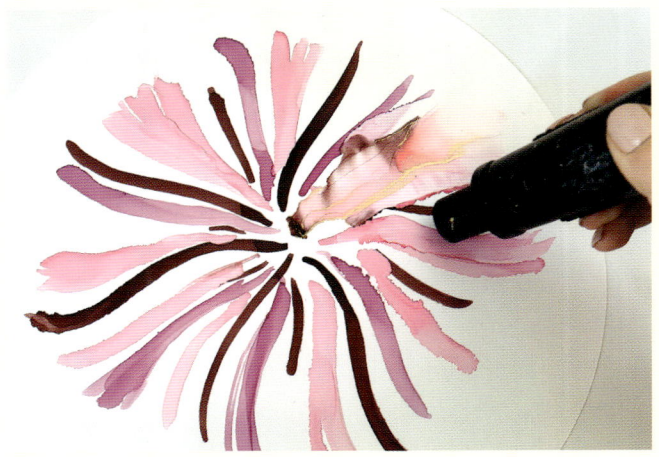

Step 2

To create the petals, apply a stroke of isopropyl alcohol from the outside to the center using a needle tip bottle in the same direction as the brushstrokes. Add a small stroke of gold ink mix within the wet alcohol (shake before use). For a wispy, faded look, ensure only clear alcohol is on the outside without any ink color. If needed, add more alcohol on the outside for the faded effect. Use a silicone tip tool or small brush to shape the petal, especially to create a pointed edge toward the center. Work relatively fast because the inks will spread quickly.

Step 3

While the ink is still wet, move the heat tool from the outer edges toward the center on the long side of the wet ink, first on one side of the petal then the other (not on top). Depending on the strength of your heat tool, keep it 1 to 3 inches (3 to 7.5 cm) away from the ink. Position the heat tool along the side of the wet area (not directly above it). Move slowly enough to dry the outer edges before moving to the other side. The gold will stick to the dried edges. Repeat this process until the inks travel toward the center. If there's too much of the wet ink left, use a cotton swab or paper towel to pick up the remaining ink toward the center. Keep moving the heat tool until all the ink is dry.

Abstract wispy floral technique

Need to see how to create an abstract wispy floral in action? Scan the QR for a video of this technique.

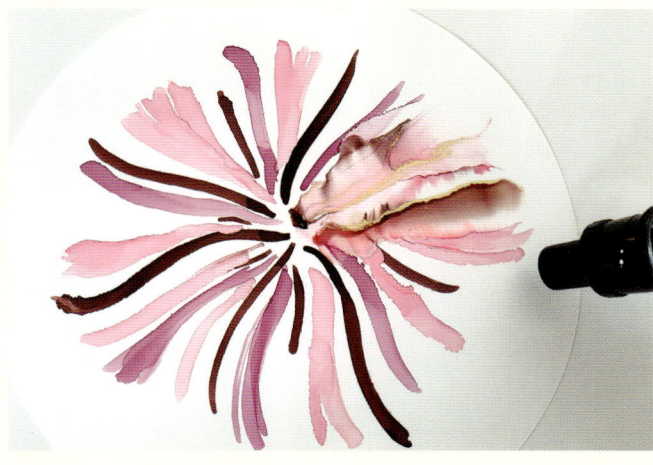

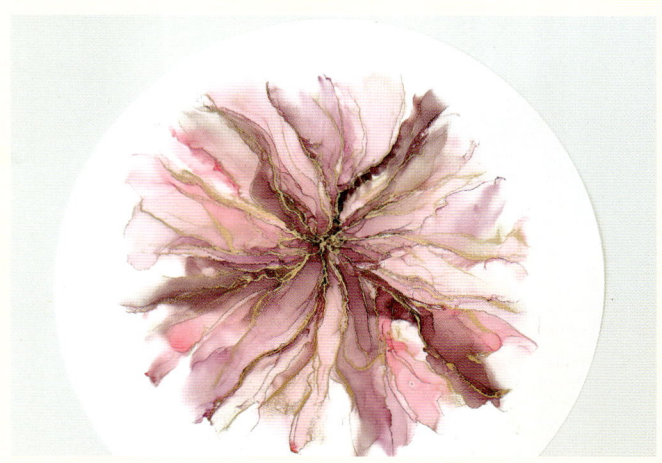

Step 4

Repeat steps 2 and 3 by applying another stroke of the isopropyl alcohol and gold ink mix right next to the previous petal shape. The petal may partly overlap the previous petal, but don't worry about this. This technique is tricky in the beginning, and it takes time to learn and control the inks. Watch how the inks behave so you can react to them. For example, if ink flows too much to one side, move the heat tool there to bring the inks back. A silicone tip tool or brush helps guide wet ink into the desired shape. This requires some multitasking. You can also vary the amount of isopropyl alcohol used for each petal until you find the ideal amount.

Step 5

Keep repeating steps 2 and 3 and work your way all around the center to create a full bloom. If a petal is too large or messy, use a paper towel with isopropyl alcohol to remove it, reapply ink, dry it, and blow out the petal again using the technique from steps 2 and 3. If the petal turns out too small, move over it a second time. If the gold alcohol ink sticks at the bottom, use a brush to loosen it so it floats in the mix. Continue until you are pleased with the floral design.

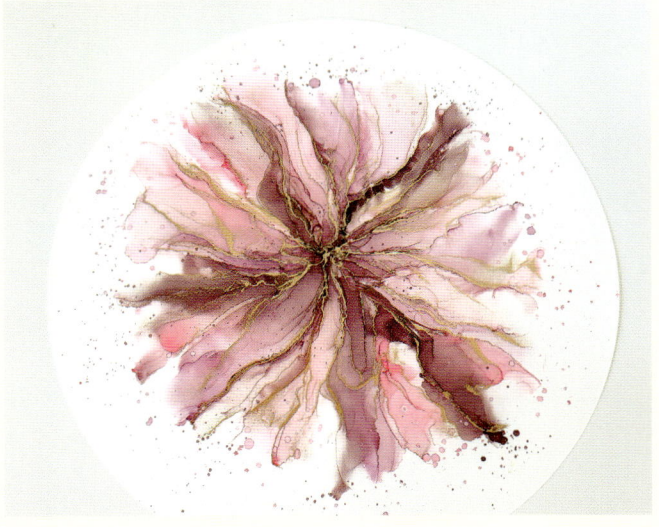

Step 6

Use a cotton swab with alcohol to clean any messy edges of the petals. To finish, load a brush with the desired ink color and gently tap it with another brush or tool to create splatters around the floral design until you're satisfied with the overall look. You can also add gold splatters using your gold ink mix.

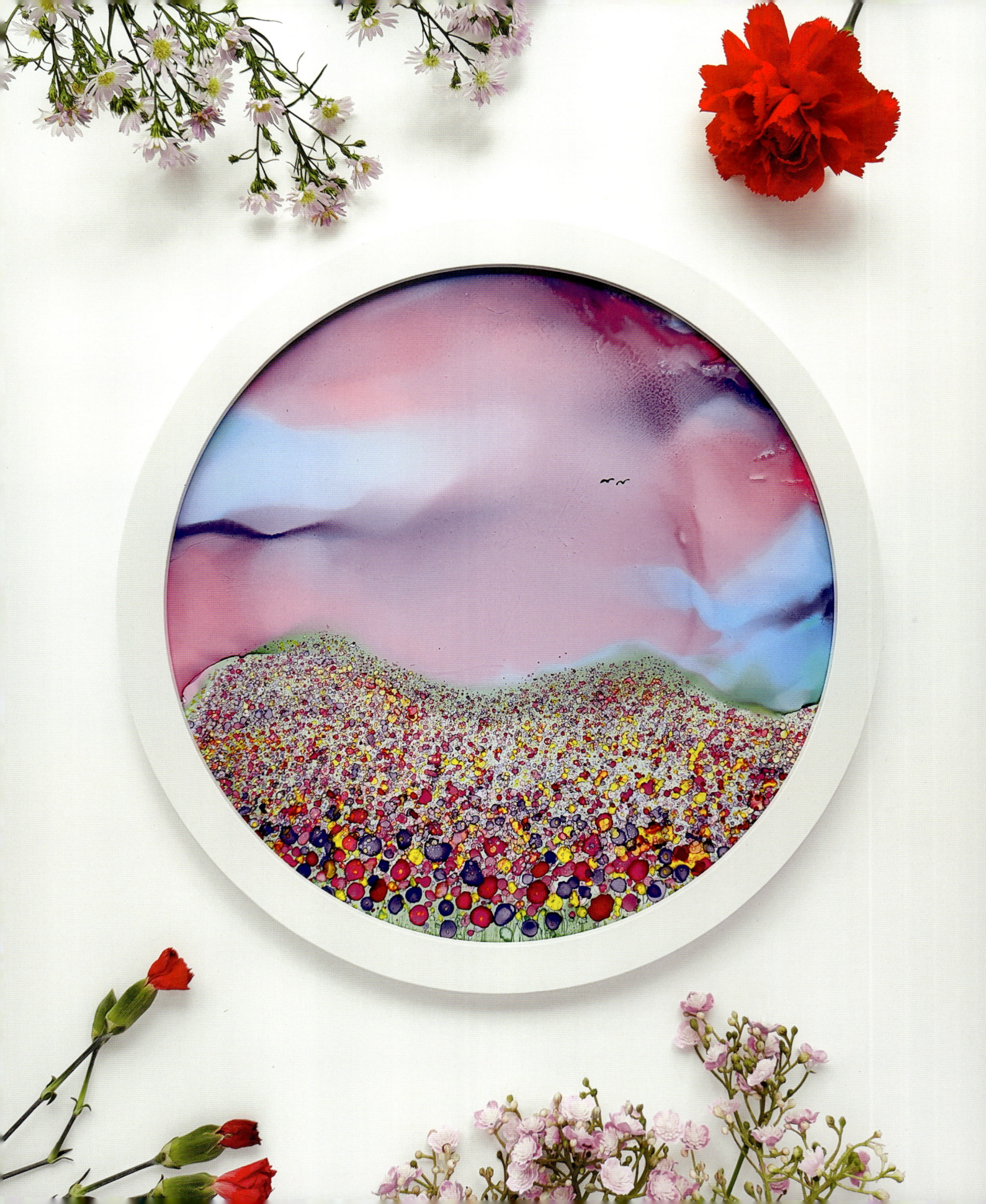

flower field

The beauty of art is that we can create our own imaginary worlds, in this case an endless flower field beneath a serene pastel sky that we can dream away in. And the best part: It doesn't need to be difficult to create! First, you'll learn how to create the pastel sky background using a tilting technique. Then, we'll have fun creating various layers of splatters to resemble a flower field.

LEVEL: BEGINNER
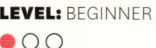

materials

- Alcohol inks in two shades of green, lilac, purple, bright pink, light blue, yellow, and black
- 91% or 99% isopropyl alcohol in a needle tip bottle
- Synthetic paper round or square 12 × 12 inches (30 × 30 cm)
- Glazed ceramic tile for practicing (optional)
- Set of miniature round synthetic brushes, 000 to 4.0 mm, plus a fan brush

- Painter's tape (optional)
- Heat tool (optional)
- Paint palette or parchment paper
- Cup with isopropyl alcohol to clean brushes (optional)
- Paper towels
- Safety supplies

Step 1

Make sure the paper is flat. Begin by wetting the entire surface of the paper with alcohol and spreading it evenly using a large brush. Working quickly, apply strokes of ink from the bottle left to right, using the light blue, lilac, purple, and bright pink at the top half to create the pastel sky. Leave space between the ink strokes so they don't mix into each other right away. For the bottom half, use the two shades of green, but only use a little of the green ink to get a light color. For a hill-like effect, use a curved line where the green meets the sky and leave some space between the sky and the field. Keep in mind there's a relatively small working time since the inks will start drying quickly.

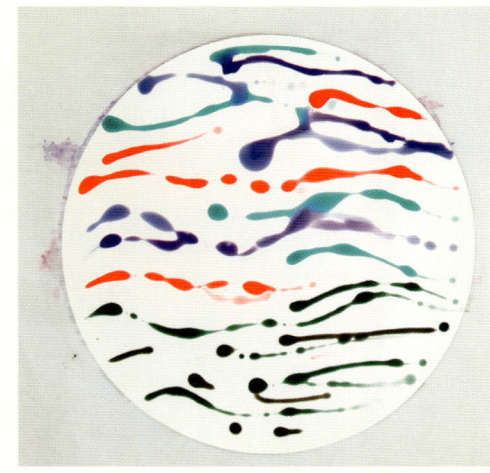

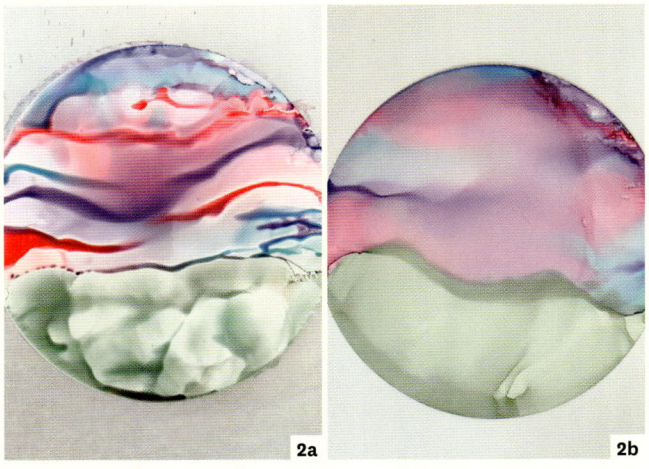

2a 2b

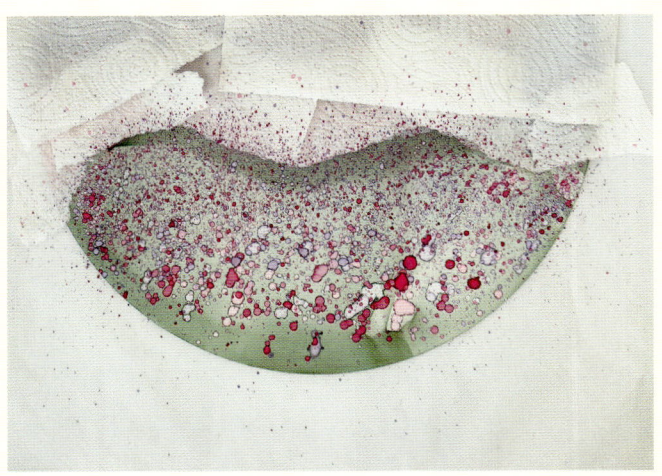

Step 2

While the background is still wet, use a fan brush to spread the inks from left to right, ensuring they don't mix too much and use separate brushes (or clean the brush) for the top and the bottom. Then, tilt the surface from left to right to softly blend the colors (2a). Fill in any empty spots with more ink and repeat the process as needed. Since the surface will start drying relatively quickly, don't overthink this step and don't keep reworking it for too long. Use a paper towel to pick up or remove inks if they build up into a puddle (usually toward the middle or edges) and if the green and pink have mixed into a muddy color. Apply more ink in the empty spots if needed. Allow it to air-dry for a soft gradient; this may take up to 60 minutes (2b). Once it's almost dry, you can use your heat tool to speed up the drying process.

Step 3

Cover the sky with a paper towel to protect it from ink splatters. Add the pink, purple, lilac, and yellow ink to your palette. If needed, add a few drops of isopropyl alcohol to dilute the ink colors for a lighter color. Load a brush with the bright pink ink and gently tap it with another brush or tool to create splatters across the green field. Start by making large splatters at the bottom, and when the brush loses ink, it will create smaller splatters suitable for the top, creating depth in the flower field. Using larger brushes will result in larger splatters, while smaller brushes will produce smaller ones. Avoid concentrating too many splatters in one spot to prevent forming a large ink blob.

Change things around!

Create your own landscape by varying the colors for the landscape and flowers. Try a sunset sky with red, orange, and yellow or a blue clouded sky. For the flower field, go for a poppy, lavender, or tulip field. Let your imagination guide you!

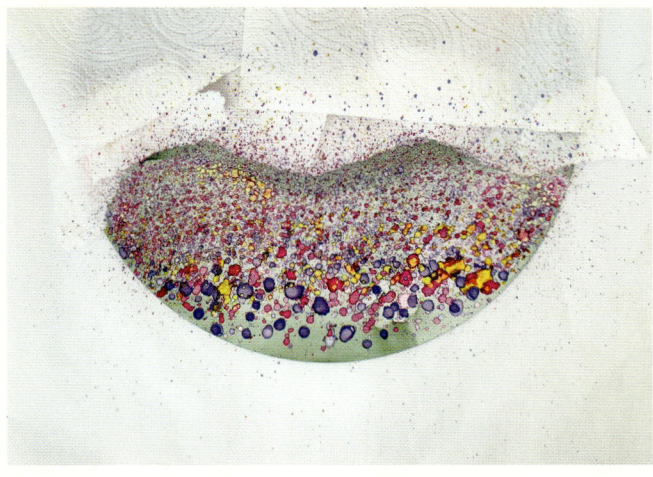

Step 4

After a layer of bright pink ink splatters, repeat the process with the other ink colors. Only add the layer of yellow ink toward the end as mixing the yellow with the pink and purple may result in a muddy color. Allow each layer of splatters to dry and continue layering until there is a nice full coverage, while keeping some green visible.

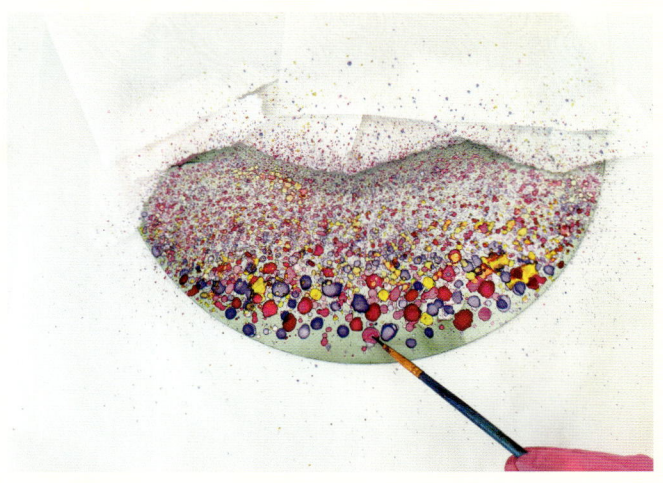

Step 5

To create more saturated, bigger flowers at the bottom, load a small brush with ink and dab it softly in several spots. Dry each layer before adding another color until you achieve a nice coverage in the foreground.

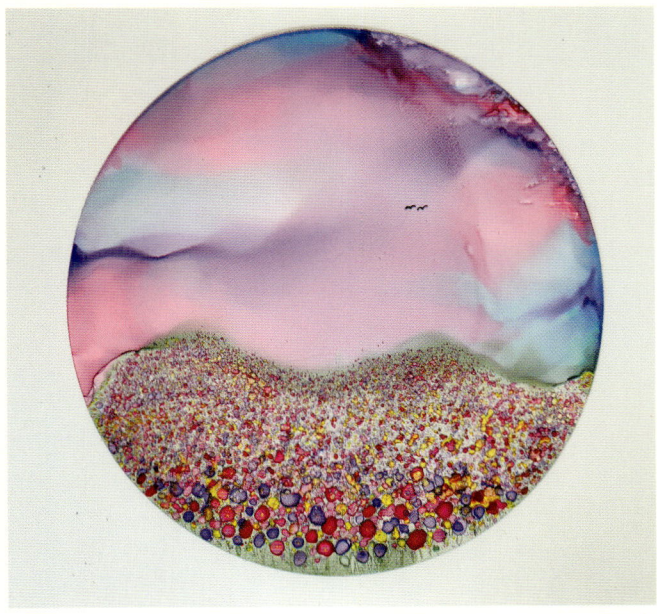

Step 6

Remove the paper towel to reveal the sky. Add a few drops of green ink to your palette and load a fine brush with the green ink to draw tiny strokes for stems and leaves in the foreground. We are going for an abstract look, so don't make it very precise, but instead draw some loose, small stokes here and there. Finally, add one drop of black ink to your palette. Load the fine brush with black ink and draw two C-shapes connected in the sky to indicate small birds in the distance.

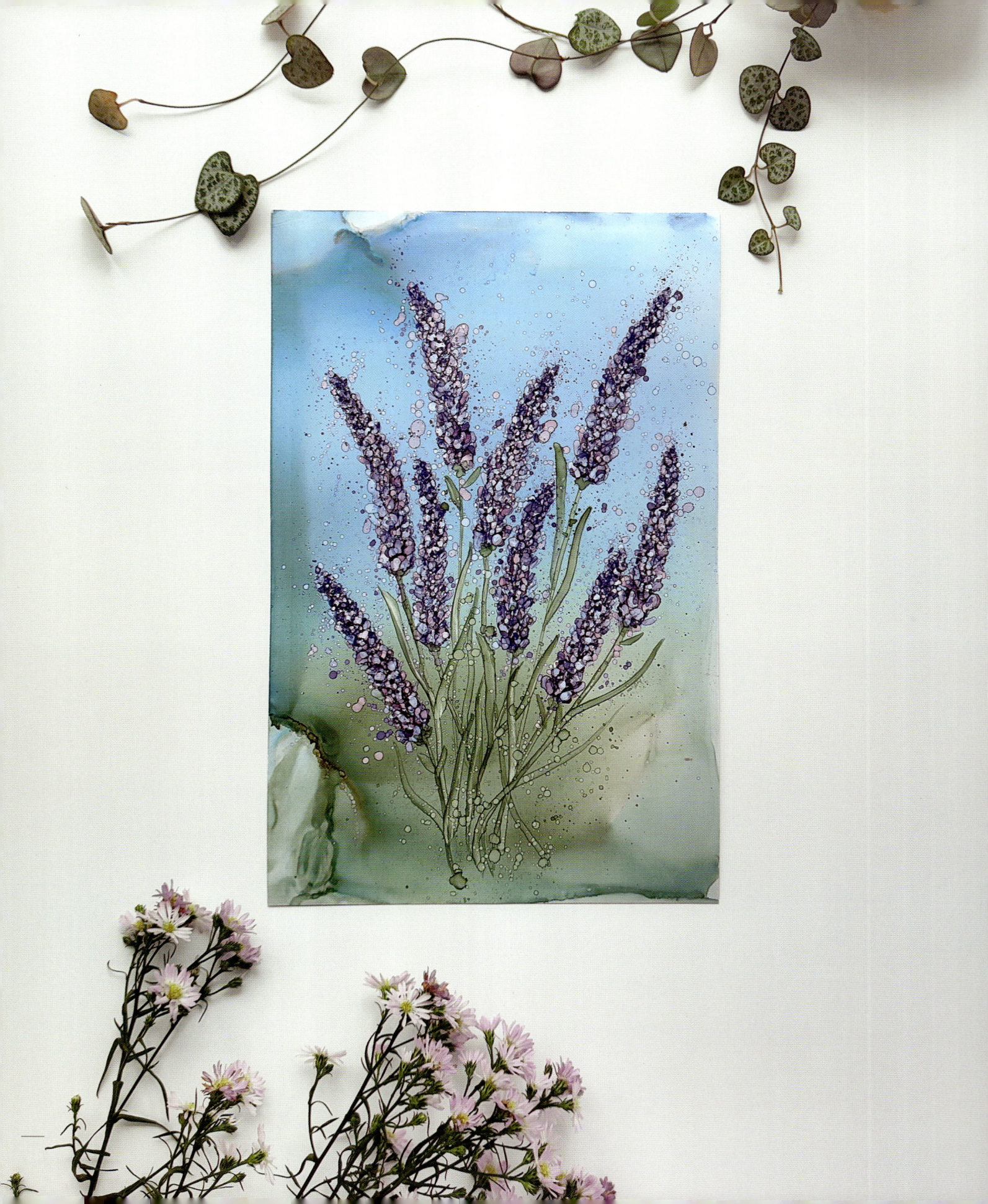

lavender

There's nothing like the fresh, comforting smell of lavender flowers. For this project, we'll first work on an ink background with a soft gradient and then use a simple dabbing and dotting technique to layer several shades of purple to create the lavender flowers, as if they are popping out of the background. You can almost smell them from your paper!

LEVEL: BEGINNER
● ○ ○

materials

- Alcohol inks in light green, light blue, lilac, lavender, and purple (or several shades of purple)
- 91% or 99% isopropyl alcohol in a needle tip bottle
- Synthetic paper 10 × 12 inches (20 × 30 cm)
- Glazed ceramic tile for practicing (optional)
- Ink air blower

- Heat tool (optional)
- Set of miniature round synthetic brushes, 000 to 4.0 mm
- Paint palette or parchment paper
- Painter's tape
- Paper towels
- Safety supplies

Step 1

Make sure the paper is flat or tape it down with painter's tape while making sure the paper can still be lifted up to tilt it. Add enough isopropyl alcohol to cover the paper entirely. Use a large brush to spread it out evenly. Create a background with a soft blue and green gradient by applying multiple drops of the light blue ink at the top and light green ink toward the bottom. Add more isopropyl alcohol on top and tilt the paper around to create a soft gradient or use an ink air blower to spread the inks around. Fill in any empty spots with more ink and repeat the process as needed. Allow it to air-dry completely. This may take up to 60 minutes.

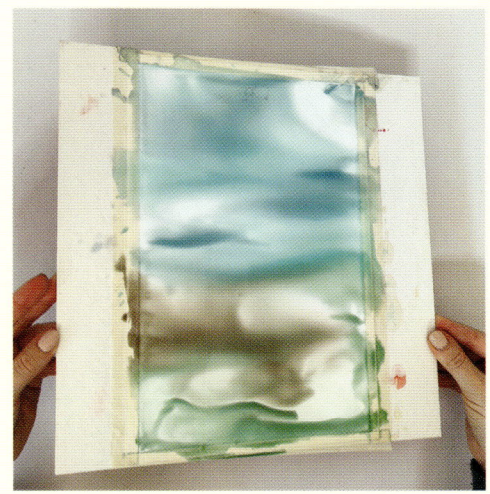

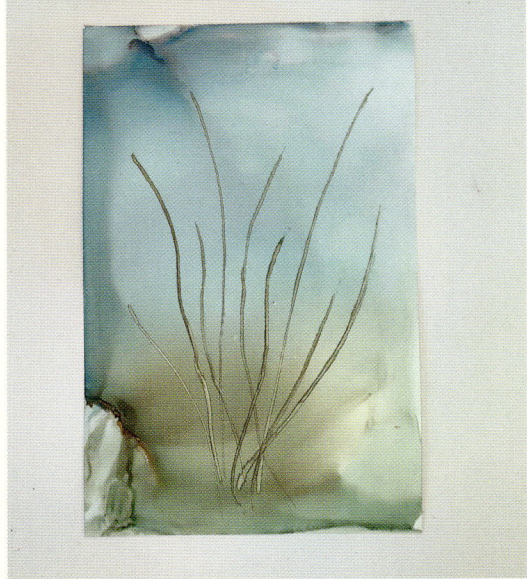
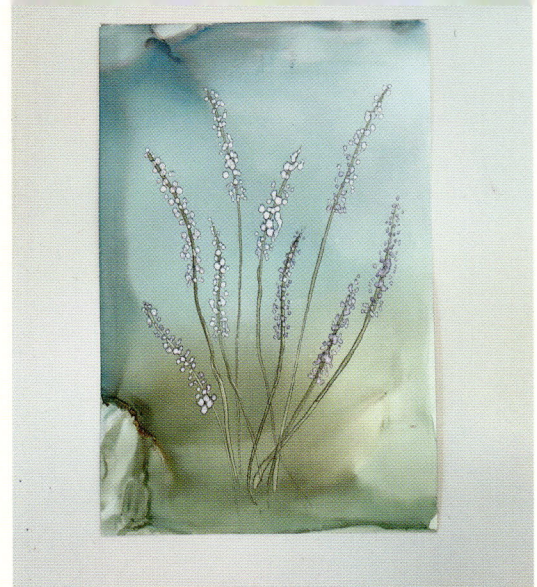

Step 2

Remove the painter's tape and trim the edges if needed. Add the light green ink to your palette and use a fine brush with the green ink to draw nine long, small stems to indicate where the lavender flowers are going to be.

Step 3

Add the purple ink shades to your paint palette. Load a small brush with the lightest purple ink and working from bottom to top, softly dab it onto the paper and apply short, upward strokes along the stems to form tiny petals. Create bigger strokes toward the bottom and smaller ones toward the top, leaving empty spots along the stem.

Mix your own lavender or lilac shade

If don't have any light lavender or lilac ink available, mix your own by adding one or two drops of white ink to your purple ink and add isopropyl alcohol to dilute the thick white ink down.

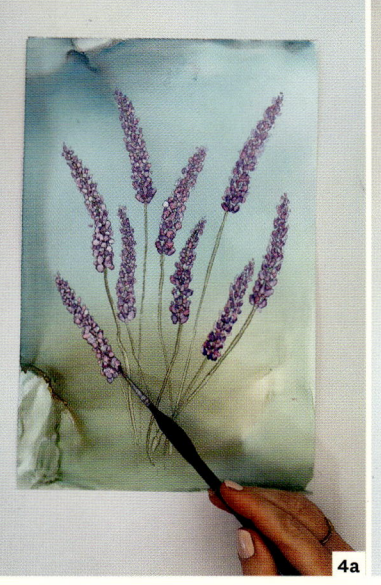 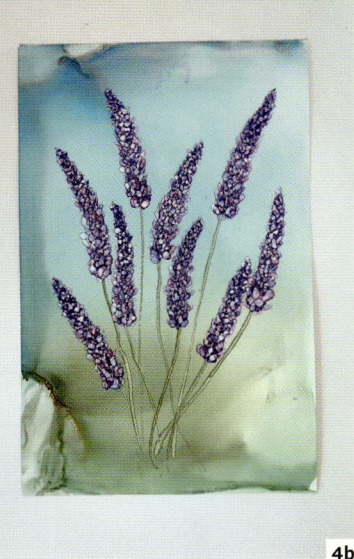

4a **4b**

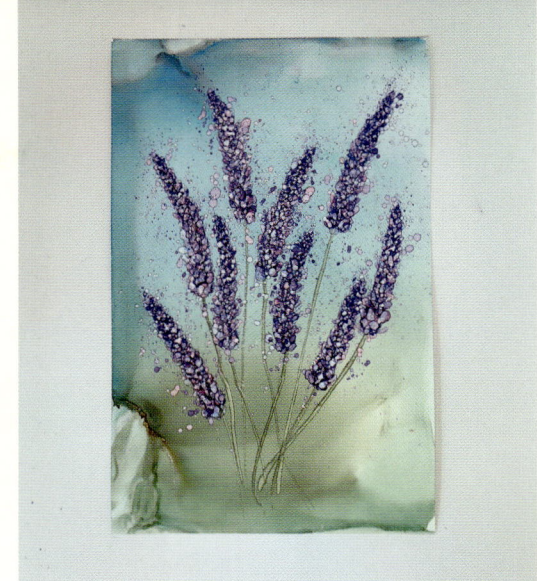

Step 4

Continue adding new layers of small petals, varying the colors from the lightest purple to the darkest (4a). Ensure that the top of the lavender flower is narrower. If necessary, dry each layer with a heat tool before applying the next one. Apply a layer of clear alcohol dabs to blend the colors softly or to lighten them if they become too dark. Load the brush with a small amount of ink or alcohol to avoid large blobs on your lavender. If a large blob appears, let it dry and apply new layers to cover it up. Add more of the purple inks to your palette if needed. Don't overthink it and just have fun creating various layers. Keep repeating this process until you have a nice variation of the purple colors (4b).

Step 5

To finish the lavender flowers, add purple splatters on top and around the lavender petals so they look like they pop out from the background. Load a brush with purple ink and gently tap it with another brush or tool to create splatters around the lavender until you're satisfied with the overall look.

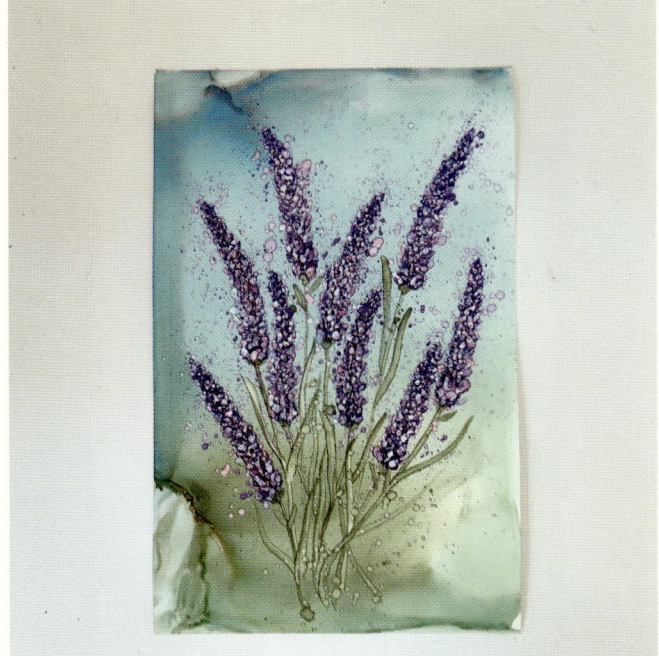

Step 6

To finish the composition, reactivate the light green ink on your palette. Add small narrow leaves by loading your small brush with some green ink, then softly touch the paper with the tip of your brush. Press down lightly for a broader stroke, then lift your brush to create a narrow leaf attached to the stem. Add one or two leaves to each stem and a few smaller ones toward the top. Load a brush with the desired ink color and gently tap it with another brush or tool to create green splatters around the stems and leaves to finish.

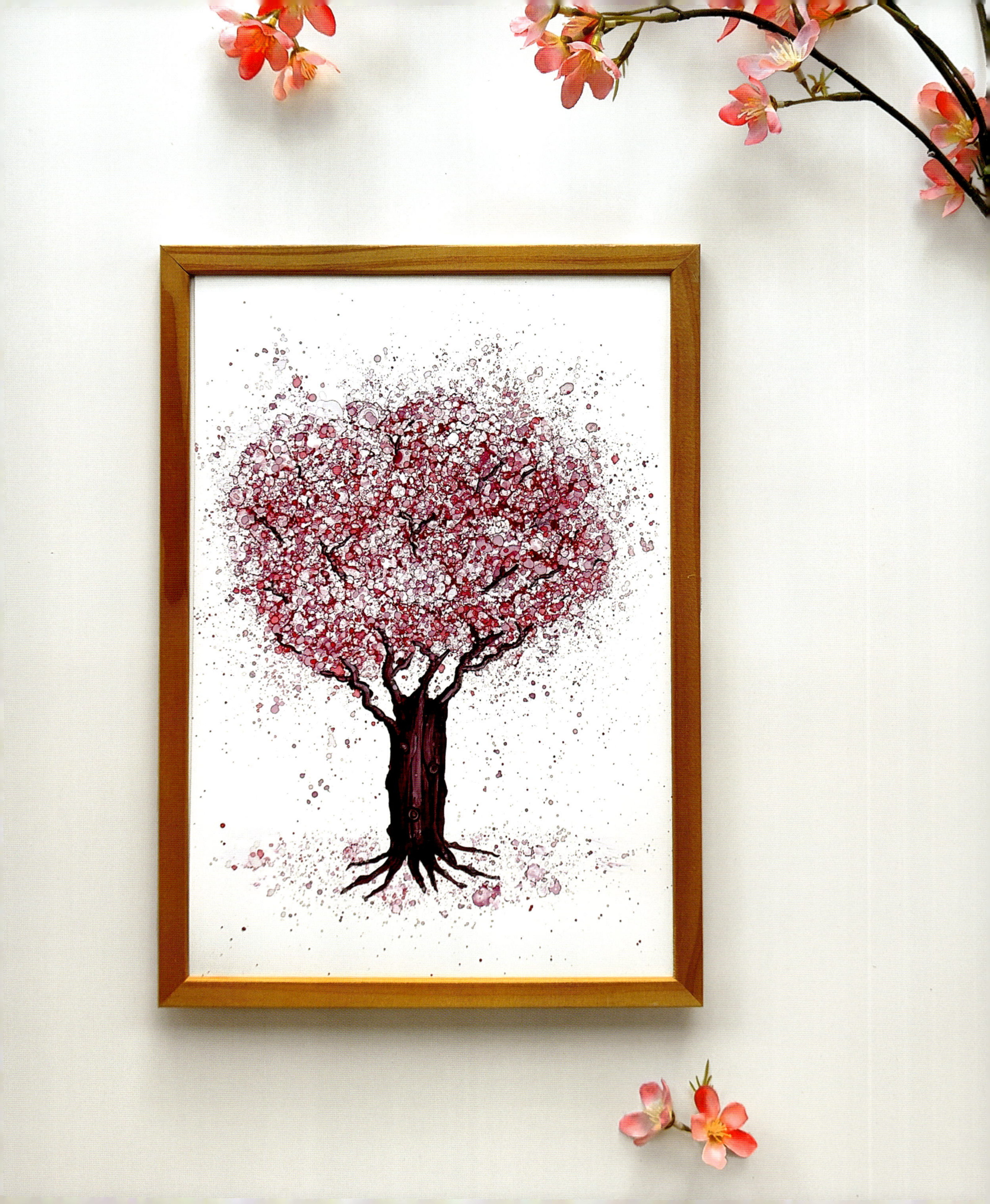

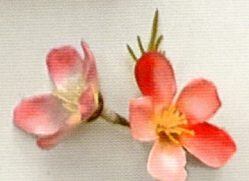

cherry blossom tree

Spring is my favorite season, and there's nothing like the explosion of cherry blossoms to signal spring is here. In this project, we'll create an abstract version of this beautiful tree with clouds of pink blossoms by using a splattering technique. Let's get to it!

LEVEL: BEGINNER
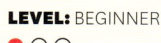

materials

- Alcohol inks in light pink, bright pink, deep pink (or 3 different shades of pink), and brown
- 91% or 99% isopropyl alcohol in a needle tip bottle
- Synthetic paper 10 × 12 inches (20 × 30 cm)
- Set of miniature round synthetic brushes, 000 to 4.0 mm
- Paint palette or parchment paper
- Paper towels
- Safety supplies

Step 1

Add the three pink inks to your paint palette and use the same amount of ink and isopropyl alcohol for each color and mix it (e.g., five drops each). Start with your first layer of splatters with the lightest pink color. Load your brush with the light pink ink and start tapping it with another brush or tool to create splatters. Splatter in an oval shape at the top half of the paper. Keep your brush relatively close to the paper (about a fist away) so you have some control over layering the splatters in an oval shape. You can also layer small pieces of paper towel around the oval shape to shield it from the splatters.

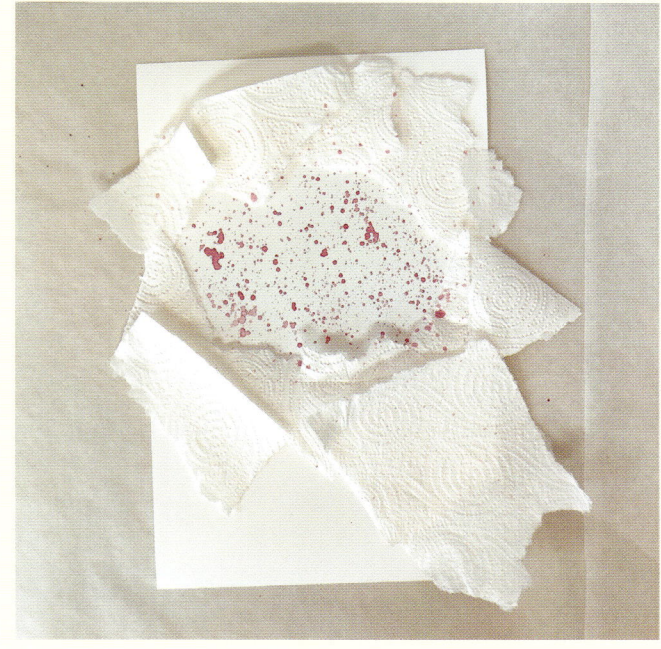

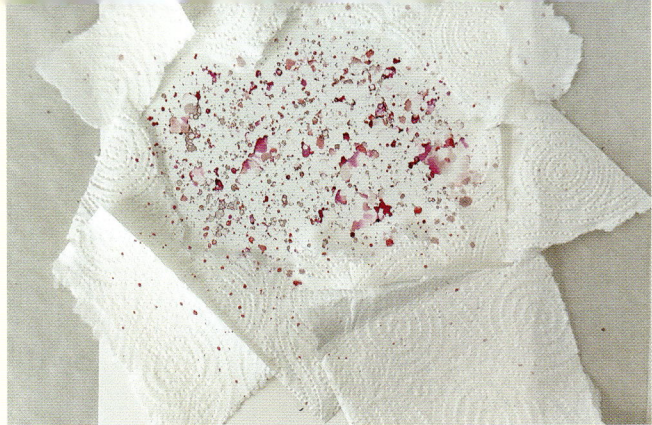

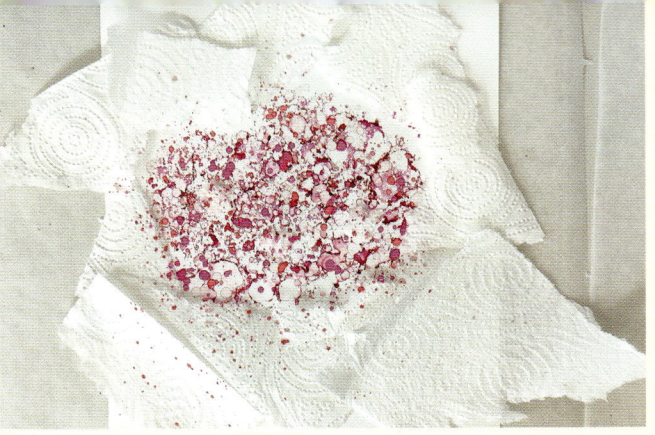

Step 2

Now, it's time for the second layer. Load a clean brush with the bright pink ink. Create a second layer of splatters following the same technique as step 2. Follow with a third layer of splatters with the deep pink ink. To blend the pink ink colors together, follow with a fourth layer of splatters using just isopropyl alcohol. You don't have to wait for a previous layer to dry. Splatters that are still a bit wet can create beautiful ink blends. Be cautious that the splatters don't turn into one big puddle of inks. If this happens, you can always go over them once they dry to create smaller splatters on top.

Step 3

Keep adding new layers of splatters. Follow each layer of pink color with a layer of clear alcohol splatters to mix them into each other a little more. If you want one dominant color, use more splatters of that pink color as compared to the others. Add more clear alcohol splatters to lighten up the colors underneath and blend them together. You can also alter splattering with softly dabbing the brush onto the paper. Vary the brush sizes to create various sizes of splatters. Don't overthink it and just have fun creating various layers.

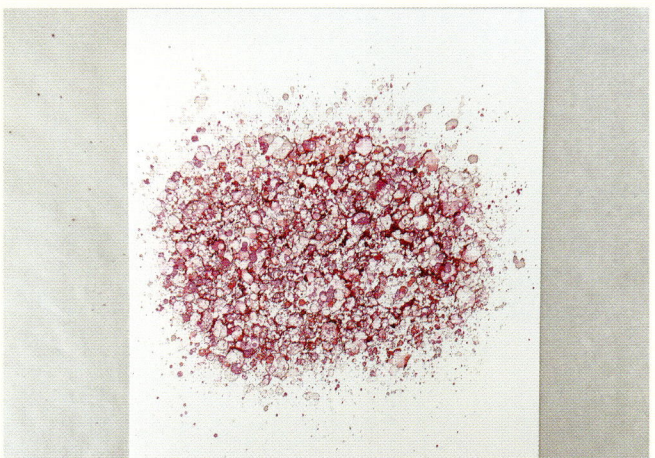

Step 4

Repeat step 3 until you have a nice coverage in an oval shape. Don't create a perfectly round pattern of blossoms because that doesn't look natural. If you had pieces of paper towel covering part of the paper, you can remove it at the end and just add some more splatters on the empty spots and outside of the oval shape to make it blend with the background better. Be patient; it may take a while before the tree is full of blossoms.

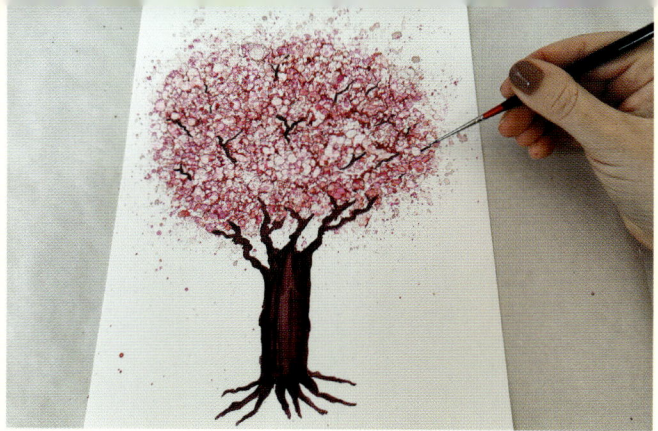

Step 5

To create the tree trunk and branches, add a couple of drops of brown ink to your palette and mix it with just one drop of the bright pink ink to match the brown color with the blossom colors. Use a large brush to outline where the tree trunk is going to be at the lower half of the paper. Don't add too much ink to your brush as it may spread fast. Use a small brush to add smaller branches that will move from the top of the tree trunk up to the blossoms. Use a zigzag motion with your brush to create crooked branches. Also add some side branches to the main branches. At the bottom of the tree trunk, paint smaller lines to form the tree roots. After you have outlined the tree trunk, branches, and roots, you can go over it multiple times with your brush to fill the shape and add texture in the tree trunk. You can also load your brush with some clear alcohol to create lighter parts in the tree trunk and add small rings on the trunk that resemble knots. Then, use a fine brush to add small branches within the pink blossom splatters that peek through.

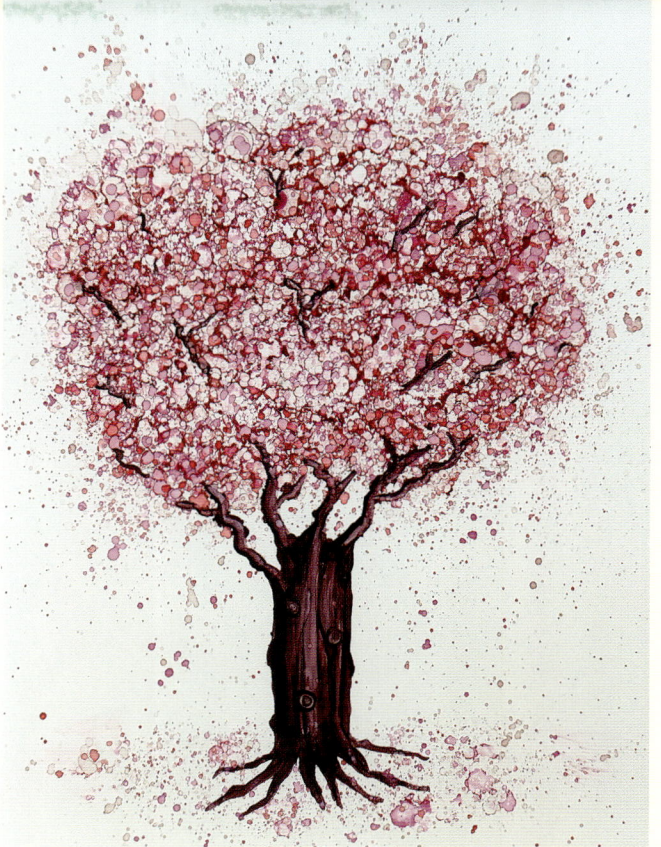

Step 6

As a final touch, I like to add splatters toward the roots of the trunk where the blossoms have fallen to the ground. Using the technique from step 2, add a few layers of splatters in various pink colors around the roots of the tree. To be safe, cover the tree trunk with a paper towel so the splatters don't end up on there. Keep going until you're happy with the result!

 tip

Cherry blossom tree technique

Need to see how to create the cherry blossom tree in action? Scan the QR for a video of this technique.

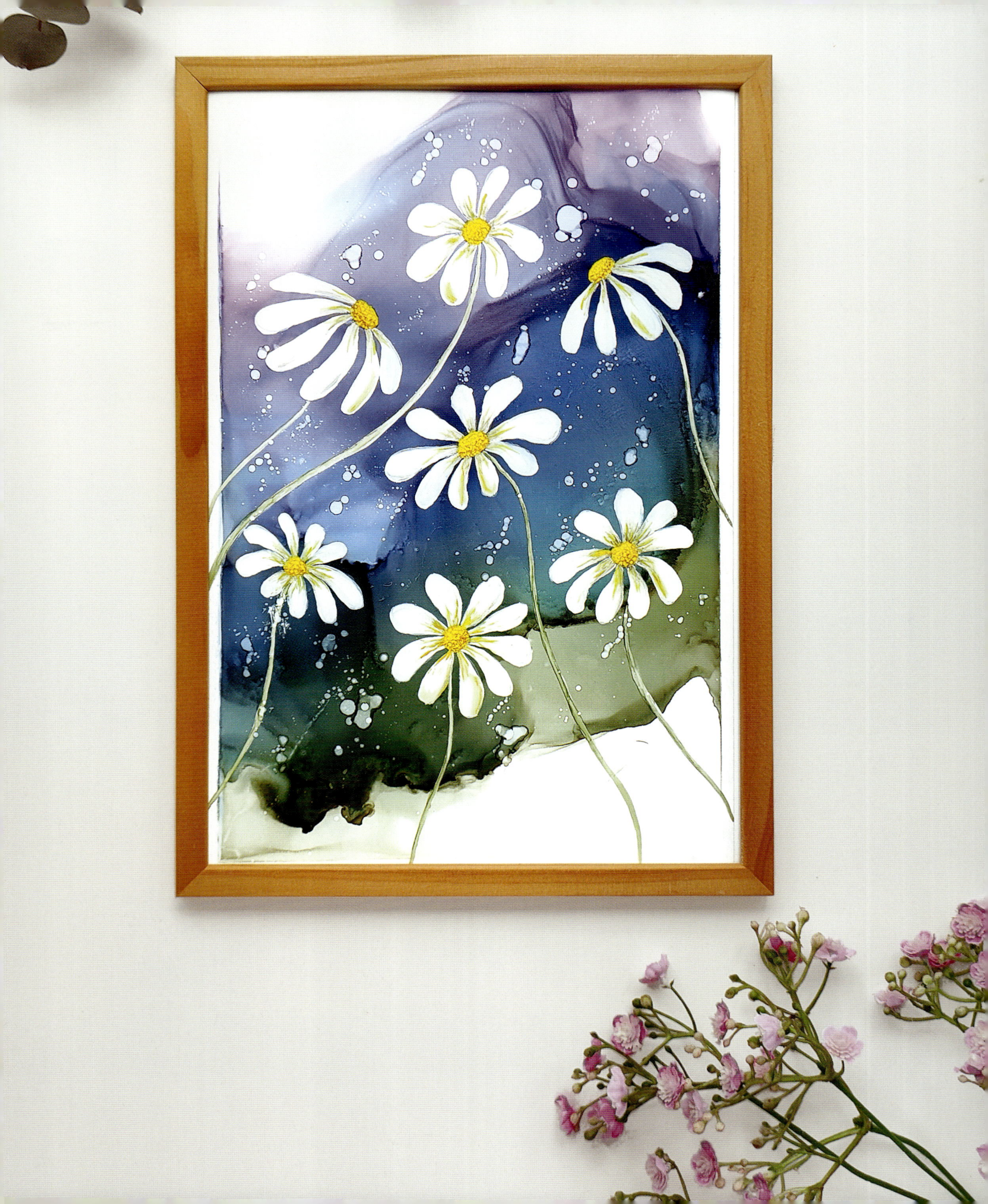

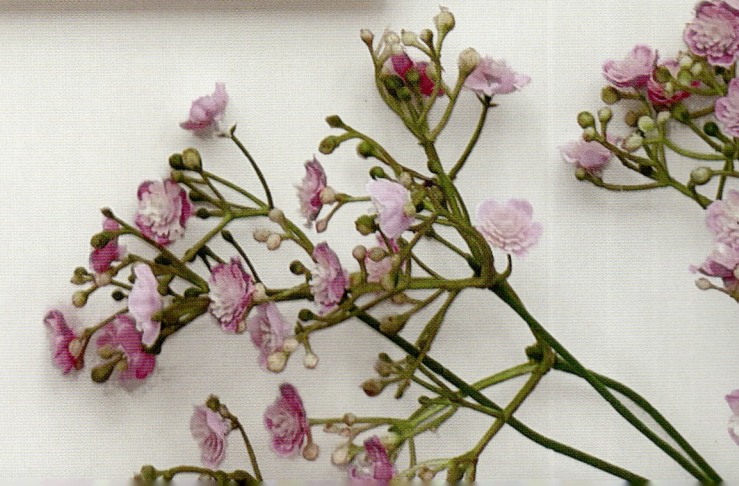

daisies

Is there anything more happy and cheerful than a field of white daisies? In this project, we'll use masking fluid to create our daisies. Masking fluid is super handy for keeping parts of your paper white. In this project, it helps us keep the daisy petals white while we have fun adding color to the background. Removing the masking fluid and seeing the daisies appear from the ink background is magical!

LEVEL: BEGINNER
● ○ ○

materials

- Alcohol inks in two shades of green, two shades of blue, two shades of purple, yellow, gray, and white
- 91% or 99% isopropyl alcohol in a needle tip bottle
- Synthetic paper 10 × 12 inches (20 × 30 cm)
- Glazed ceramic tile for practicing (optional)
- Ink air blower
- Heat tool (optional)
- Masking fluid in small cup

- Cup of water
- Set of miniature round synthetic brushes, 000 to 4.0 mm plus an old brush (to apply the masking fluid)
- Silicone tip tool (optional)
- Paint palette or parchment paper
- Painter's tape (optional)
- Pencil
- Paper towels
- Safety supplies

Step 1

Start by sketching daisies from various angles. For front-facing daisies, draw a small circle for the center and a larger circle around it to guide the length and shape of the petals. Sketch elongated, teardrop-shaped petals around the center. For tilted daisies, draw horizontal ovals with a smaller oval in the center and add petals using the oval as a guide. For side-facing daisies, use a horizontal oval with teardrop-shaped petals coming from the top to the bottom. Add a small oval at the top for the center. Draw S-shaped stems from between petals to the side or bottom of the page. When finished, erase the petal guidelines.

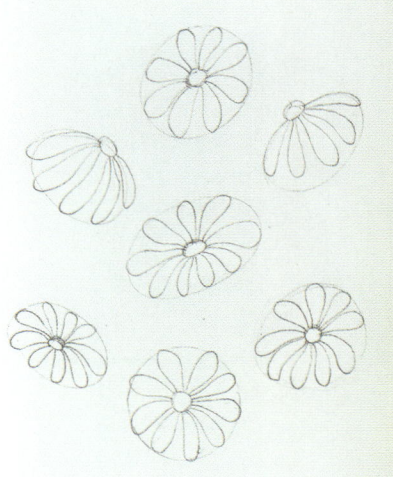

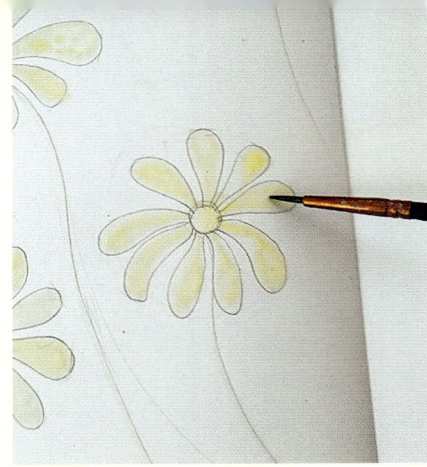
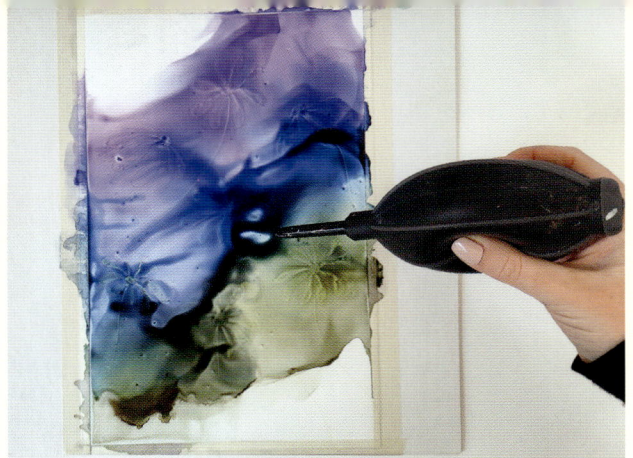

Step 2

Apply a small amount of masking fluid to a small cup. Use an old brush (masking fluid can damage it) to fill the daisy center and petals. Moisten the brush with water, dab it on a paper towel, then load with masking fluid. First fill the center of the daisy and then outline and fill the petal shapes carefully. Clean your brush with water after each daisy and work from top left to bottom right to avoid smudging the wet masking fluid. Paint the stems last. Please note the masking fluid will start drying relatively quickly, so there's not a lot of working time for each flower. Clean your brush immediately after use. Let the masking fluid dry completely before proceeding to step 3; this may take up to an hour.

Step 3

Make sure the paper is flat or tape it down with painter's tape. Apply a generous amount of isopropyl alcohol and tilt it around to cover the entire surface. Starting at the lower right corner, apply several drops of the two green ink shades. In the middle, apply the two blue shades across the paper and apply the purple shades toward the top. I left negative space in the bottom-right and upper-left corner. Apply more isopropyl alcohol on top and make them softly blend by either using your ink air blower or by tilting the paper around. Apply more inks and isopropyl alcohol if needed. For a faded effect, add some isopropyl alcohol to the edges (at the bottom right and top left) and push it inward with the ink air blower. Let it air-dry completely before moving to step 4. Be patient; this may take up to an hour. Once it's almost dry, you can use your heat tool to speed up the drying process.

 tip

Alternatives to masking fluid

Instead of masking fluid, you can use white acrylic paint to create the daisies on top of your ink background and skip step 2. Acrylic paint is opaque, so you'll be able to paint over the ink background.

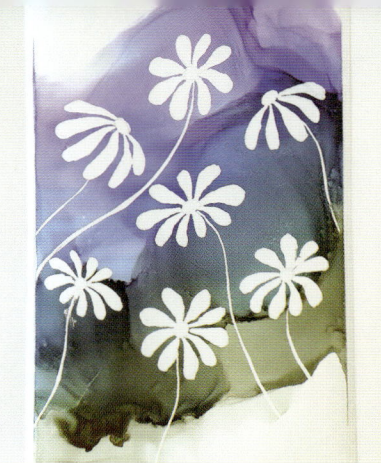

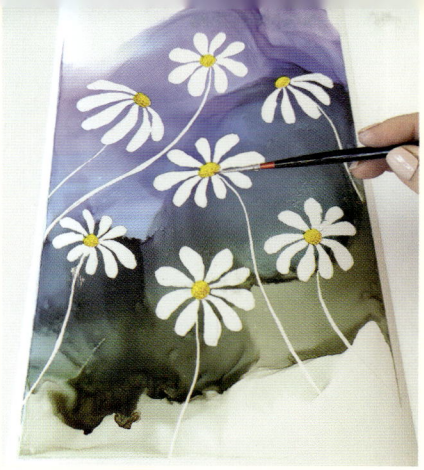

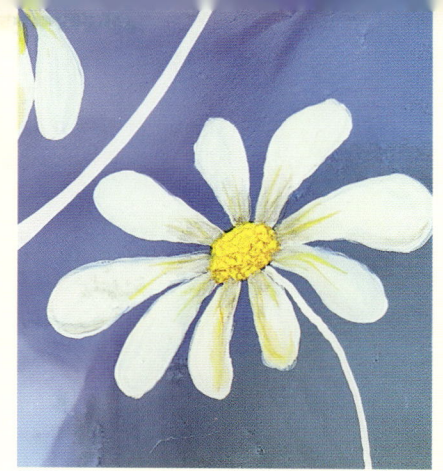

Step 4

This is the most fun step! Use your finger or a small eraser to softly rub over the areas where the masking fluid is applied to remove it. Be careful as it's possible to damage the ink background. The daisies will now magically appear from the background. Remove the painter's tape if used.

Step 5

To bring the daisies to life, first add the two shades of yellow to your palette. Use a small brush to fill the center with the lightest yellow. Dry it with your heat tool. Add small dots with your brush across the circle using the lightest yellow. Dry it again and repeat this step a couple of times with the two shades until you have a dotted center.

Step 6

Add the white, yellow, gray, and light green inks to your palette. Load a small brush with the white ink and carefully fill in the petal shapes for each daisy flower. After finishing all the petals, use the small brush or silicone tip tool with the yellow and/or gray ink and add some small brushstrokes from the center outward into the petal to give the petals more depth. Apply more white ink on top to create a faded effect. Load a fine brush with the light green ink and fill in the stems with the green (as always: Don't apply too much ink). Let the inks dry or use your heat tool to speed up the drying process.

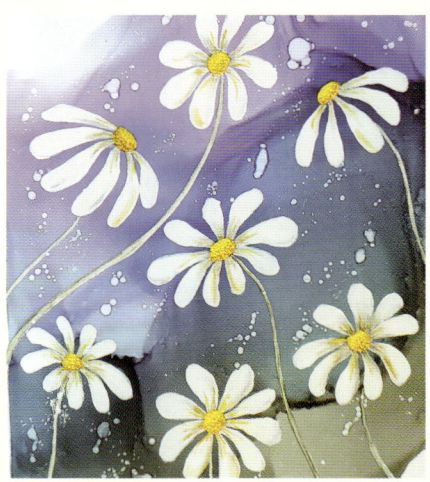

Step 7

Finish the composition with splatters of clear isopropyl alcohol for a playful effect. Load your large brush isopropyl alcohol and dab it with another brush or tool to create splatters across the paper until you're satisfied with the overall look! Protect your daisies with small pieces of paper towel if you don't want splatters ending up on top of the flowers.

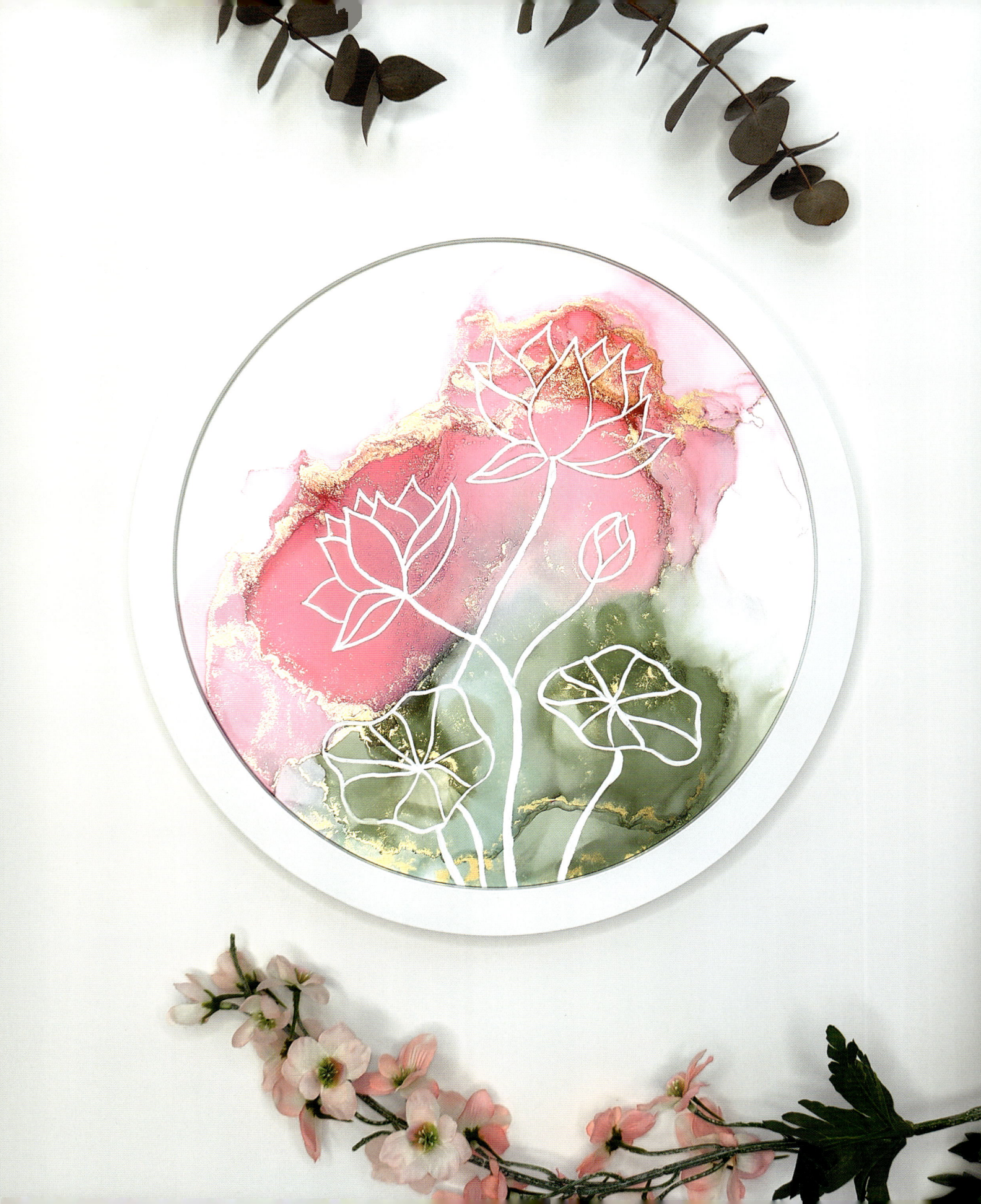

lotus flowers

The sight of pink lotus flowers magically arising from a pond is magnificent. In this project, we'll create a lovely line drawing of lotus flowers that will also magically appear from underneath our ink background. We'll start by creating our line drawing using masking fluid and then cover it with inks to create a beautiful gradient from which the lotus flowers will appear!

LEVEL: BEGINNER

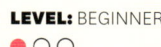

- Alcohol inks in light and dark green, light pink, and bright pink
- Gold alcohol ink and isopropyl alcohol mix in needle tip bottle at a 50/50 ratio
- 91% or 99% isopropyl alcohol in a needle tip bottle
- Synthetic paper square or round 12 × 12 inches (30 × 30 cm)
- Glazed ceramic tile for practicing (optional)
- Masking fluid in small cup
- Cup of water
- Ink air blower

- Heat tool (optional)
- Set of miniature round synthetic brushes, 000 to 4.0 mm plus an old brush (to apply the masking fluid)
- Soft pencil (6B or higher) for transferring design
- Hard pencil
- Painter's tape (optional)
- Small eraser (optional)
- Paper towels
- Safety supplies

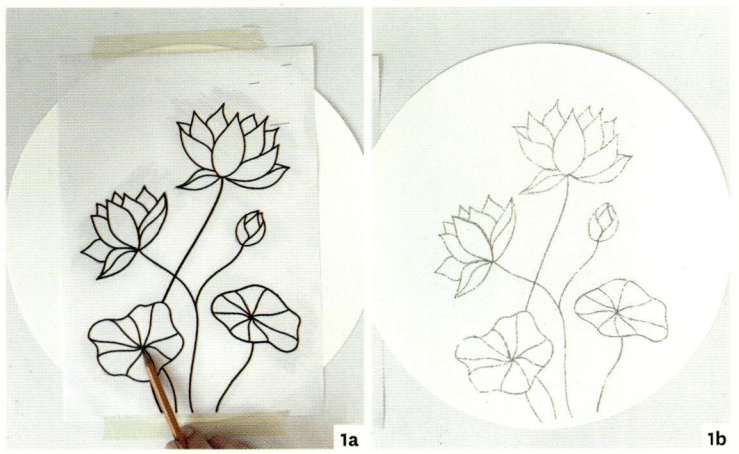
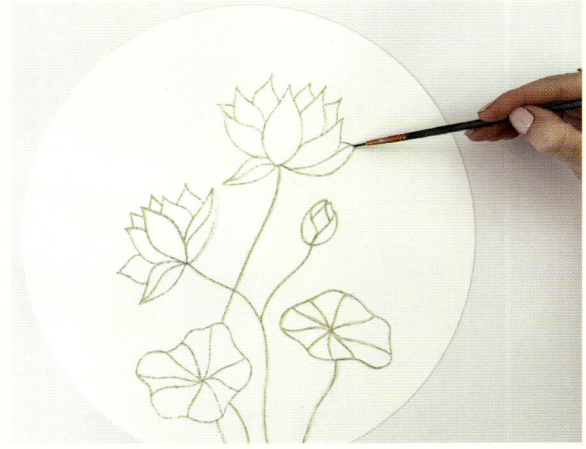

Step 1

Start by drawing the composition of lotus flowers on your paper using a pencil. To simplify this process, download the printable PDF via the QR code and print the file on printer paper. Next, color in the back side of the printout with a 6B or higher graphite pencil. Then, place the printout, graphite-side down, on the synthetic paper and secure it with painter's tape. Use a hard pencil to trace the lotus flower design, transferring the graphite onto the synthetic paper (1a) (1b). Alternatively, you can use carbon paper, or if you feel comfortable, sketch the design yourself or create your own.

Step 2

Add a small amount of masking fluid to a small cup and use a fine, old brush (masking fluid can damage the brush) to trace the pencil drawing from step 1. First, moisten your brush with a little water and then dab it on a paper towel. Use the damp brush and load it with a bit of the masking fluid. First, trace the lotus flower petals, then the leaves, and finish with the stems. Clean your brush with water in between and dab it on the paper towel so it's not too wet before continuing. Since masking fluid will start drying relatively quickly, work fast and avoid touching any part that is already drying as it may lift the masking fluid. After finishing, clean your brush right away; otherwise, the masking fluid is difficult to remove. Let it dry thoroughly before moving to step 3. Please note this may take up to an hour.

Lotus flowers printable pdf

Need some help with sketching the composition of lotus flowers? Scan the QR for a printable PDF to trace onto your synthetic paper.

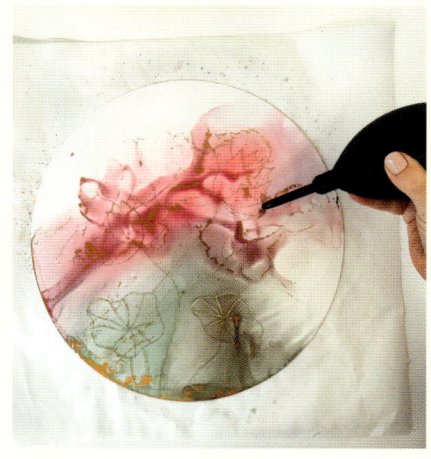 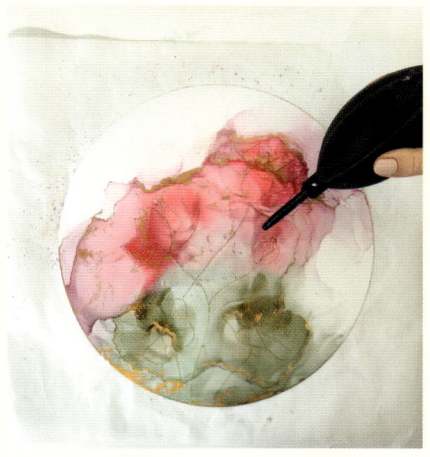 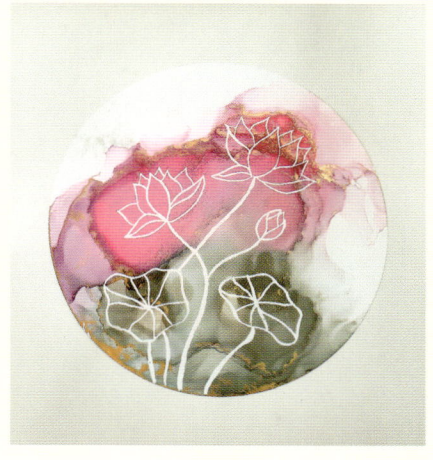

Step 3

Ensure the paper is flat and level, taping it down with painter's tape if necessary. Cover the paper with a generous amount of isopropyl alcohol using a small brush or by tilting it around.

Begin by applying light pink ink on top of and around the lotus flowers and light green ink at the bottom part, around the leaves and the lower end of the stems. Add a few drops of the gold ink mix on top, then apply more isopropyl alcohol to spread the inks. Use your ink air blower to spread the inks and make the pink and green softly blend into each other. You can also tilt the paper around to create a soft gradient. Since pink and green may not combine well, avoid excessive blending to prevent creating a muddy color. I keep some negative space around the composition, but you can also choose to fill the entire background with inks.

Step 4

While the ink is still wet, add a couple of drops of the bright pink to the lotus petals and dark green to the leaves to increase the saturation. Apply more gold ink mix and isopropyl alcohol as needed and use an ink air blower to spread it. For a faded effect, apply alcohol to the edges and push inward with the blower. Allow the paper to air-dry for 30 to 60 minutes. You can use a heat tool to speed up the drying process once it's almost dry.

Step 5

Now, it's time to reveal the lotus flower drawing! Gently rub over the masking fluid areas with your finger or use a small eraser. Be careful as it's possible to damage the ink background. The design will now magically appear from the background. Use a soft, clean brush to clear any remaining masking fluid particles from your paper. If the pencil lines are still visible, carefully remove them using a small eraser.

 Alternative to masking fluid

Instead of masking fluid, you can use a white acrylic paint marker to create the lotus flower composition on top of your ink background. Skip step 2 and trace the line drawing after step 3 using your acrylic paint marker.

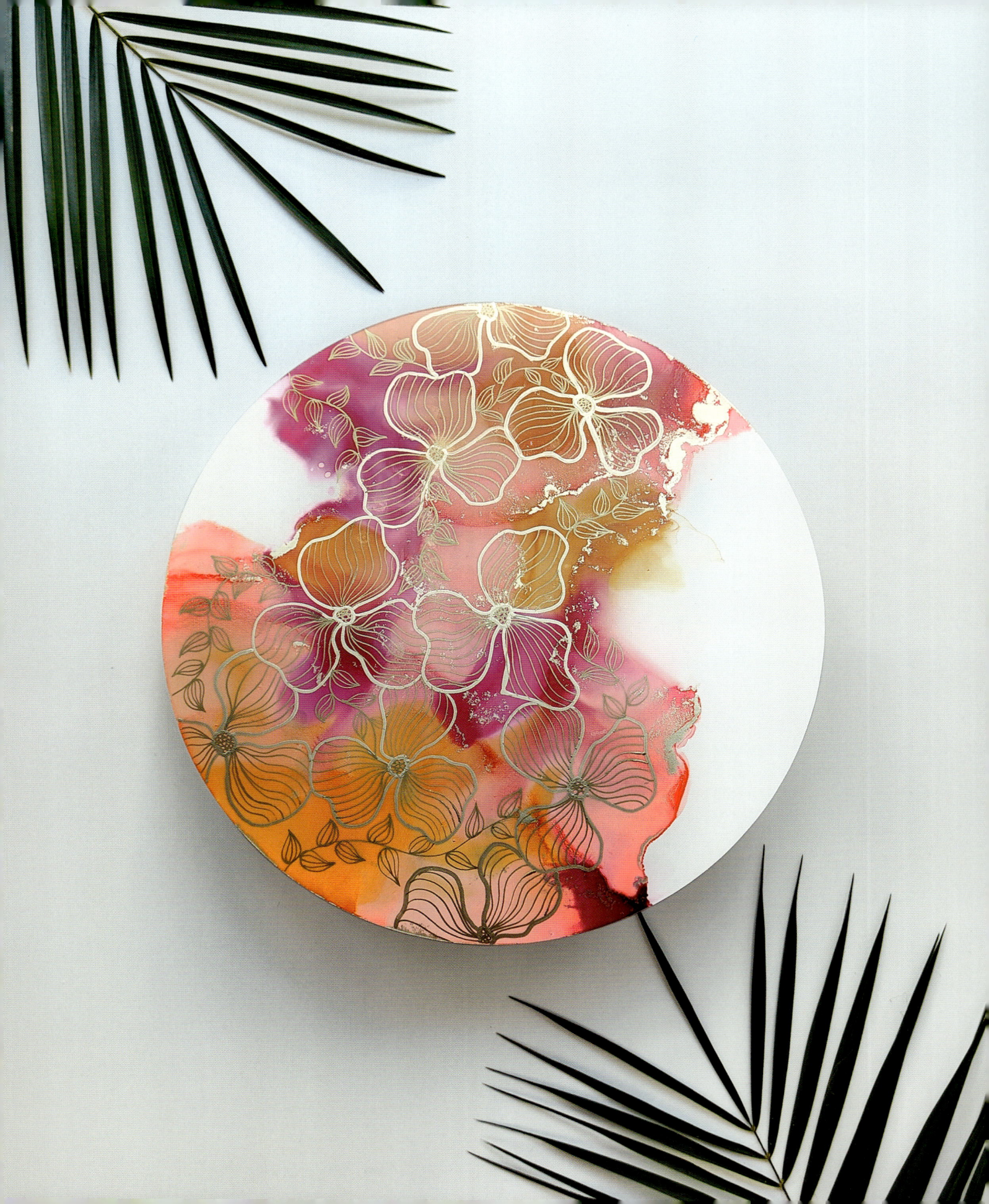

abstract floral doodles

Let your creativity bloom with these Abstract Floral Doodles! In this beginner-friendly project, we'll work on a vibrant alcohol ink background and let the inks softly blend into each other. The background will serve as an inspiration to fill the composition with floral doodles and foliage using gold acrylic paint markers. Let your own imagination guide you or follow my example!

LEVEL: BEGINNER

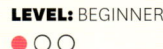

materials

- Alcohol inks in deep pink, light pink, and orange
- Gold alcohol ink and isopropyl alcohol mix in needle tip bottle at a 50/50 ratio (optional)
- 91% or 99% isopropyl alcohol in a needle tip bottle
- Synthetic paper round or square 12 × 12 inches (30 × 30 cm)
- Glazed ceramic tile for practicing (optional)

- Ink air blower
- Medium to broad gold paint marker (1 to 2 mm) and fine gold acrylic paint marker (0.8 mm) or a white or black acrylic paint marker
- Painter's tape (optional)
- Paper towels
- Safety supplies

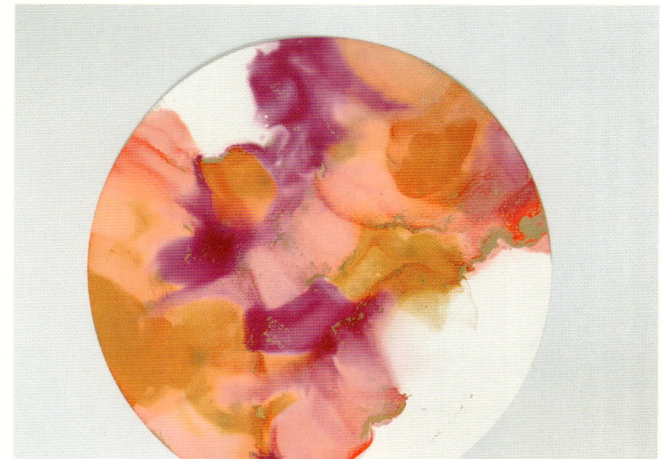

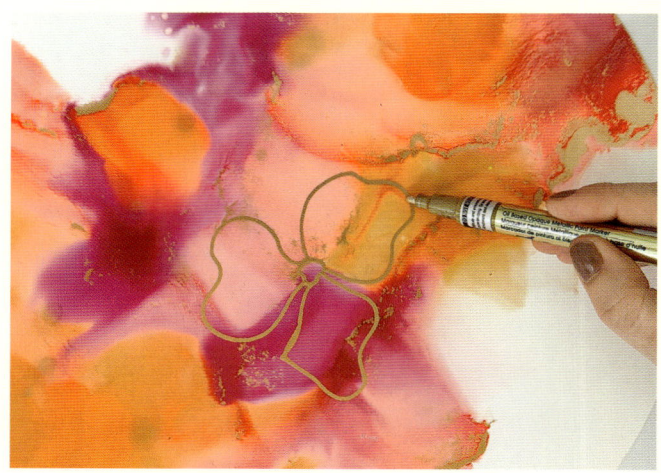

Step 1

Ensure the paper is flat and level, taping it down with painter's tape if necessary. Cover the paper with a generous amount of isopropyl alcohol using a large brush. Drop several drops of each of the three ink colors, evenly distributing them across the paper. I like to work in a diagonal line and leave some negative space on both sides of the paper. If you'd like metallic accents in the background, also add several drops of gold ink mix. Add three drops of isopropyl alcohol on top of each ink drop to spread the inks. Add more isopropyl alcohol to spread the inks further if needed and fill any empty spots with more ink drops and alcohol. Let the inks blend naturally or use an ink air blower to help spread the inks. Try not to manipulate it too much. For a faded effect, apply alcohol to the edges and push inward with the ink air blower. Finally, allow the paper to air-dry. Be patient; this may take up to 30 minutes.

Step 2

Use the medium to broad gold paint marker to draw the floral doodles. Begin with a small circle in the center of the paper and add three petals using curved lines, keeping space between the petals. You can also create your own floral doodles from your imagination. Let the placement of the colors in the background guide the positioning of the flowers. For instance, floral doodles can be created where multiple colors merge so the petals have different colors, or they can be centered within one color to achieve single-colored flowers.

 tip

Abstract floral doodles technique

Need to see how to create the background of step 1 in action? Scan the QR for a video of this technique.

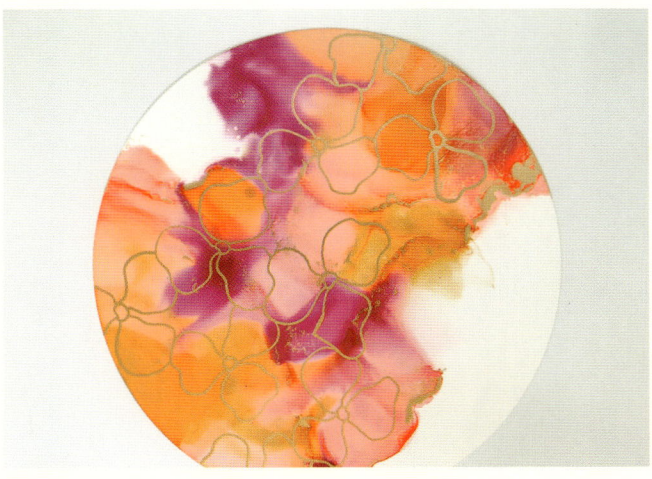

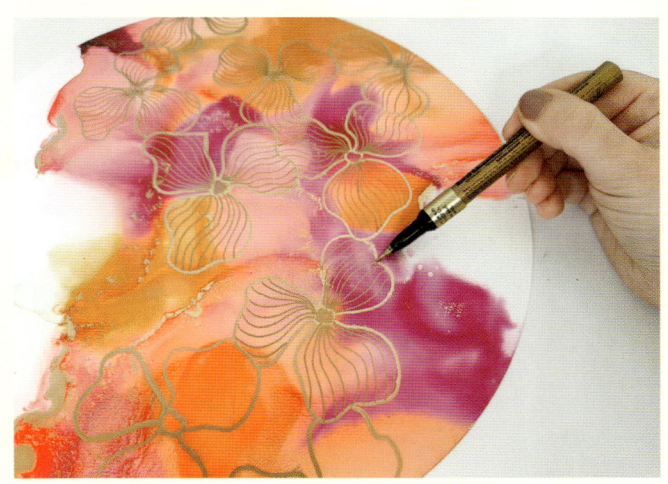

Step 3

Fill the background with floral doodles by repeating step 2 and making the petals of one floral doodle slightly overlap with the one next to it so they're all connected. Use half florals at the edges where they fall off the page. Arrange the doodles along a diagonal line and keep some negative space on the sides and within the florals.

Step 4

Use the fine marker to fill the floral doodles with linework. Draw a line in the center of the petal from the outside of the petal toward the center of the flower. Add parallel lines on both sides to fill the petal with lines. Repeat this process for every floral. Create the stamen by drawing small circles in the center.

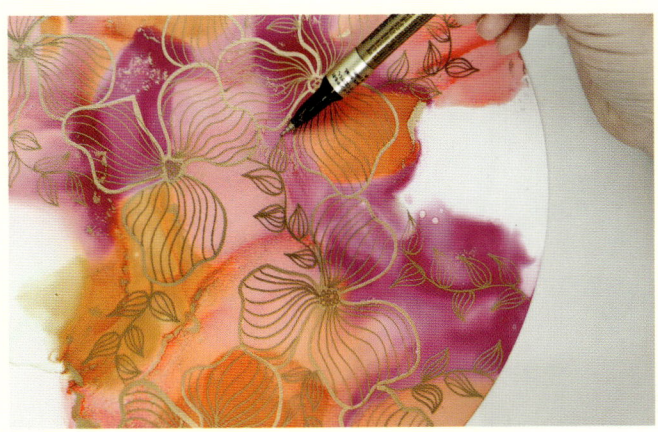

tip

Make your doodles 3D

For a fun effect, use relief paint or 3D liners for textured lines instead of the paint markers.

Step 5

To finish the composition, add foliage by using the small marker to draw curved lines from one floral doodle to another (or toward the edge of the paper) and add small, pointed oval shapes as leaves and fill them with line work. Fill up the empty spots with foliage until you are satisfied with the overall composition.

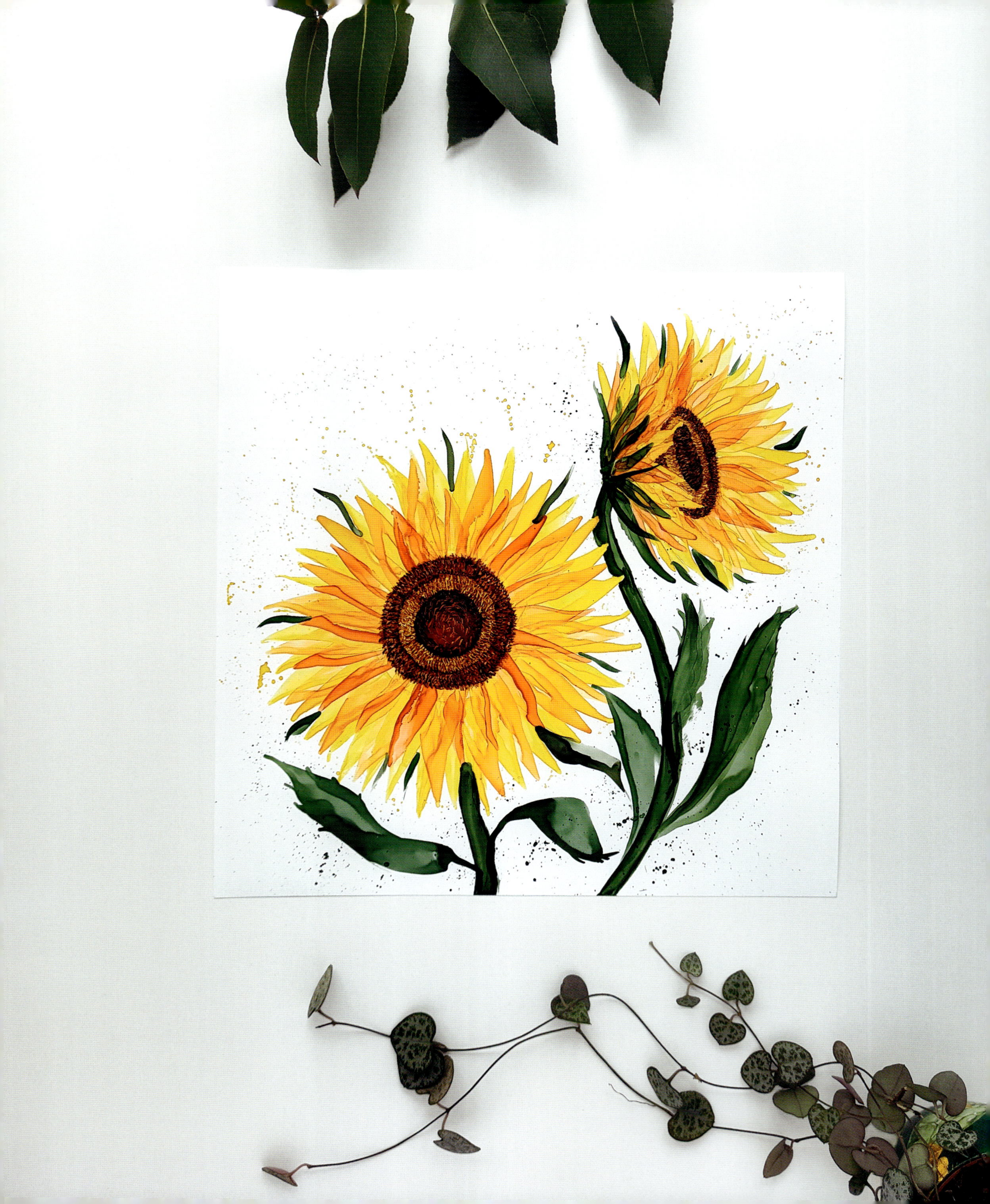

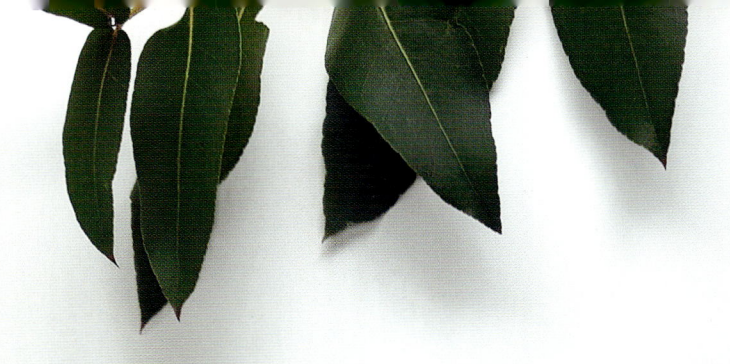
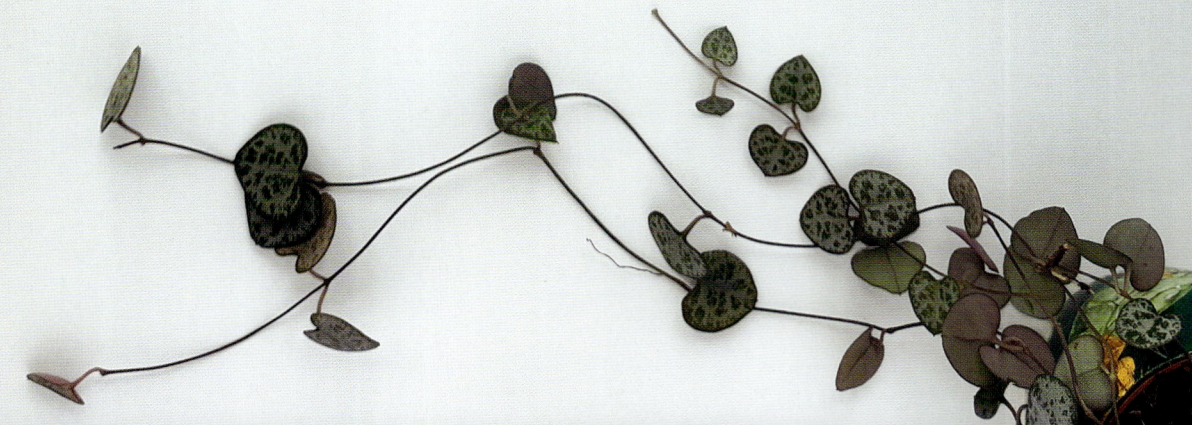

sunflowers

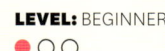

The name *sunflower* originates from the tendency of the flower to position itself toward the sun, so most of us are like sunflowers, aren't we? These majestic flowers with their beautiful hearts are a work of art on their own and can feel challenging to re-create. In this Flower Project, we'll use a palette knife as a new tool to create flower petals relatively quickly and easily. Instead of a palette knife, you can use a catalyst wedge, silicone spatula used for baking (dedicated solely for non-food use), a wide silicone brush used for resin or nail art, or even a credit card. You can also refer to the technique used in the project Gerbera Daisies (page 91) to blow out the petals using a heat tool.

materials

- Alcohol inks in yellow, orange, orange brown, light brown, brown, and green
- 91% or 99% isopropyl alcohol in a needle tip bottle
- Synthetic paper round or square 12 × 12 inches (30 × 30 cm)
- Scrap paper to practice on
- Plastic palette knife with diamond shaped blade

- Set of miniature round synthetic brushes, 000 to 4.0 mm
- Silicone tip tool (optional)
- Parchment paper
- Cup with isopropyl alcohol to clean palette knife
- Paper towels
- Safety supplies

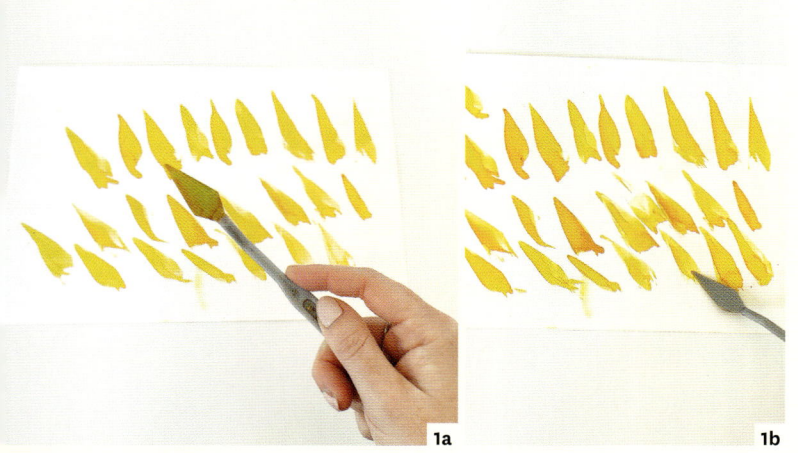

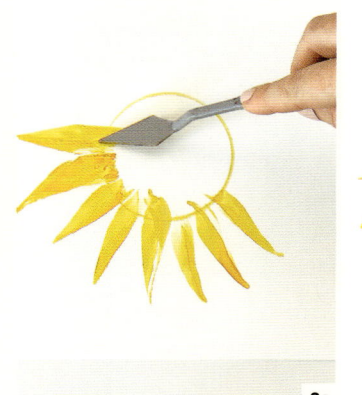
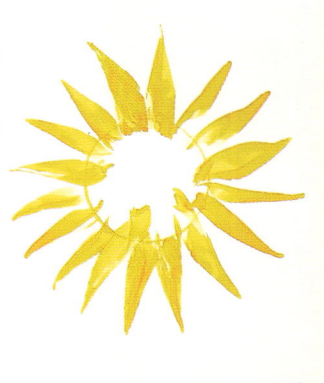

1a · 1b · 2a · 2b

Step 1

It's best to first practice using the palette knife on a piece of scrap paper before creating the sunflowers. Add a few drops of yellow ink to your parchment paper and load the back of the palette knife with the yellow ink. To create a long and narrow petal, softly touch the tip of your palette knife to the paper, press it down completely, and then pick it up again to the tip of the palette knife, while making a downward motion (1a). This motion is like creating a narrow leaf with pointed tips using a brush. Keep your index finger on top of the blade of the palette knife to control the pressure (1b). Practice this motion a couple of times until you get a feel for the technique.

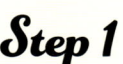 **tip**

Sunflower palette knife technique

Need to see how to create the sunflowers in action? Scan the QR for a video of this technique.

Step 2

To create the first sunflower, use a small brush loaded with a bit of the yellow ink and draw a circle of about a 3-inch (7 to 8 cm) diameter slightly off-center to the left of the paper. Find a round object of this size to trace to simplify this process. This is going to be the center of the sunflower. Create the first round of petals using the technique from step 1 (2a). Create a full ring of petals but keep enough distance between them so they don't touch each other (2b). Work from the outside toward the inside of the circle; this helps in creating an equal length for each of the petals. To simplify the process of creating the petals, rotate the paper around for a good hand coordination. Don't worry about the inks getting messy within the circle, as this won't be visible in the end. You can easily move over a petal a second time if needed or remove it with some paper towel if it turned out too big or wide. Ensure the petals are dry before moving to step 3.

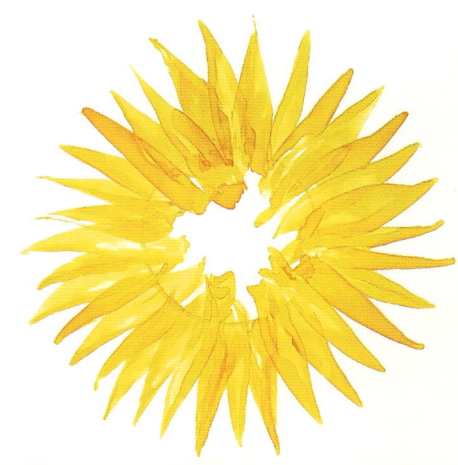

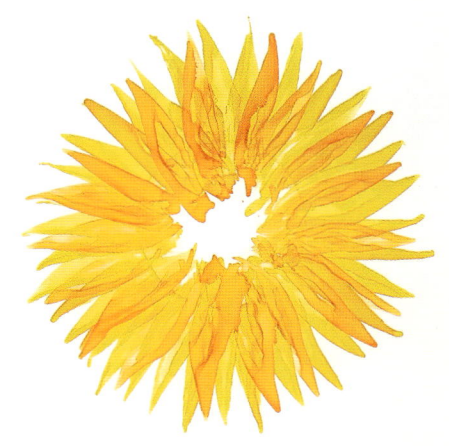

Step 3

Create another layer of petals by placing each new petal between two petals from the previous layer, using the technique from step 1. Add more yellow ink to your parchment paper whenever needed and scrape the inks together to make it easier to pick up the ink. Ensure the petals are dry before moving to step 4.

Step 4

Add orange ink to your parchment paper. Clean the yellow ink from your palette knife using isopropyl alcohol and a paper towel. Create a new layer of petals using the technique from step 1, this time picking up the orange ink and filling in some of the empty spots.

Palette knife petals tips

- Make sure there's not too much ink on the palette knife, or else it will spread out too much.
- The technique is easiest when the inks are relatively thick, so only add a little isopropyl alcohol to your inks.
- Make the motion relatively quickly so the ink does not have time to spread out too much.
- The more you press the palette knife down, the wider the petal shape will become and vice versa.
- Vary the shapes of the petals by creating different motions, from more straight petals by using a straight motion to using S-shaped motions for a curved look.

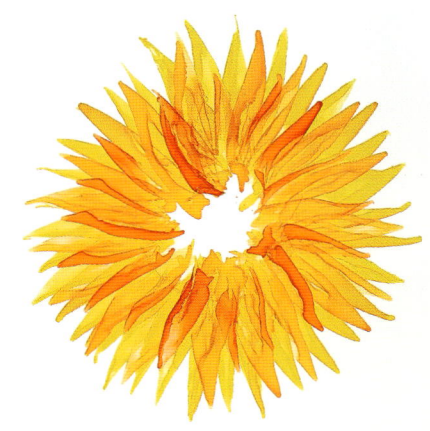

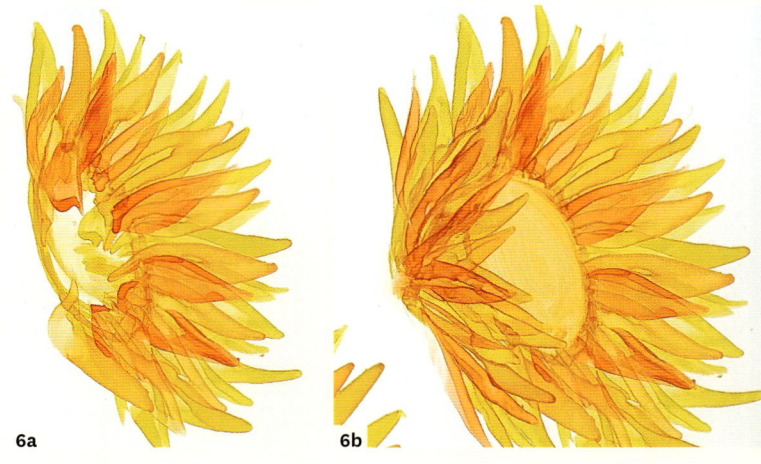

6a **6b**

Step 5

Add the orange-brown ink to your parchment paper. Clean the remaining ink from your palette knife using isopropyl alcohol and a paper towel. Create a new layer of petals using the technique from step 1, this time picking up the orange-brown ink and creating smaller petals to create more depth. You can also choose to leave this color out.

Step 6

To create a side-facing sunflower, start by drawing an oval shape facing the upper right of the paper using a small brush loaded with yellow ink. Repeat steps 2 to 5 to create the sunflower petals. First, create the petals emerging from the right side, making them extend outward from the right edge of the oval. Also add a few top- and bottom-facing petals (6a). Then, remove the petals overlapping the center of the sunflower using isopropyl alcohol and a paper towel. Now, create the petals on the left side. Some of these petals will partly overlap the heart of the sunflower, while others have a more diagonal angle (6b). Create them so they start about 1 inch (2.5 cm) from the left edge of the oval. Use a paper towel with some isopropyl alcohol to remove any excess ink on the left side of the sunflower. Alternatively, you can choose to add another front-facing sunflower to simplify the process.

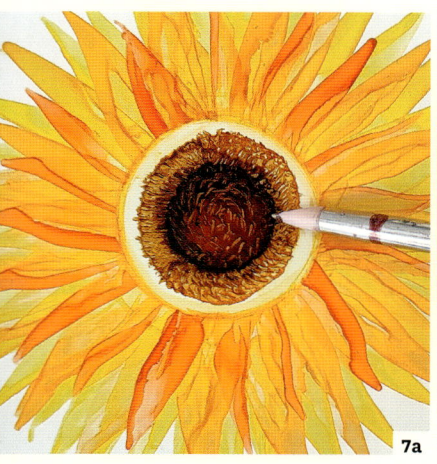 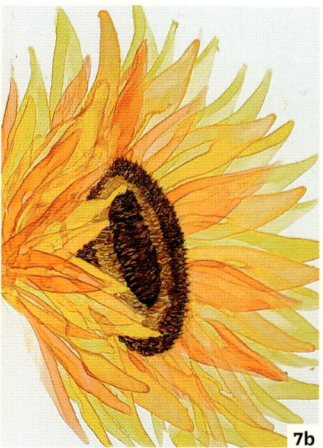

7a 7b

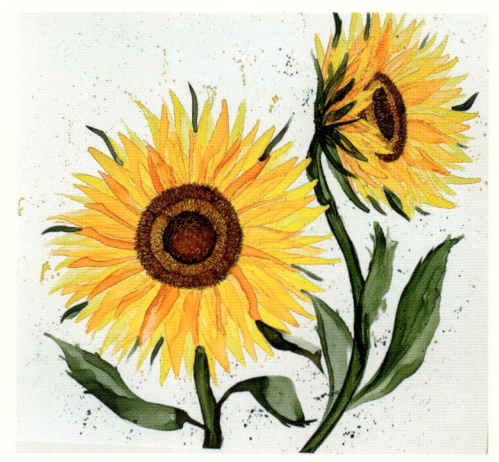

Step 7

To create the center of the sunflower, first clean any excess ink in the center of the front-facing sunflower using isopropyl alcohol and a paper towel. Then, use a small brush with yellow ink to outline two circles within the center of both sunflowers (using an oval shape for the side-facing sunflower). Start with the front-facing sunflower. Add a few drops of brown ink to your parchment paper and load your brush with the brown ink. Fill the circle with the ink, creating a thick layer. Use a silicone tip tool or the edge of the palette knife to draw small strokes in the inner circle from the outside toward the inside (7a). By applying pressure, you can create texture within the inks to create a hairy look while the inks are drying (it may take a few seconds before the texture can be created). Next, repeat this process for the middle ring using a mix of the orange ink with a bit of brown. For the outer ring, use orange-brown ink. For the side-facing sunflower, follow the same process but create small strokes from left to right and draw the center around the petals (7b). Alternatively, use a fine brush to create the center using small brushstrokes.

Step 8

To add the stems and leaves, add green ink to your parchment paper. First, draw the stem with a medium brush. Use a straight line for the front-facing sunflower from between the petals toward the bottom and an S-curved stem for the side-facing sunflower from the left side of the sunflower downward. Note that the stem may be positioned behind the petals of the front-facing sunflower. Second, load your palette knife with green ink and use the same technique from step 1 to add a few small narrow leaves that emerge from outside the sunflower petals. For the side-facing sunflower, add a few narrow leaves over the petals on the right side. For bigger leaves attached to the stems, use the same technique but press the palette knife down more to create a wider shape. It can be helpful to practice this on scrap paper first. As always, finish the flowers with splatters if you like. Cover the center of the sunflower with a small piece of paper towel to protect it. Load a brush with the desired ink color and gently tap it with another brush or tool to create splatters until you are satisfied with the overall look. Add yellow splatters outside the sunflower petals and green splatters where the stems and leaves are.

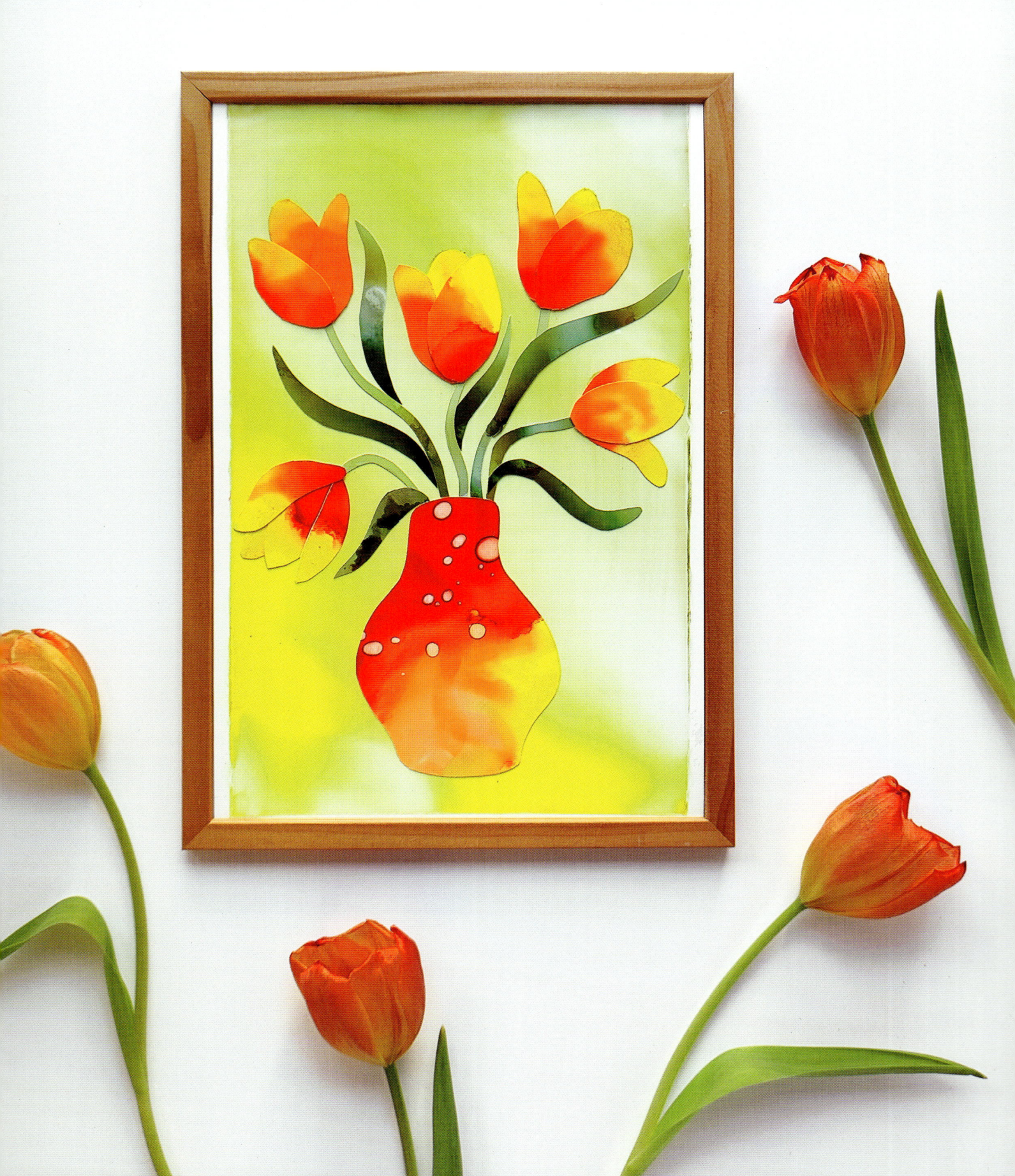

tulips in a vase

In this project, we'll work on a colorful vase of tulips using an easy collage technique. Being Dutch, I needed to include tulips in this book because they are the national Dutch flower and can be found everywhere in spring. We'll start by creating several ink backgrounds, and then we'll use those to cut out the shapes of the vase and tulips and assemble it into a playful composition!

LEVEL: BEGINNER
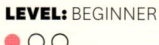

tip

Follow along with my composition or create your own!

Sketch your composition first or play with creating a composition by arranging the cut out shapes in different ways.

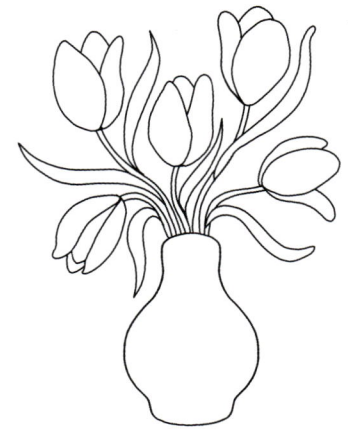

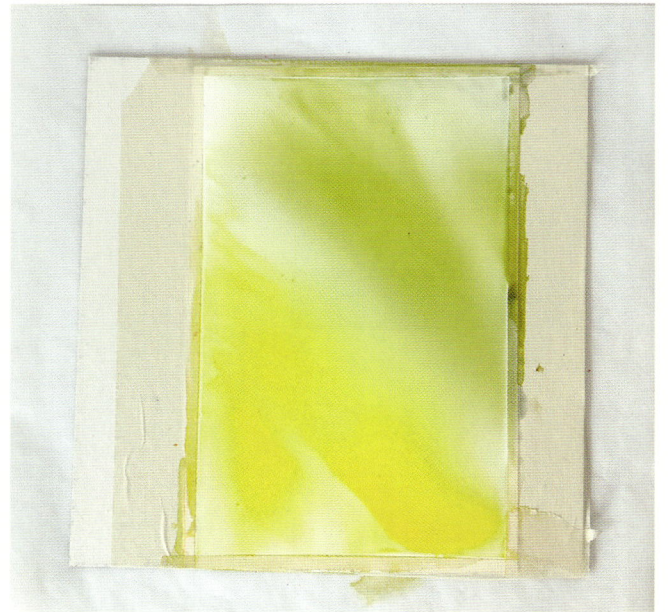
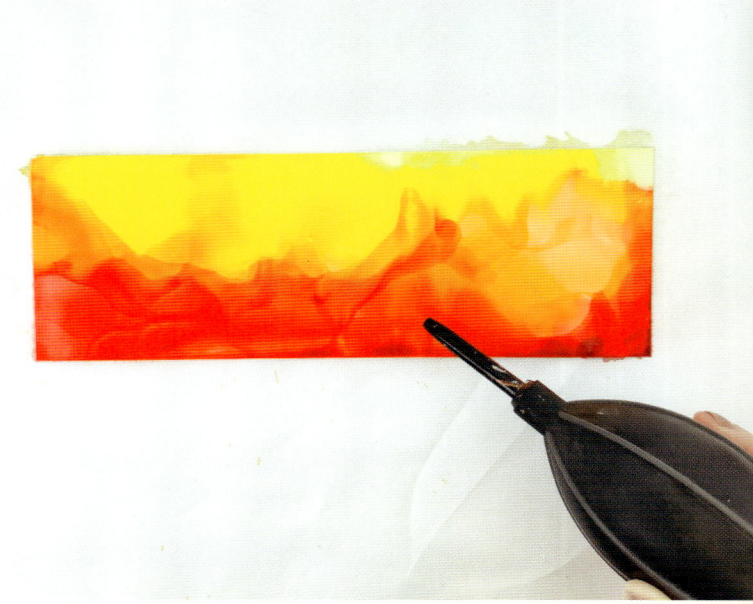

Step 1

Use one sheet of synthetic paper to create the background for your collage. Make sure your paper is flat so the inks won't move in different directions. If needed, use painter's tape to secure the sides. Add enough isopropyl alcohol to cover the paper entirely. Use a large brush to spread it out evenly. To keep the background color light, only add five drops of the green on the upper half and five drops of the yellow on the lower half. Add more isopropyl alcohol on top and tilt the paper around to make the inks cover the entire background or use an ink air blower to spread the inks. If the wet inks build up toward the edges, use a paper towel to lift some of the ink. Allow it to air-dry completely.

Step 2

Cut the second sheet of paper in half across the long edge. For the tulip petals, I like to create a gradient from yellow to orange to red. Add enough isopropyl alcohol to cover one half of the paper entirely, spreading it out with a large brush if needed. Add three lines of ink along the long edge of the paper, starting with yellow, orange, and then red at the bottom. Add more isopropyl alcohol on top to help the colors spread. Use an ink air blower to spread and softly blend the inks into each other. Let the inks air-dry.

Use the remaining half of the sheet for the vase. Repeat the same instructions as for the tulip petals. Let it air-dry. Add a few splatters of isopropyl alcohol across the paper to create a speckled effect.

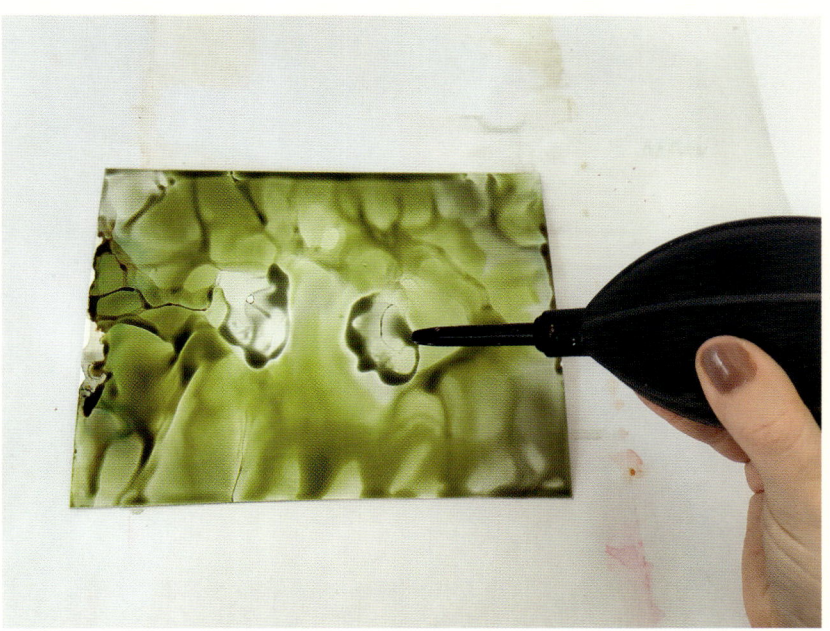

Step 3

Cut the third sheet in half across the short edge to use for the stems and leaves. Again, add enough isopropyl alcohol to cover the paper and spread it out with a large brush. Use two shades of green ink and apply them across the paper. Add more isopropyl alcohol to help the colors spread. Use an ink air blower or tilt the paper around to blend the colors softly. Let it air-dry.

 tip

Recycle scrap paper or failed pieces!

Scrap paper on which you tested some ink colors or techniques or failed pieces can be great to recycle for a flower collage. Leave them as is and let the colors inspire you or reactivate the inks and add more to make them fit your project. Leftovers from this project can also be used for future collages.

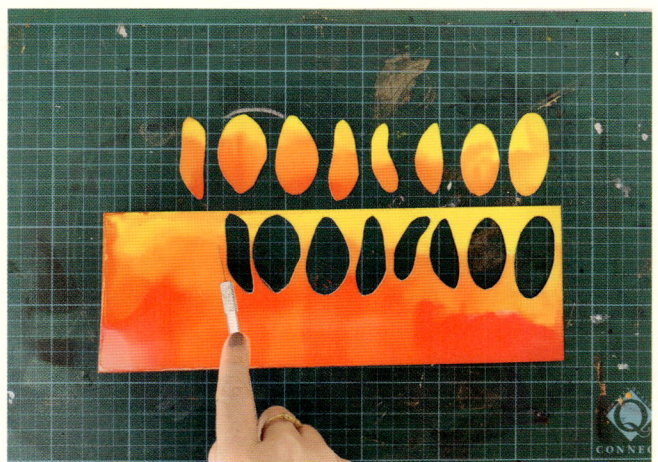
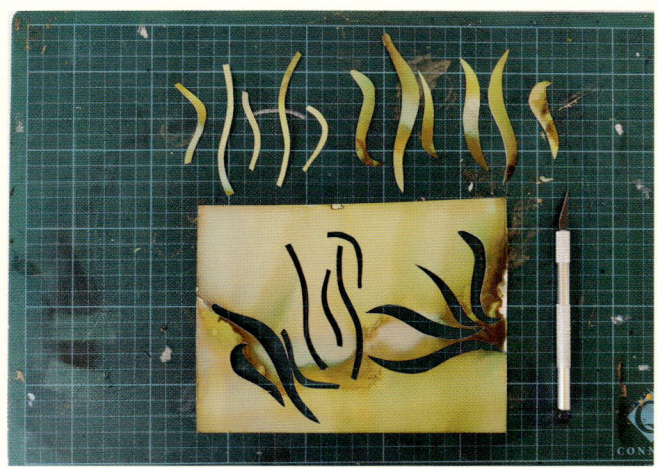

Step 4

Use the first sheet from step 2 to cut out the tulip petals. Draw elongated, teardrop shapes with a rounded tip in various sizes and cut them out using a craft knife and a cutting mat. Make sure your petals cover the gradient from red on the bottom to yellow at the top to create multicolored tulip petals. For a design with five tulips, you will need fifteen to twenty petals (three or four per tulip). Refer to my example for the shapes, but feel free to use your own imagination. For additional help, scan the QR code on the opposite page to access a printable PDF that can be used to cut out the shapes and trace them onto paper.

Use the second sheet from step 2 to draw and cut a vase in the desired shape; I chose a rounded vase with a narrow top and bottom.

Step 5

Use the sheet from step 3 to cut out the stems and leaves. Draw and cut long thin, S-shaped lines for the stems in various lengths. You need one stem per tulip (so five in total). For the leaves, draw and cut out long, narrow shapes with a pointed tip and rounded bottom. For five tulips, you need five to seven leaves.

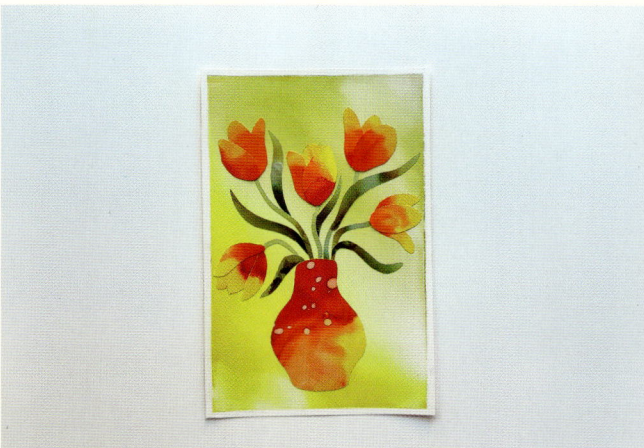

Step 6

If necessary, remove the painter's tape from the background and leave the edges white or trim them. Arrange the vase, stems, leaves, and tulip petals on the background sheet until you find a composition you like. Refer to my example for inspiration or create your own unique design. Allow the tulip petals to overlap naturally and trim the stems to the appropriate length if needed. Once satisfied with the layout, glue the vase shape to the background using gel medium and a brush. Then, glue the stems and leaves, ensuring they appear to emerge from the vase. Position the tulip petals at the top of the stems; glue them in place, starting with the petals in the back and progressing to those in the foreground. When finished, cover the collage with parchment or tissue paper, stack books on top to ensure the shapes adhere well to the paper, and allow it to dry overnight.

Tulip shapes printable pdf

Need some help with the shapes of the tulips and vase? Scan the QR for a printable PDF to cut out the shapes and trace them onto your ink backgrounds.

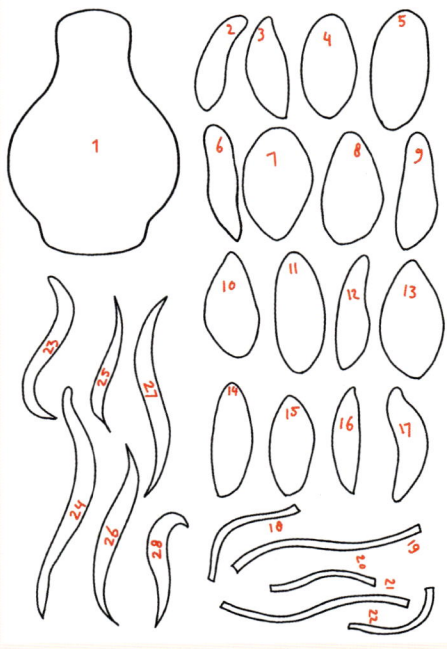

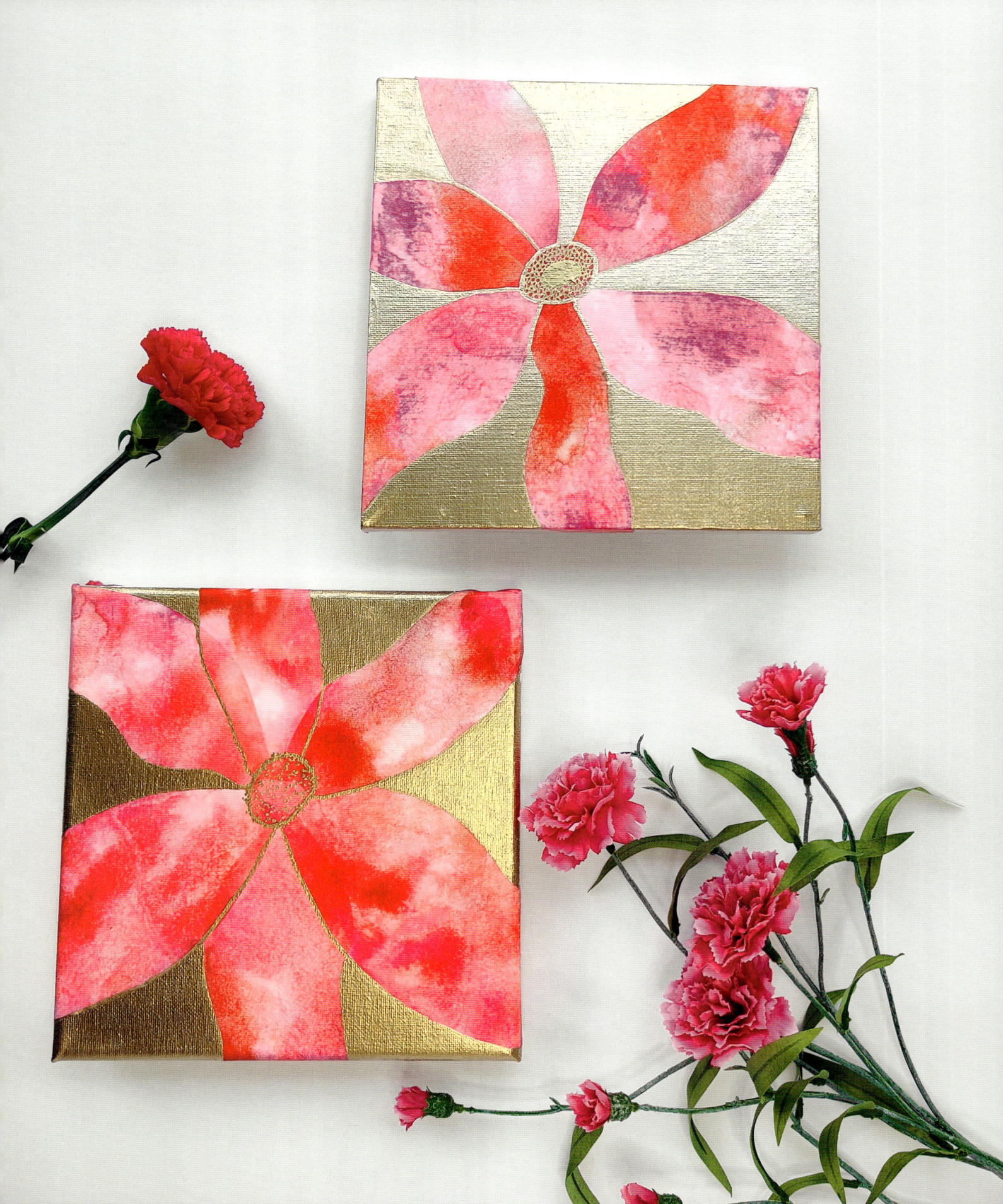

tissue paper flower

For the final project, we will integrate several projects into one by working with ink backgrounds, collage, markers, and a new material: tissue paper. We'll use this to create a big flower on canvas inspired by the Big Bloom project. You can also choose to use your imagination and create your own flower design using the same technique!

materials

- Alcohol inks in bright pink, light pink, and bright red
- 91% or 99% isopropyl alcohol in a needle tip bottle
- White tissue paper 10 × 12 inches (20 × 30 cm) or synthetic paper
- White canvas 10 × 10 inches (20 × 20 cm) or synthetic paper
- Heat tool

- Large foam brush or old brush
- Medium to broad gold paint marker (1 to 2 mm) or a white or black acrylic paint marker
- Decoupage glue
- 2 pieces of parchment paper
- Scissors or craft knife and cutting mat
- Paper towels
- Safety supplies

Step 1

Apply several drops of each of the three ink colors across the parchment paper and leave space between them. Add a generous amount of isopropyl alcohol on top of the inks to help them spread. Ensure the inks cover an area suitable for a 10 × 12-inch (20 × 30 cm) sheet. Carefully place the tissue paper on top of the inks on the parchment paper and use your fingers or a foam brush to gently press the tissue paper down and make the inks spread across the entire surface. As an alternative, you can use synthetic paper instead of tissue paper and follow the same steps. Wear nitrile gloves to prevent ink stains on your hands, as the inks penetrate tissue paper. Lift the tissue paper carefully (1a), turn it over, and place it on a second, clean sheet of parchment paper. Use a heat tool to dry the tissue paper from both sides, or alternatively, allow it to air-dry (1b). Handle the tissue paper with care, as it's fragile.

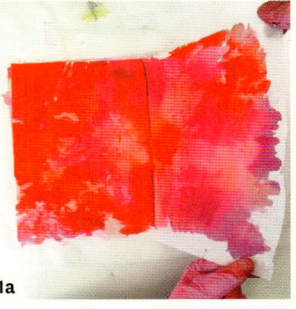

1a

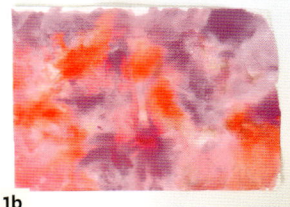

1b

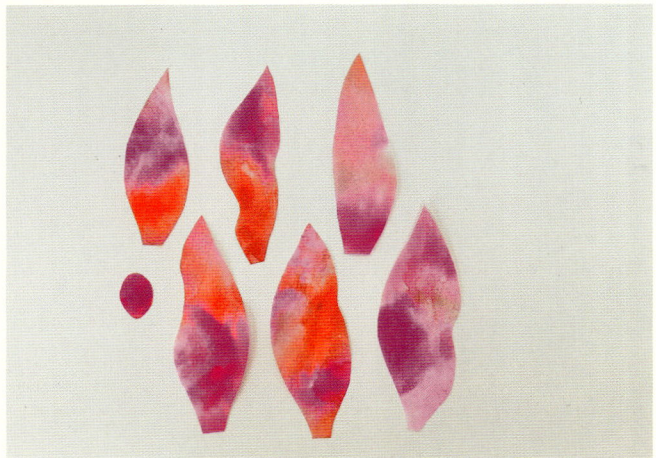

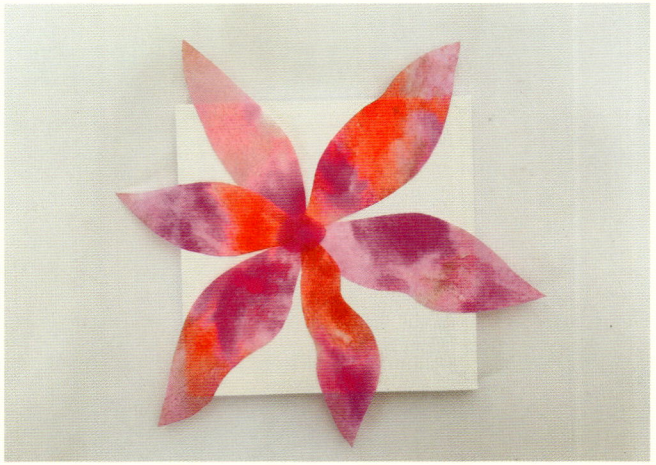

Step 2

Divide the tissue paper (or synthetic paper) from step 1 into six equal parts using your scissors. Next, cut one long, large petal shape of about 6 inches (15 cm) out of each part (six petals in total). Vary the width and curviness so each petal is different. Cut out one small circular shape from the leftover tissue paper to serve as the center of the flower.

Step 3

To create a composition, arrange the shapes from step 2 onto your 10 × 10-inch (20 × 20 cm) canvas or synthetic paper to create a flower design you like. I used the Big Bloom project as inspiration for the composition of this project. First, place the round shape slightly off-center to create an asymmetrical composition. Then, arrange three evenly spaced petals around the circle and place the remaining three in between them. Don't worry about the petals extending beyond the edges; these will be trimmed off later. Once you're happy with the arrangement, move it aside for placement in step 4.

Use your own creativity!

Create different flowers by cutting out various smaller petals. Let the other Flower Projects like Poppies, Daisies, and Tulips in a Vase inspire you. Enjoy experimenting with this technique!

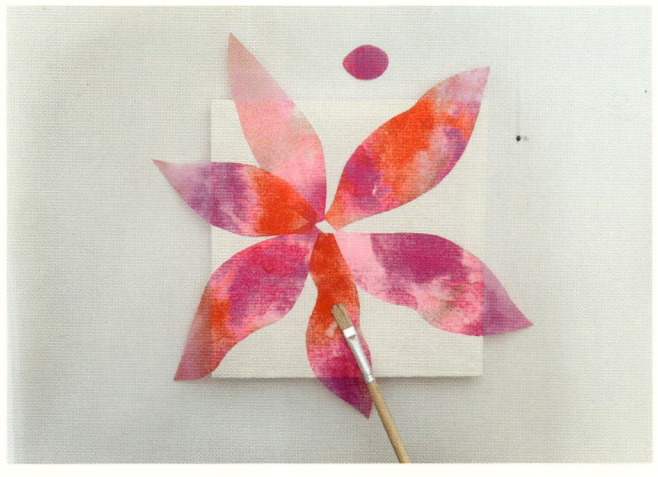

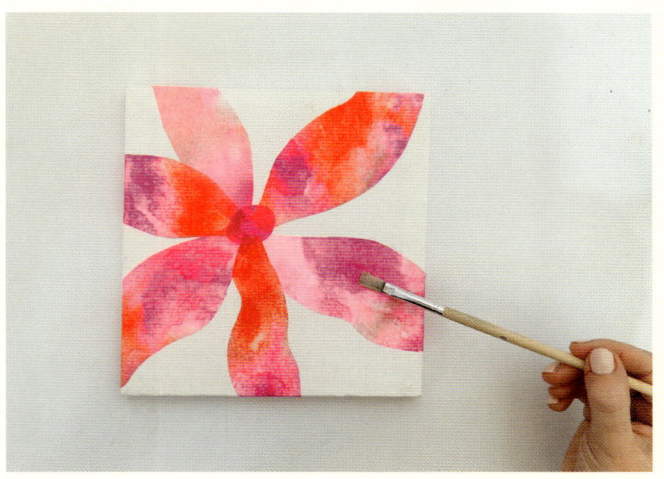

Step 4

Cover the entire canvas or synthetic paper with decoupage glue using a large foam brush. Place the petals on the wet surface, pressing gently from the center outward. Use a clean brush on top and softly stroke it from the center outward to remove any bubbles. Arrange the three background petals first, then the three top petals, and finally the center shape. Apply more decoupage glue if necessary to ensure all the petal edges stick to the canvas.

Step 5

Skip this step if you are working with synthetic paper. When working on a canvas with tissue paper, apply an additional layer of decoupage glue along the edges of the canvas to secure the petals on the edges. Allow the adhesive to dry before trimming any excess petals. Apply another coat of decoupage glue on top of the petals using a foam brush to seal them. Be aware that the adhesive may partially reactivate the underlying inks, staining the brush. Allow the project to dry thoroughly overnight.

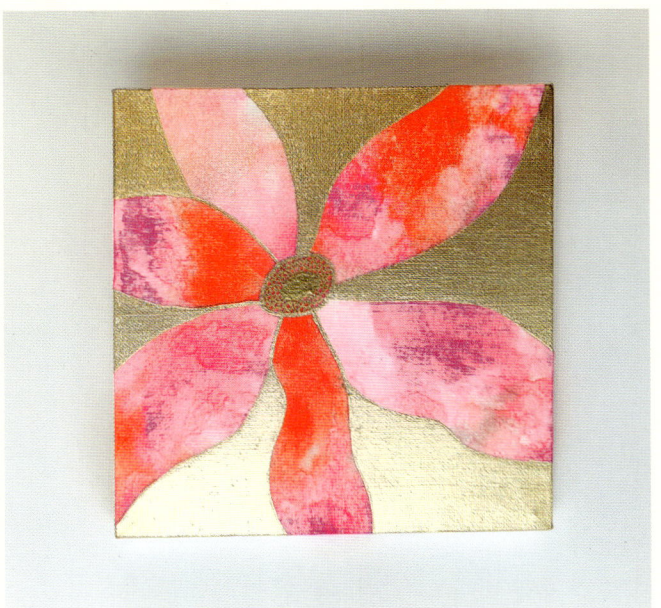

Step 6

Once dry, trim the petals extending beyond the canvas or synthetic paper using scissors or a craft knife. To complete the flower, use a gold paint marker to outline the flower's center and petals. You can fill the background with the gold paint marker, or leave it white, according to your preference. If you are working on canvas, ensure to paint the sides gold as well.

resources

Amsterdam All Acrylics
Relief paint
amsterdam-acrylics.com

ArtResin
Epoxy resin
artresin.com

3M
Protective gear
3m.com

BaByliss
Heat tools
babyliss.com

Copic
Alcohol inks
copicmarkers.com

DecoColor
Gold paint markers
uchida.com

edding
Gold paint markers
edding.com

Grafix
Synthetic paper
grafixarts.com

Jacquard Products
Alcohol inks and varnish
jacquardproducts.com

Kamenskaya
Alcohol inks, synthetic paper, and varnish
kamenskaya.store

Krylon
Varnish
krylon.com

Mod Podge
Decoupage glue
themodpodge.com

MOLOTOW
Metallic alcohol inks
molotow.com/en

Montana
Varnish
montana-cans.com

NARA
Alcohol inks and synthetic paper
narasyntheticpaper.com

Octopus Fluids
Alcohol inks
octopus-fluids.de/en

Pebeo
Relief paint
pebeo.com

PIXISS
Alcohol inks
pixiss.com

POSCA
Acrylic paint markers
posca.com

Ranger Tim Holtz
Alcohol inks and ink air blower
rangerink.com

Revlon
Heat tools
revlonhairtools.com

Sakura
Gold paint markers
sakuraofamerica.com

Sennelier
3D liners
sennelier-colors.com

Talens
Varnish
royaltalens.com

Winsor & Newton
Masking fluid and varnish
winsornewton.com

YUPO
Synthetic paper
yupousa.com

ANNE ROOS SMINK
Original art, online courses, and other alcohol ink resources
anneroosart.com

Learn more in my online courses!

I hope this book has sparked your creativity and helped you create beautiful alcohol ink flowers! If you're eager to dive deeper and explore even more techniques, I'd love to invite you to join my online courses.

In these courses, you'll get access to step-by-step video demonstrations where I guide you through the process of creating stunning flowers from start to finish.

As a special thank you for being a reader of *Creative Alcohol Ink Flowers*, use coupon code CREATIVEFLOWERS at checkout for 20 percent off your purchase!

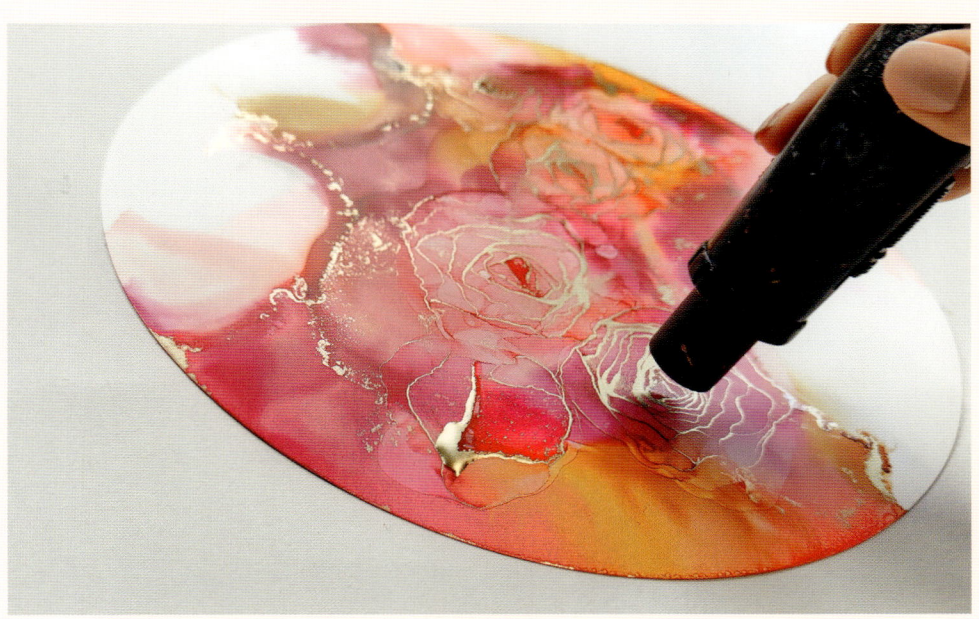

Website: alcoholinkartclub.thinkific.com
Scan the QR to go directly to the website.

acknowledgments

It was a joy bringing this book to life, and I want to thank my editor Salwa Jabado in believing in this project and guiding me through the process of creating this book. I also want to thank Elizabeth Weeks and the design team for making this book a reality with its beautiful design that captures my projects so well.

I want to thank my parents for always being my number one supporters and encouraging me to follow my own passions and dreams. Lastly, I'd like to thank my partner Bas, for always supporting and encouraging me in my creative endeavors!

about the artist

Anne Roos Smink is a Dutch alcohol ink artist renowned for her mesmerizing floral art, particularly her signature roses, that beautifully blend abstract and floral elements. Originally from an academic background, Anne discovered alcohol inks as a creative outlet to relieve stress, which quickly evolved into a passion and a new artistic path. Her true joy lies in teaching and inspiring others to discover their creativity through alcohol ink art, sharing her work with over 140,000 Instagram followers (@anneroosart). Through her online courses, Anne has helped thousands of creatives worldwide transform simple blobs of ink into stunning floral art.

Website: anneroosart.com
Instagram: @anneroosart

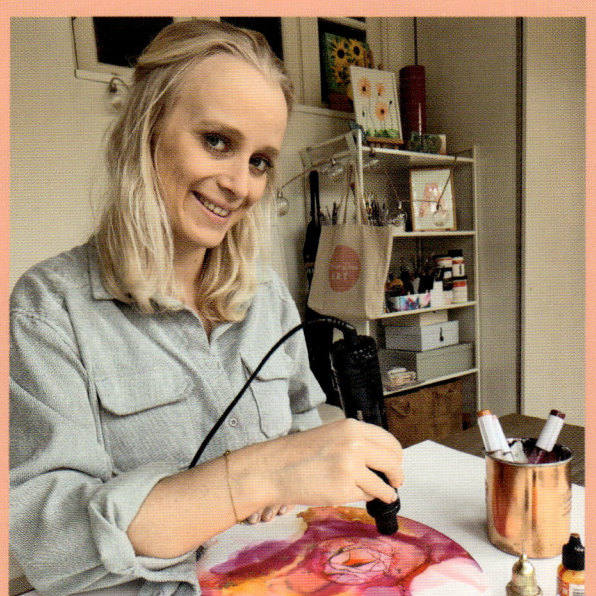

index